The Ethical and Legal Consequences of Posthumous Reproduction

Posthumous reproduction refers to the procedure that enables a child to be conceived using the gametes of a dead person. Advances in reproductive technology mean it is now possible to assist in creating a life after you die, and in recent years the number of women who have attempted to get pregnant using posthumous reproduction has increased. However, the law in many jurisdictions has not put regulations in place to deal with the ethical and legal consequences that arise as a result of posthumous reproduction.

This is the first book to exclusively focus on posthumous reproduction. The book comprehensively explores the legal and ethical issues surrounding posthumous reproduction in a number of jurisdictions including the US, Israel, the UK and France. The book looks at a number of issues including: ascertaining the wishes of the dead and protecting the reproductive rights of men who have deposited frozen sperm in clinics prior to their deaths; cases involving people who want to acquire fresh sperm from deceased or incompetent men and determining who should have the right to accept the sperm; identifying the parents of the posthumously conceived child; and discussing the need to promote the best interests of the child. The book critically examines the current laws that are in place and proposes additional regulations and policies in order to effectively regulate posthumous reproduction.

Browne Lewis is the Leon and Gloria Plevin Professor of Law and Director, Center for Health Law & Policy at Cleveland-Marshall College of Law, Cleveland State University, USA.

Biomedical Law and Ethics Library
Series Editor: Sheila A.M. McLean

For a full list of titles in this series, please visit www.routledge.com

Scientific and clinical advances, social and political developments and the impact of healthcare on our lives raise profound ethical and legal questions. Medical law and ethics have become central to our understanding of these problems, and are important tools for the analysis and resolution of problems – real or imagined.

In this series, scholars at the forefront of biomedical law and ethics contribute to the debates in this area, with accessible, thought-provoking, and sometimes controversial ideas. Each book in the series develops an independent hypothesis and argues cogently for a particular position. One of the major contributions of this series is the extent to which both law and ethics are utilized in the content of the books, and the shape of the series itself.

The books in this series are analytical, with a key target audience of lawyers, doctors, nurses, and the intelligent lay public.

Available titles:

Assisted Dying
Reflections on the Need for Law Reform
Sheila A.M. McLean

Medicine, Malpractice and Misapprehensions
V.H. Harpwood

Euthanasia, Ethics and the Law
From the conflict to compromise
Richard Huxtable

About the Series Editor

Professor Sheila A.M. McLean is Professor Emerita of Law and Ethics in Medicine, School of Law, University of Glasgow, UK.

The Ethical and Legal Consequences of Posthumous Reproduction

Arrogance, Avarice and Anguish

Browne Lewis

Routledge
Taylor & Francis Group
LONDON AND NEW YORK

First published 2017 by Routledge

2 Park Square, Milton Park, Abingdon, Oxfordshire OX14 4RN
52 Vanderbilt Avenue, New York, NY 10017

Routledge is an imprint of the Taylor & Francis Group, an informa business

First issued in paperback 2018

British Library Cataloguing in Publication Data
A catalogue record for this book is available from the British Library

Library of Congress Cataloging-in-Publication Data
Names: Lewis, Browne, author.
Title: The ethical and legal consequences of posthumous reproduction : arrogance, avarice, and anguish / Browne Lewis.
Description: Abingdon, Oxon [UK] ; New York : Routledge, 2017. | Series: Biomedical law and ethics library | Includes bibliographical references and index.
Identifiers: LCCN 2016029627| ISBN 9781138021358 (hbk) | ISBN 9781315767901 (ebk)
Subjects: LCSH: Artificial insemination, Human—Law and legislation. | Artificial insemination, Human—Moral and ethical aspects. | Fertilization in vitro, Human—Law and legislation. | Human reproductive technology—Law and legislation. | Posthumous children—Legal status, laws, etc. | Estates (Law)
Classification: LCC K3611.A77 L49 2017 | DDC 346.01/7—dc23
LC record available at https://lccn.loc.gov/2016029627

ISBN: 978-1-138-02135-8 (hbk)
ISBN: 978-0-367-07563-7 (pbk)

Typeset in Galliard
by Apex CoVantage, LLC

Contents

Introduction

A necessary means

Sigmund Freud said, "it would be one of the greatest triumphs of humanity, one of the most tangible liberations from the constraints of nature to which mankind is subject, if we could succeed in raising the responsible act of procreating children to the level of a deliberate and intentional activity and in freeing it from is its entanglement with the necessary satisfaction of a natural need."[1] Freud can rest easy. Procreation has been set free from sexual intercourse. The natural need Freud referenced was the need to have sex. He saw procreating children as just a by-product of sexual desire. For many people, the compulsion to have children has become a natural need. Science is helping people to satisfy the yearning to procreate. As a consequence of the advances in assisted reproductive technology, people can now procreate intentionally. This ability to family plan goes beyond the simple use of oral contraceptives and other birth control devices. For example, the availability of gestational surrogacy permits a woman who has lost her uterus to a hysterectomy to procreate. The ability to purchase donor eggs gives a postmenopausal woman the opportunity to conceive a child. As this book will reveal, not even death can prevent a person from procreating.

This book is about posthumous reproduction. This book is both timely and necessary because the number of requests for posthumous reproduction is increasing. Posthumous reproduction is the process of conceiving children using the gametes of men and women who are dead or in a vegetative state.[2] It involves fertilizing the gametes of the dead person in order to produce a child.[3] This book deals primarily with the posthumous use of sperm but acknowledges that, in some cases, the oocytes of a dead woman may be used to conceive a child. The sperm may be removed from the man prior to his death or immediately after his death. In the case of post-mortem sperm retrieval, the sperm is surgically removed from the testes, epididymis and vas deferens then preserved in nitrogen vapor. In order for the sperm to be viable, it has to be retrieved within 24 to 36 hours of the man's death.[4] Posthumous reproduction is different from posthumous birth where a child is conceived when his or her father is alive and born after the man dies.[5] The end result is the same – the child is born fatherless. Nevertheless, from a public policy perspective, the latter may be more acceptable than the former.[6]

No one would argue that a pregnancy should be terminated after the death of the unborn child's father. In fact, the public appears to be comfortable with doctors going to great lengths to ensure that a child is born alive. For example, there have been a few cases where a pregnant woman has been kept on life-support in order to permit her to gestate her unborn child to viability.[7] Some jurisdictions in the United States even have laws that require health care providers to ignore the provisions of living wills and other health care directives for comatose or vegetative patients who are pregnant.[8]

Advances in assisted reproductive technology that have led to the availability of posthumous reproduction exist because of the rising epidemic of infertility. This book is about more than posthumous reproduction. It is about the desire to procreate by any means necessary. It is about the determination, and sometimes the desperation, to preserve and/or protect fertility. Therefore, a brief examination of the infertility problem provides a helpful prelude to taking up the discussion of posthumous reproduction. Even though this book is mostly about sperm, I talk about infertility from a female perspective to highlight the pressure that is put on women to conceive. That subtle coercion which may come from society, family and friends may contribute to women seeking to procreate using the sperm of dead husbands and significant others.

Infertility and the need to procreate

The changing conversation

In their late teens and early twenties, women spend a lot of time trying not to get pregnant. They use birth control pills and other types of contraceptives. They make sure that their sexual partners wear condoms. In the event that passion overtakes common sense and she has unprotected sex, the woman may attempt to protect herself from pregnancy by taking the over the counter (OTC) "morning-after" pill. The most popular "morning-after" pill is called the Plan B pill. Plan A is to not have unprotected sex. In the event of an unexpected pregnancy, the woman has the legal right to choose to get an abortion.[9] Numerous resources have been expended to ensure that a woman does not have to deal with an unplanned pregnancy. Each year, men and women spend millions of dollars to reduce and/or eliminate the chances of an unwanted pregnancy.[10]

The conversation about a woman's right not to procreate is consistently a part of the national conversation. Regardless of which political party occupies the White House or controls Congress, a woman's ability to control her reproductive organs remains a hot topic. At times, it seems like the nation is obsessed with reducing the odds of a woman getting pregnant. During the Clinton Administration, one of the things that motivated the proponents of welfare reform was the desire to discourage teenagers and low-income women from having children. In order to achieve that goal, the law gives states the authority to refuse to award additional money to a family who has another child while already receiving welfare benefits.[11] To further discourage pregnancy, the law requires a woman to work in order to be eligible for welfare and restricts the number of years the woman can remain on welfare.[12]

In 2012, then Georgetown law student, Sandra Fluke, spoke to House Democrats about the need to require health insurance providers to cover contraceptives.[13] In 2013, Texas Senator Wendy Davis, relying on *Depends* and pink running shoes, talked for almost thirteen hours to successfully filibuster a law that would have banned twenty-week abortions and resulted in the closure of most of the abortion clinics in the state.[14] The anti-pregnancy conversation has not been limited to teenaged girls. For example, the Chicago Department of Public Health's Office of Adolescent and School Health created an advertising campaign featuring pictures of teenaged boys that were digitally altered to make it look like the boys were pregnant. The goal of the campaign was to emphasize that teenage pregnancy negatively impacts boys as well as girls. The campaign organizers hoped that the advertisements would discourage young people from having babies.

The conversation about reproduction changes when women enter their thirties and forties. At that time, the focus of the conversation shifts from the right not to procreate to the desire to replicate. The conversation also becomes more solitary and intimate. There is no public discussion about the steps society can take to make it easier for women and men to have children. In order to help combat the trend, *Redbook* magazine and RESOLVE, the national fertility association in McLean, Virginia, created "Truth About Trying", an online video campaign designed to start a public dialogue about infertility.[15] That campaign is just one of the small steps being taken to shine the light on infertility in the United States. The public has been slow to join the infertility conversation, so men and women who are unable to conceive children without reproductive assistance remain in the shadows.

The term "birth control" is narrowly used to refer to the practice of preventing unwanted pregnancies. If it is about control, birth control should be defined to include any practice a person engages in to control his or her reproductive activities, including using assisted reproductive technology to conceive a child. After a woman tries unsuccessfully to get pregnant, she is left to suffer in silence or, if she is lucky, to seek comfort from close relatives and friends. The United States Supreme Court's holding that a person has a fundamental right to procreate brings the infertile man or woman no solace. In fact, the Supreme Court cases dealing with the right to procreate only restricts the government's ability to interfere with a person's decision to procreate. Nothing requires the government to provide resources to help infertile people conceive children. Thus, the fundamental right is to have children without governmental interference. If there was truly a fundamental right to procreate, the government might have to take steps to ensure that every person who wanted a child would be able to have a child. For example, the government might be compelled to make procedures like in vitro fertilization (IVF) available to all infertile people. Even groups that advocate for insurance companies to pay for contraceptives have not demanded that those companies be forced to cover assisted reproductive procedures like posthumous reproduction.[16] Supporters of Planned Parenthood insist that the organization is necessary to assist low-income women in their quest to avoid unexpected pregnancies.[17] However, even the most progressive person would probably reject the idea that the government should pay for an infertile low-income person to use assisted reproductive technology to conceive a child.

It is difficult to have a public conversation about infertility when private conversations about the subject are limited. Infertility is a silent epidemic. If asked whether or not he or she knows someone who is infertile, the average person would probably answer in the negative. Infertile people rarely tell friends and family members about their condition. The shame of infertility makes conversations about the subject taboo. There are no public service announcements (PSAs) about infertility like there are about other medical conditions. Since infertility has not been classified as a disease in the United States, a person suffering from it cannot expect to get the same sympathy as someone who has been diagnosed with a disease like cancer. As a result, the infertile person remains silent about his or her inability to conceive.

For religious reasons, some infertile people are afraid of being judged if they discuss the steps they are taking to resolve the issue. If the infertile woman is Catholic, she has to contend with the fact that the Vatican has denounced the use of IVF and certain other fertility treatments.[18] The Church has not yet officially spoken on posthumous reproduction, but, based on its stance on assisted reproductive technology, there is no doubt that the procedure would be condemned.[19] Protestant women and Jewish women who are being treated for infertility may fear having their faith questioned. Women of those faiths would have heard the story of God blessing infertile Sarah with a child in her old age and may have to justify the fact that they are not waiting on God to give them a miracle baby.[20] People struggling with infertility have to deal with the fact that there is always a possibility that the infertility treatment will fail. Thus, they may be afraid of disappointing family and friends if their quest to conceive a child is unsuccessful. In some cultures, a woman's worth is connected to her ability to have children. As a result, the infertile woman may be afraid of being ostracized by her community and/or being divorced by her husband.[21] The equation of a woman's worth with her fertility may be one of the reasons why posthumous reproduction is so prevalent in Israel. Until people are more comfortable talking about infertility, it will be difficult to change the topic of the national conversation from pregnancy avoidance to reproductive assistance. In the meantime, women should be encouraged to talk about all aspects of their reproductive journeys.

The three talks

The moment that a young girl has her first menstrual cycle her parents live with the fear that she may become pregnant. To lessen the chances of that happening, parents talk to their young girls about sex and explain in detail the true source of babies. The "first talk" is about the changes a woman's body goes through as the result of menstruation. The media helps people to be comfortable when it comes to discussing a woman's menstrual cycle. For example, the public is inundated with advertisements for feminine hygiene products like *Kotex* and *Midol.* A key component of that "first talk" is to explain to the girl the dangers of having unprotected sex. Traditionally, the parents enumerated the virtues of abstinence and encouraged the girl to refrain from having sexual intercourse. Today, parents are more realistic about the libidos of young adults, so, as a part of the "first talk," parents advise their daughters to avoid pregnancy by using contraceptives. Middle schools often show videos in physical education classes focusing upon the changing female body. Pregnancy is indirectly discussed through school projects like the one that requires the students to care for an "egg baby".

In 2012, Kimberly Clark, the owner of the *Poise* feminine hygiene brand, attempted to start a public conversation about menopause. The company created a line of products made for the fifty million American women who are or will soon go through menopause. The television commercials featuring the new products encouraged women to have what the company referred to as the "second talk." The "second talk" is about the changes a woman's body goes through as a consequence of menopause. It is ironic that the "talks" focus upon the beginning of a woman's childbearing years and the end of a woman's childbearing years. The silence in-between is deafening.

The real "second talk" should be a conversation about the changes that occur in a woman's body between menstruation and menopause. That talk should focus upon the possibility that the woman may be unable to reproduce during her child-bearing years. The infertility talk is necessary because, according to the Center for Disease Control and Prevention's webpage, approximately eleven percent of women of reproductive age are unable to conceive or carry a baby to term.[22] The infertility talk is needed because women do not realize that infertility is a possibility until they try to have children. I regularly speak with young women who say that they plan to have their first child when they turn a certain age. These women make their declarations without doubt. They assume that getting pregnant will be just as easy as obtaining a degree and finding a husband. For the sake of all women, hopefully in the near future, the fertility talk will become as commonplace as the menstruation and menopause talks because infertility is a growing problem that can touch the lives of people from all walks of life.

The complex face of infertility

A true public conversation about infertility will not be possible until the public cares about the problem. For that to happen, the public must be made aware of the problem. Members of the public must be informed that infertility does not have a particular face. The women and men[23] suffering from infertility reflect the melting pot that is America. The condition afflicts women and men from all races, classes and socio-economic statuses. Women of color like Padma Lakshmi, Tamar Braxton and Angela Bassett have spoken candidly about their fertility problems. Other women of color like Janet Jackson, Grace Hightower and Mariah Carey have encountered difficulties conceiving after postponing motherhood.[24]

Being physically fit does not protect a woman from infertility. In a *Redbook* article, Dr. Robert Gustofson, medical director of Colorado Center for Reproductive Medicine, stated: "Regardless of how well you take care of yourself ovaries age at a consistent rate, and there's nothing you can do to halt it. That clock ticks on."[25] Jillian Michaels, arguably one of the fittest persons in the world, has stated that she has several medical conditions, including endometriosis, which makes it difficult for her to get pregnant. Instead of trying to conceive, Michaels adopted a child.

Being physically beautiful does not prevent a woman from having to confront the ugly truth about infertility. The condition even impacts supermodels. For instance, supermodel Naomi Campbell was infertile for years before having corrective surgery in 2008. Likewise, supermodel Cindy Margolis battled infertility for years. As a result of that struggle, Margolis was led to write her book, *Having a Baby...When the Old Fashioned Way Isn't Working.*[26] After publicly discussing her fertility problems, supermodel Tyra Banks had a son using a surrogate.[27] Infertility goes beyond the inability to get pregnant. Some women are capable of conceiving a child, but fail to bring the child to term. For example, supermodel Christine Brinkley suffered three miscarriages while going through IVF before she gave birth to her youngest child.

Having a sense of humor does not negate the fact that infertility is not a laughing matter. Comedian Sherri Shepherd endured two years of fertility treatments before she got pregnant at the age of 38. After years of infertility, funnyman Tom Arnold became a dad for the first time at the age of 53. Nia Vardalos, the star of *My Big Fat Greek Wedding*, suspended her acting career to deal with the emotional pain caused by her battle with infertility. Vardalos stated that she had to grieve. She returned to acting after she adopted a three-year-old girl. Even women with the gift of the gab, like former talk show host Elizabeth Hasselbeck and anchorwoman Giuliana Rancic have found it difficult to talk about their struggles with infertility. The public watched as Rancic tried unsuccessfully to have a baby for almost two years before becoming a mother via surrogacy. Reality television is a cultural phenomenon that affords the public the opportunity to witness the daily lives of previously unheard-of people. The television audience watched as reality television stars Kandi Burruss and Rosie Pope discussed their infertility problems. The availability of reproductive technology has brought hope to a new generation of women. Some of those women are determined to conceive and they will not let a little thing like death get in their way.

Reasons for posthumous reproduction

Jack Kerouac was quoted as saying, "I hope it is true that a man can die and yet not only live in others but give them life, and not only life, but that great consciousness of life." A person who loses a loved one may share Kerouac's sentiment. That hope of creating life from the dead may lead a man's survivors to select posthumous reproduction. The reasons for the increased demand for posthumous reproduction are as varied as the people who seek to use the procedure to have a child conceived. Persons seeking to conceive children using posthumous reproduction may be motivated by arrogance, avarice or anguish. Nevertheless, the person's request may be an act of self-sacrifice.

Arrogance or vanity may cause a woman to go to great lengths to create a mini-version of herself using the sperm of her dead husband or significant other. The woman may reject the option of adoption because she wants to have a child that is genetically related to her. This desire may be magnified if the woman is older when her husband or significant other dies. The woman may hear her biological clock ticking and see posthumous reproduction as her last chance to procreate. She may not want to wait to find another man that she considers to be "father material." The woman may reason that, since she has sperm readily available to her, she should use it to conceive a child. Instead of an act of narcissism, the woman's incentive for using posthumous reproduction to conceive a child may be altruistic. She may be honoring the wishes of the dead man. Prior to his death, the man may have frozen his sperm and asked the woman to use it to conceive his child. It is not unusual for a dying man to think about his legacy. A part of that legacy may be the creation of a child who will carry on his bloodline.

Spouses and significant others are not the only ones who can act selfishly. Parents who seek to have their dead sons' sperm extracted and frozen may feel that they are entitled to a grandchild. For example, Missy Evans got a court order to have twenty vials of her dead son's sperm harvested and donated his heart, liver, kidneys and pancreas. In response to critics, Evans stated: "He helped five people live that day. If you can say I am no longer in charge, how can I give five gifts? I am happy about that, but why can't I have a gift? Why do I lose everything?"[28] Evans' statement indicates that she feels that the universe owes her a grandchild because she lost her only child. Some parents may take drastic steps to achieve their goals of becoming grandparents. For example, the mother of a man who committed suicide allegedly only agreed to donate her dead son's organs if some of his sperm was harvested.[29]

Avarice or greed may also lead a person to conceive a child relying on the gametes of a deceased person. For example, a spouse or significant other may create an heir in order to receive an inheritance from a wealthy man. With regards to persons of modest means, a spouse or significant other may have or facilitate the conception of a dead man's child, so that he or she can receive Social Security Survivors' benefits, Veteran's benefits or other government benefits. Rapacity can go beyond the desire for money. A spouse may want a child by his or her dead husband or significant other in order to have someone to love and nurture. The fear of loneliness may cause the person to have the sperm of the dead man retrieved.

Finally, as a result of anguish or grief, a person may want to have a child conceived from a dead person's gametes. Posthumous reproduction cannot occur without death. Death causes sorrow. When a person is told that his or her husband is dead or a significant other is informed about the death of his or her significant other, that person experiences unimaginable grief. One way of dealing with that misery is to attempt to retain a piece of the decedent. For instance, some people are consoled by being able to keep the ashes of their cremated loved ones close. In cases involving posthumous reproduction, that piece is sperm. Even if the sperm is never used to conceive a child, the survivors may be comforted by the fact that the sperm is available if necessary. This is similar to the reassurance that a terminally ill patient gets from having a prescription for a lethal dose of medication the patient can use to end his or her life if the suffering becomes unbearable. People often idealize the dead. After a person dies, everyone usually has something positive to say about them. For example, in the wake of a tragedy, television interviews often feature people singing the praises of the dead victims. It is not unreasonable for a person to think that his or her perfect loved one deserves to be reproduced.

The loss of a child is a heartbreaking experience. In the natural course of things, parents are not meant to bury their children. Consequently, when a child dies, a parent is paralyzed with grief. That heartache may lead a parent to make decisions that appear to be illogical.[30] There have been several cases where a mother, like Missy Evans, reacts to losing her child by seeking to have his sperm harvested, so she can have a grandchild. It is all about keeping the dead child alive. We have seen this phenomenon in cases involving parents who donate their children's organs. The story of Heather Clark is illustrative. Heather Clark's son, Lukas, died in 2013 when he was just seven months old. Clark donated Lukas' organs. Jordan Drake, a fifteen-month-old girl who was born with a heart condition, received Lukas' heart. When Jordan was four years old, her mother, Esther Gonzalez, arranged for Clark to hear Jordan's heartbeat. Afterwards, Clark stated: "The sound was so strong, I could feel him there with me. He is continuing on through her, no doubt." Jordan gave Clark a teddy bear containing a recording of her heartbeat.[31] Guilt is another emotion that might follow the death of a child. This is especially true if the child dies in an accident. The parent may try to ease his or her feelings of grief by honoring the dead person's memory with a child. From an ethical perspective, a person's motives may be irrelevant. However, the legal consequences of posthumous reproduction may be impacted by the reason the person seeks the procedure.

Outline of the book

This book examines the impact of the use of reproductive technology to conceive children using the gametes of dead persons. In this book, I will mainly focus upon the use of sperm because that practice is more common than creating children using the eggs of dead women. Nonetheless, the book will include information on surrogacy because parents seeking to produce grandchildren using the sperm of their dead sons must rely on egg donors and surrogates. In addition, surrogacy is relevant to the posthumous conception of children using the eggs of dead women. In the book, I will analyze the pertinent ethical consequences and legal issues that occur because of the use and availability of posthumous reproduction. Unlike other books on this topic, this book relies on legal principles from contract law, family law, probate law and property law, to recommend the legal steps that can be taken to address the ethical concerns raised. The book is written in a way that acknowledges the fact that gender restrictions have been removed from marriage. Nevertheless, in cases where it is appropriate, I will discuss issues in the context of a marriage between a man and a woman. During those times, I am not negating the fact that a man may use his dead husband's sperm to conceive a child. The book is divided into four parts and eight chapters.

Part I–Ethical concerns and legal regulations

Part I of the book includes two chapters. This part contains a discussion of the potential ethical problems that can occur if posthumous reproduction becomes a commonly accepted practice. It also discusses some of the ethical arguments that can be made in support of the procedure. In addition, the current attempts to legally regulate postmortem sperm retrieval and the posthumous conception of children are analyzed.

Chapter 1–Ethical concerns

This chapter starts with a discussion of the ethical arguments that can be made against and in favor of the use of posthumous reproduction. Those arguments will be evaluated using the four principles of bioethics-autonomy, nonmaleficence, beneficence and justice. Since the law has incorporated aspects of those principles into the doctrine of informed consent, I will analyze the different types of legal consent that may be relevant to posthumous reproduction. The chapter also looks at the arguments through the lens of deontological and consequential theories.

Chapter 2–Legal regulations

This chapter contains a brief summary of the current legal landscape with regards to the use of the sperm of a dead man to conceive a child. The chapter identifies the countries that have explicitly prohibited the procedure and the countries in which it is legal. I analyze the legal regulations and policies that are in place in countries that permit the conception of children through posthumous reproduction. In addition, I discuss the legal treatment of posthumous reproduction in countries that have not enacted laws to govern the use of the procedure. In particular, I examine the approaches that may be taken in those countries to determine whether or not to allow posthumous reproduction.

Part II–The sperm

Part II of the book consists of two chapters dealing with the acquisition and use of the sperm of men who are dead or in vegetative states. This part includes a chapter that explores approaches the courts can take to help health care providers decide what to do with the man's frozen sperm after he dies. The second chapter in this part examines cases where the health care provider is faced with the task of deciding whether to extract fresh sperm from the body of a man who is dead or in a vegetative state.

Chapter 3–Frozen sperm (thaw it out or throw it out?)

This chapter will analyze cases involving women who seek to gain possession of frozen sperm that their husbands or significant others have deposited in clinics prior to their deaths. In those cases, the physician or the fertility clinic has to decide whether to thaw out the sperm – so that it can be used to conceive a child – or whether to throw out the sperm. The chapter will start out with an examination of some of the reasons why men store their sperm for future use. Then, I will discuss the manner in which frozen sperm is treated when the man leaves written instructions expressing his wishes with regards to the use of his sperm in the event of his death. Those written instruments may be contained in a will or in an agreement between the man and the fertility clinic.

I will also explore instances where the man dies without indicating a preference as to the treatment of his frozen sperm. In those cases, the physician or fertility clinic has the difficult task of deciding whether the dead man would want his sperm to be discarded or used to conceive his child. Prior to his death, the man did not give specific instructions with regards to the frozen sperm. Hence, the physician or fertility clinic has to rely upon extrinsic evidence to determine the decedent's intent and upon legal precedence to decide whether to thaw out or throw out the sperm. I will explore whether or not a substituted judgment approach will assist the health care provider in making that decision.

Chapter 4–Fresh sperm (extract and release?)

The more recent posthumous reproduction cases have involved requests for the sperm of dead men to be harvested within hours of their deaths. When faced with these types of cases, health care providers must first decide whether or not to extract the sperm from the dead man's body. This decision has to be made fairly quickly because the body must be protected in order to preserve the viability of the sperm. Doctors cannot release the body so that it can be embalmed and they must place ice on the testicles as soon as feasible. Further, in order for the sperm to be useable, it has to be retrieved from the body within 36 hours after the man dies. In most cases, to protect themselves from liability, doctors will not remove the sperm without a court order. Given the urgency of the situation, if the person requesting the sperm is the spouse or the parent, doctors may be willing to extract the sperm. The doctors' decisions become even more difficult when the requests involve retrieving sperm from a man who is comatose or in a vegetative state. Once the doctor extracts the sperm from the dead man, he has to decide if and to whom to release the sperm. The potential recipients include the man's spouse, significant other or parents.

Part III–The child

Part III of the book contains two chapters addressing the needs of the posthumously conceived child. One of the chapters deals with the child's need to have legal parents who can provide emotional, psychological and financial support. That chapter discusses the importance of the legal parent-child relationship. It also includes an analysis of the methods legislatures and courts have used to adjudicate legal maternity and paternity. The other chapter focuses upon the inheritance rights of the posthumously conceived child. In addition, the chapter explains the legal connection between the child's right to inherit and his or her right to receive governmental benefits like Social Security Survivors' benefits and Veteran's benefits.

Chapter 5–Posthumously conceived children (adjudicating the parents)

This chapter will address the importance of identifying the parents of the posthumously conceived child. The chapter will be divided into two parts. The chapter will begin with a discussion of the reasons why establishing the parent-child relationship is critical to the well-being of the child. Some posthumously conceived children are gestated by surrogates. This may occur when parents obtain the sperm of their dead son and select a surrogate to be the child's biological mother. Thus, in the first part of the chapter, I will discuss the tests that courts apply to designate a woman as the legal mother of a child conceived as the result of a surrogacy arrangement. In the second part of the chapter, I will examine how the manner in which courts adjudicate the paternity of the men involved in the artificial insemination process may be relevant to determining the legal father of a posthumously conceived child.

Chapter 6–Posthumously conceived children (allocating financial support)

This chapter will deal with the necessity of providing financial support to posthumously conceived children. That support usually takes two forms. As a result, this chapter will be divided into two parts. At the beginning of the chapter I will discuss the adverse impacts that receiving financial support from just one parent can have on a child. Then, I will analyze the cases, including the recent United States Supreme Court case, putting forth the circumstances under which the posthumously conceived child is eligible to receive Social Security Survivors' benefits and other government benefits. In the second part of the chapter, I will discuss the steps courts and legislatures have taken to define the inheritance right posthumously conceived children have under the intestacy system. This discussion is crucial because the United States Supreme Court has given states the authority to establish the circumstances under which posthumously conceived children can receive government benefits through their deceased fathers.

Part IV–The balance

The final part of the book includes one chapter which has two objectives. First, I attempt to balance the interests of the dead man and the posthumously conceived child to determine if posthumous reproduction should be an option for persons who want to conceive using assisted reproductive technology. After answering that question in the affirmative, I devote the remainder of the chapter to laying out my proposals. My proposals are premised on the belief that as long as the necessary legal regulations are put in place, posthumous reproduction can be performed in a way that respects the rights of the dead or incapacitated man and promotes the best interests of the resulting child or children.

Chapter 7–Finding the balance

This chapter will deal with the safeguards that need to be put in place to protect the reproductive rights of dead men. The chapter will begin with a discussion of the need for uniformity. In this chapter, I will discuss the importance of ensuring that the man has consented to the use of his sperm to conceive his child after he dies. Then, I will put forth my proposal and explain how it will address some of the main ethical and legal consequences of posthumous reproduction. In addition, I will put forth guidelines that need to be put in place to protect the welfare of the children after they are born. As long as posthumous reproduction is permitted, the law has an obligation to ensure that the children conceived as a result of the process are supported both emotionally and economically.

Notes

1 Sigmund Freud cited in Ch. 12 "Selective Acts of Procreation," Richard W. McCaty, *Sexual Virtue: An Approach to Contemporary Christian Ethics* (New York: SUNY Press, 2015).
2 Cynthia E. Fuchtman, Tales From the Crib: Posthumous Reproduction and ART, 33 Whittier L. Rev. 311, 313 (Winter 2012) (discussing several definitions of posthumous reproduction).
3 *Id.*
4 Charles P. Kindregan, Jr., Genetically Related Children: Harvesting of Gametes From Deceased or Incompetent Persons, 7 J. Health & Biomedical L. 147, 157 (2011).
5 John A. Robertson, Posthumous Reproduction, 69 Ind. L.J. 1027, 1027 (Fall, 1994).
6 The Ethics Committee of the American Society for Reproductive Medicine, Posthumous Reproduction, 82 Suppl. 1 Fertility and Sterility S260, S260 (September 2004).
7 Hope E. Matchan and Kathryn E. Sheffield, Adding Constitutional Depravation to Untimely Death: South Dakota's Living Will Pregnancy Provision, 37 S.D.L. Rev. 388, 394–395 (1991/1992).
8 At least one professor prefers a broard definition of posthumous reproduction that includes cases involving pregnant women who are placed on life support until the fetus is fully gestated. See Hilary Young, Presuming Consent to Posthumous Reproduction, 27 J.L. & Health 68, 71 (2014).

9 *Roe v Wade*, 410 U.S. 113 (1997).
10 Christopher G. Kuhn, An Epic Oversight: Why the Current Battle For Access to Contraception Will Not Help Reduce Unintended Pregnancy in the U.S., 17 Health Matrix 352–353 (2007).
11 Rebekah J. Smith, Family Caps in Welfare Reform: Their Coercive Effects and Damaging Consequences, 29 Harv. J. L.& Gender 154–155 (2006).
12 Karen Syma Czapanskly, Parents, Children and Work-First Welfare Reform: Where is the C in TANF?, 61 Md. L. Rev. 328–329 (2002).
13 Remarks of Sandra Fluke, Panel 1-The ACA's Other Mandate: Contraceptive Coverage, Conscientious Objection, and Reproductive Rights, 23 Alb. L.J. Sci. & Tech. 481, 481–488 (2013).
14 The law eventually passed, but the conversation continues. Manny Fernandez, Abortion Restrictions Become Law in Texas, but Opponents Will Press Fight, http://mobile.nytimes.com/2013/07/19/us/perry-signs-texas-abortion-restrictions-into-law.html (July 18, 2013). The United States Supreme Court invalidated the law in 2016. Adam Liptak, Supreme Court Strikes Down Texas Abortion Restrictions, www.nytimes.com/2016/06/28/us/supreme-court-texas-abortion.html (June 27, 2016).
15 www.redbookmag.com/truthabouttrying (accessed July 22, 2016).
16 But see Jean Hayes, Female Infertility in the Workplace: Understanding the Scope of the Pregnancy Discrimination Act, 42 Conn. L. Rev. 1299, 1326 (May 2010).
17 Katherine R. Dieterich & Janet L. Dolgin, The "Other" Within: Health Care Reform, Class, and the Politics of Reproduction, 35 Seattle U.L. Rev. 407–410 (2012).
18 Emma Reynolds, Pope tells infertile couple to shun "arrogant" IVF treatment as sex between husband and wife is the "only acceptable" way to conceive, www.dailymail.co.uk/news/article-2106392/Pope-Benedict-XVI-tells-infertile-couple-shun-arrogant-IVF-treatment-sex-husband-wife-acceptable-way-conceive.html (February 25, 2012). See European Society of Human Reproduction and Embryology (ESHRE), Task Force on Ethics and Law 11: Posthumous assisted reproduction, 21 Human Reproduction 305, 305 (2006) (opining that "Roman Catholics will reject this application because it separates human reproduction from sexual intercourse and implies insemination of a single woman.")
19 Helen M. Alvare, Catholic Teaching and the Law Concerning the New Reproductive Technologies, 30 Fordham Urb. L.J. 116–119 (2002).
20 Genesis 1–2; Keith Alan Byers, Infertility and In Vitro Fertilization, 18 J. Legal Med. 266–267 (1997).
21 S.J. Dyer, N. Abrahams, M. Hoffman, and Z.M. van der Spuy, "Men Leave Me As I Cannot Have Children": Women's Experiences With Involuntary Childlessness, 17 Human Reproduction 1663 (2002).
22 www.cdc.gov/reproductivehealth/infertility (last updated June 20, 2013).
23 7 to 10 percent of men are infertile.
24 In 2016, Janet Jackson announced by video on the Internet that she was suspending her tour because, at the age of 49 she and her husband were trying to start a family. She stated that doctors told her that she had to rest up and indicated that time was of the essence in regards to her having a baby. Mariah Carey had a miscarriage before conceiving her twins with the help of IVF.
25 Norine Dworkin-McDaniel, The Invisible Pain of Infertility, www.redbookmag.com/health-wellness/advice (February 29, 2016).
26 Cindy Margolis, *Having A Baby When the Old Fashioned Way is Not Working* (New York: Penguin Group 2008).
27 Emanuella Grinberg, Tyra Banks shows off newborn son in photo, http://edition.cnn.com/ (February 15, 2016).

28 Susan Donaldson, Sperm Retrieval: Mother Creates Life After Death, at http://abcnews.go.com/Health/Wellness/mother-murdered-son-hopes-create-grandchild-post-mortem/story?id=9913939 (February 23, 2010).
29 Raziel, Arieh, Friedler, Shevach, Stassburger, Deborah, Kaufman, Sarit, Umansky, Ana, and Ron-El, Raphel, Nationwide use of postmortem retrieved sperm in Israel: a follow-up report, 95 Fertility and Sterility 2693, 2693 (June 30, 2011).
30 Some persons have proposed given a quarantine period after postmortem sperm retrieval has occurred and before the sperm is used. Laborde, Eric, Sandlow, Jay and Brannigan, Robert E., Postmortem Sperm Retrieval, 32 Journal of Andrology 467–469 (September/October 2011). This approach has been implemented in Israel.
31 Rose Minutaglio, California Mom Hears Dead Son's Heartbeat Through 4-Year-Old Transplant Recipient: The Sound Was So Strong at www.people.com (February 1, 2016).

Part I

Ethical concerns and legal regulations

1 Ethical concerns

For some, the ethical argument against posthumous reproduction can be summed up by the sentiment expressed by bioethicist Arthur Caplan who said: "the core principle is not to reproduce anyone without their permission."[1] From a legal perspective, an expert had asked: "Is it appropriate to consciously bring a child into the world with a dead father?"[2] Posthumous reproduction has been hailed as a medical breakthrough that can give comfort and hope to men who freeze their sperm to maintain the possibility of being fathers; to people who want to have children for the men they love; and to parents who seek to fulfill their dreams of becoming grandparents. Nevertheless, posthumous reproduction is not without its critics. The arguments against using posthumous reproduction to conceive children are aimed at the existence of the procedure and the impact its use has on the parties involved. Most of those arguments are made by bioethicists relying on the principles of bioethics and/or philosophical theories.

Arguments based on biomedical ethics principles

Every semester, I begin my health law and ethics class with a discussion of Beauchamp and Childress' four principles of biomedical ethics.[3] Those principles are autonomy, nonmaleficence, beneficence and justice.[4] Adherence to these principles helps physicians to remain true to the provisions of the Hippocratic Oath.[5] Furthermore, all of these principles have influenced the legal regulation of the field of medicine. The need to protect patient autonomy led to the development of legal torts like medical battery[6] and lack of informed consent.[7] To ensure that physicians adhere to the principles of nonmaleficence and beneficence, the tort law system was created. Anti-discrimination laws like the Americans with Disabilities Act (ADA) are in place to bring about justice and fairness in the health care system. For instance, persons with physical and mental disabilities are entitled to the same quality of health care as similarly situated non-disabled patients.[8]

Autonomy

The autonomy principle is synonymous with patient self-determination. The legal recognition of individual autonomy permits patients to make voluntary medical decisions, including the decision to withdraw life-sustaining treatment.[9] Doctors must respect medical decisions of their patients.[10] In the legal context, autonomy is the driving force behind the development of the informed consent doctrine. Therefore, the main ethical objections to posthumous reproduction revolve around the issue of consent. The dead or vegetative man is the patient whose autonomy must be protected. Consequently, it is unethical to use his frozen sperm or to extract his fresh sperm without his consent. By respecting the man's autonomy, the fertility clinic also protects itself from liability for torts like medical battery and lack of informed consent. In some jurisdictions, if a fertility clinic releases a man's frozen sperm without his consent, it may be sued under the torts of bailment and conversion. Consent may be expressed, presumed, inferred or substitutional.

Expressed consent (oral/written)

Prior to his death, the man may explicitly give his consent to posthumous reproduction orally or in writing. Under certain circumstances, it may be appropriate for courts to deem the man's oral consent to be satisfactory. The man may not be given the opportunity to give his written consent with regards to the use of his sperm in the event of his death. For example, the fertility clinic agreement may not contain a provision asking the man to state the manner in which he wants his sperm disposed of if he dies before it is used. In addition, the man may not feel that promises he makes to his spouse or significant other need to be in writing. An emergency situation may also prevent a man from giving written consent to the retrieval and use of his sperm. For instance, a young man who has not contemplated death but who has expressed an oral desire to have children, may die or become incapacitated. Given his age and good health, the man may not have felt that he needed to put his wishes in writing. The man should not be deprived of the opportunity to procreate because his clearly expressed agreement to posthumous reproduction was not provided in writing.

The main problem with oral consent is evidentiary. At the time the dispute arises, the man will be dead or incompetent, so he will not be able to state his position with regards to posthumous reproduction. Thus, the court will have to learn the man's intentions from the person seeking to obtain his sperm. Even if that person's testimony is credible, it would be self-serving. A decision as important as whether or not to reproduce a person should not be based solely on this type of evidence.

The only way to make sure that posthumous reproduction is consistent with the desires of the dead or incompetent man is to require that his consent be in writing. The best way to avoid conflicts and problems regarding the disposition of the man's sperm after he dies or becomes incapacitated is to have his written consent. Therefore, this is the preferred type of consent. In some countries, including the United Kingdom, the gametes of a dead or incompetent person cannot be extracted and/or used for conception without that person's written consent.[11] This approach is also recommended by the Ethics Committee of the American Society for Reproductive Medicine.[12] Written consent has its advantages. It prevents a person from obtaining a man's sperm by fraudulent means. Moreover, it assures the man that his wishes with regards to his sperm will be carried out after his death or incapacitation. Judicial economy also dictates that a man's consent be in writing. Any time there is no concrete proof of the man's intentions with regards to the use of his sperm, the possibility of litigation remains strong. Therefore, in the absence of written consent, courts will be forced to intervene whenever there is a dispute regarding the extraction and/or use of the sperm of a man who is dead or in a vegetative state. We have witnessed this type of intense litigation in cases involving the withdrawal of food and hydration from patients in vegetative states.[13]

Presumed consent

A man's consent may be presumed. The reasoning behind presumed consent is that a reasonable man would agree to have his spouse use his sperm to conceive a child. This approach may make sense in cases where the man dies while he and his spouse are undergoing IVF. The fact that the man is participating in the process indicates that he wants to have children. This theory of consent would presume that the man's death would not change his desire to procreate. Presumed consent is permitted in Israel as long as the person seeking to use the sperm is the man's wife.[14] In the United States, there are no laws regulating the process of posthumous reproduction. However, the majority of states have laws that regulate artificial insemination. Courts may rely on those laws when determining whether or not to permit a man's sperm to be used without his written consent. If a married man consents to the artificial insemination of his wife with donor sperm, he is the legal father of the resulting child.[15] In the majority of jurisdictions, the husband's consent must be in writing.[16] Nonetheless, at least one state statute authorizes courts to presume the man's consent.[17]

There are two other possible types of consent that have not yet been legally adopted. The first type is inferred or implied consent. Under this theory, a man's consent to posthumous reproduction would be implied from his actions. Those activities might include leaving property in his will for future children or making other financial arrangements for his potential offspring. Once a man is told that his condition is terminal and he does not arrange for his sperm to be destroyed, he should understand that posthumous reproduction may be a possibility. If he fails to take actions to eliminate the option, his consent to posthumous reproduction using his sperm might be implied. For instance, a cancer patient who freezes his sperm before undergoing chemotherapy should anticipate that, in the event of his death, his partner might want to conceive his child. This approach has been taken in cases involving children conceived using artificial insemination.[18]

Substitutional consent

Healthy young men do not often think about having children. In fact, even if they are married or in a serious relationship, they are often preoccupied with avoiding fatherhood. Young men may postpone fatherhood because they are not ready for the emotional and financial responsibility of having children. Unfortunately, young men are regularly severely injured and killed in accidents. Some of those men end up in a vegetative state. Because of their condition, these men are incapable of giving any type of consent. Very few young men have advanced directives indicating the type of life-sustaining treatment that they would want in the event they become incapacitated. If a man did have an advanced directive, it would probably not indicate what he wanted done with his sperm.

In London, a woman asked the court to give her the right to take some of her comatose partner's sperm, so that she could have his child. At that time, the man, who had suffered several heart attacks, was in a persistent vegetative state and was subject to a Do Not Resuscitate (DNR) order. The woman dropped her case after the media implied that she was trying to have a child in order to get some of the man's money.[19] These cases present unique problems for doctors because the man is unable to give consent. Hence, prior to extracting or releasing the sperm the clinic has to decide what the man would say if he was capable of expressing his preferences. In those types of situations, the courts may permit the doctors to rely on what I call substitutional consent.

Substitutional consent is consent that is given by someone on behalf of the incapacitated patient. The need for this type of consent is found in cases involving incompetent patients who are receiving life-sustaining treatments. Before terminating that treatment, doctors must try to ascertain the patient's wishes. This type of consent may be appropriate in cases where the sperm donor is dead or in a vegetative state. I will expand upon substitutional consent in Chapter 2. Consent is critical in determining whether or not it is ethical to use a dead man's sperm to achieve posthumous reproduction. However, it is not the only relevant factor. The other principles of bioethics may also be the basis of ethical arguments.

Beneficence, nonmaleficence, and justice

Part of the original Hippocratic Oath states: "I will apply dietetic measures for the *benefit* of the sick according to my ability and judgment; I will keep them from *harm* and *injustice.*"[20] This places a duty on physicians to work to benefit their patients, to avoid bringing harm to their patients, and to treat their patients fairly. Beneficence requires doctors to balance the benefits of treatment against the risks and costs, and to act in the best interests of their patients. As a result, only actions which will result in good for the patient are ethically desirable. In cases involving posthumous reproduction, the question to ask is whether or not the dead man will benefit from the procedure. Some scholars may give this principle a broad interpretation and suggest that it requires doctors to consider the benefits that would be derived by other parties including the resulting child. I disagree with this interpretation. The Hippocratic Oath and the principles of bioethics are designed to govern the relationships between doctors and patients. In posthumous reproduction situations, the dead man is the patient. When frozen sperm is involved, the man is usually the one undergoing the medical treatment that caused him to store his sperm. If the extraction of fresh sperm is involved, the man is the patient because he is typically the one who has been severely injured or killed.

The main ethical argument based on the beneficence principle is that the dead man does not benefit from the process because he will not know what happens after he dies. Nonetheless, the case can be made that the beneficence principle will not be violated by posthumous reproduction because the dead man may benefit from the process. The benefit may start while the man is alive and continue after his death. Therefore, he may have some idea of what he wants to happen after he dies. This is true if the man dies after a lengthy battle with an illness. A man benefits when his wishes are honored.[21] One potential benefit to the man is the opportunity to have a child to carry on his bloodline. This may be important to a man who dies while he and his wife are undergoing IVF. A man who has accumulated a lot of wealth may benefit by having a child to inherit his property instead of having it go to distant relatives or the state.[22] Even a man of modest means may get an indirect economic benefit. The money the man has paid into the Social Security system will be used by his child if certain conditions are met and not retained by the government. A man that is undergoing treatments for a terminal condition may get hope from the possibility of a future child. That hope may enable him to live longer than predicted.

Nonmaleficence directs physicians to do no harm.[23] Any actions that harm patients are unethical. Therefore, physicians must avoid causing harm to their patients. Some would argue that all actions done to the patient without his or her consent are harmful.[24] Can the dead be harmed? This question has been debated by philosophers for years. I will briefly discuss a few of those theories of harm. A thorough discussion of the arguments is beyond the scope of this book.[25] Joel Feinberg opined that a person can suffer harm after death. Feinberg characterizes harm as an invasion of interests. Because some interests can survive death a dead person can suffer harm.[26] Feinberg seems to believe that a person can be harmed without his or her knowledge, so posthumous harm can occur.[27] He gives an example using reputational harm. Feinberg contends that a person's reputation can be harmed after he or she dies.[28] He also claims that the dead can be harmed by broken promises.[29]

Ernest Partridge disagrees with Feinberg's position. He claims that a person cannot be posthumously harmed because no one can retain interests after death.[30] Partridge appears to think that, in order for a person to suffer harm, he or she must be adversely impacted by the invasion of his or her interests. With regards to posthumous reproduction, the dead man's interest would be the right to avoid forced procreation. Feinberg would say that it would be unethical to conceive a child using the dead man's sperm without his prior written consent because he would be harmed by having his right to avoid forced procreation invaded.[31] He would also opine that, if a court ignores a dead man's instructions with regards to his sperm, that man will be injured. Partridge would counter that the dead man cannot be harmed by the unauthorized use of his sperm because his interests end when he dies. Barbara Baum Levenbook took a different approach with regard to harm. Levenbook's two-fold theory was as follows: "the harmed person must lose something or be deprived of something" and "the loss or deprivation must be bad for him."[32] Levenbook argues that posthumous harm can occur because a person can lose something after death. Using the case of libel to illustrate the validity of her theory, Levenbook maintains that it is unethical to libel a dead author because the libel can cause him harm. Applying Levenbook's theory, one could argue that it is not unethical to create a child using a dead man's sperm because he is not losing anything. In fact, he is gaining a child to carry on his name.

The law does not share the position of Feinberg, Partridge and Levenbook. Posthumous defamation is not a valid cause of action. The law does not protect the dead from defamation unless a living person's interests are adversely impacted.[33] No matter how you characterize it the harm to a dead man whose sperm is used without his permission is his right to avoid forced procreation. The way to ascertain whether the dead man can be harmed by becoming a father is to determine the harm that a living man suffers when he is made a father against his will. The following case may be a good point of reference. In 2002, Layne Hardin informed his live-in girlfriend, Katherine LeBlanc, that he wanted to have a vasectomy. At that time, the couple had one son together. In order to give LeBlanc the possibility of having another child, Hardin had seven samples of his sperm frozen and stored at a fertility clinic. The agreement the couple signed with the clinic gave control over the sperm to LeBlanc. After the couple separated, Hardin started dating Tobie Devall. In 2008, Hardin and Devall went to the clinic where his sperm was stored to discuss options of having a child together. During that visit, Devall found out about Hardin's stored sperm. Hardin and Devall ended their relationship in 2009. Shortly after that time, Devall went to the fertility clinic and withdrew two vials of Hardin's sperm. In 2010, Devall gave birth to Hardin's son.[34] In response, Hardin and LeBlanc successfully sued the clinic for breach of contract and Devall for fraud.[35]

As a consequence of Devall's action, Hardin was liable for child support. Hardin also expended thousands of dollars on attorney fees while trying to terminate his parental rights. In addition to the financial harm he suffered, Hardin claimed emotional harm. The opportunity for LeBlanc to bear Hardin's child was taken away from him. He was angry at Devall for tricking him. Hardin was concerned about the negative impact the birth of Devall's child might have on his existing child. Hardin voluntarily terminated his parental rights, but expressed regret over being denied the opportunity to meet his child. Furthermore, Hardin is unsure what he will say to his son if the boy ever decides to find him. It is clear that Hardin was harmed by becoming a father without his consent. Would he have suffered that same harm if the event had occurred after his death? Because he would not know that he had become a father Hardin would not have experienced the injuries that he did. Hardin may have been harmed under Levenbook's deprivation theory. As a consequence of posthumous reproduction with his sperm, Hardin would be deprived of the opportunity to know his son. He would also be deprived of the opportunity to give his existing child a sibling who had the same mother.

The principle of justice directs doctors to treat their patients fairly. This principle may be used to argue in support of, or against, posthumous reproduction. It is unethical to treat similarly situated patients differently. Thus, it is unethical for a doctor to harvest or use a dead man's sperm without his consent because the doctor would not treat a live man in the same manner. It is unfair because the dead man is not able to object to such a medical intrusion. The principle of justice is violated if the dead man is forced to be a parent without his consent. This is in line with the manner in which the law treats other men. For example, a man who does not consent to the artificial insemination of his wife is not recognized as the legal parent. In addition, men who become legal fathers because of fraud are given the opportunity to have their paternity extinguished.[36]

Arguments based on deontological and consequential ethics theories

Some ethical concerns about posthumous reproduction appear to be deontological. Deontological or duty-based ethics are concerned with what people do, not with the consequences of their actions.[37] Duty determines the morality of an action. With regards to posthumous reproduction, a patient-centered deontological approach may be appropriate. A patient-centered deontological theory is premised on people's rights. The core right involved is the right against being used only as a means for producing good consequences without one's consent.[38] The concept of consent will play a key role in the analyses in this book. When the sperm of a dead man is used to conceive a child, it is difficult to see how he benefits. Instead of being treated like a man, he is used as a sperm dispenser. Thus, it is unethical for a dead body to be handled in that way.[39]

Another concern about posthumous reproduction is based on emotions. In the minds of most people, the conception of children is linked to sexual intercourse. Thus, the thought of the sperm of a dead man being used to impregnate a woman may be distasteful to some people. Along that same line, some may see postmortem sperm retrieval as a desecration of a corpse.[40] In order to ensure that dead bodies are respected, there are laws governing the ways in which people can dispose of them.[41] Persons embracing this position would argue that the use of assisted reproductive technology should be restricted to the use of the gametes of persons who are alive at the time that the gametes are used for conception. Doctors have a duty to obey the wishes of their patients. This duty comes from the fact that a patient has the right to refuse medical treatment even if that refusal leads to death.[42] Under that reasoning, a doctor should abide by the instructions that a dead man leaves with regards to the disposition of his sperm.

The majority of persons expressing concern about posthumous reproduction may be able to rely on consequential ethics for support. Consequentialists hold that actions are to be morally evaluated solely by the results that they cause.[43]

Rightness or wrongness of a given act is judged exclusively by consequences. Under that approach, one would argue that posthumous reproduction should not be morally permissible because it negatively impacts society, the person seeking to use the procedure, and the resulting child.

The society

From a societal perspective, posthumous reproduction is unethical because of the undesirable position in which it places physicians and other health care providers. In the case of postmortem sperm retrieval, doctors are asked to perform an invasive procedure on a person who has not consented. Some doctors may see this as violating the autonomy of a patient. This is more troubling in cases involving harvesting oocytes from dead women because the procedure is more invasive.[44] In light of rising health care costs and a shortage of doctors, it is unethical to expend finite resources on what amounts to elective surgery. A doctor's calling is to provide care for the sick and the dying. Thus, one may argue that it is unethical for physicians to waste valuable time and resources performing invasive medical procedures on dead people. Some may argue that posthumous reproduction is unethical because it adversely impacts the world's population. Currently, the world is overpopulated, so there is no good reason to conceive additional children. The foster system is full of neglected and abused children who need parents. The conception of children using posthumous reproduction may negatively impact those children by reducing the number of potential adoptive parents. In addition, the number of children living in poverty continues to increase, so it is not a good idea to add to that figure.

The children

Posthumous reproduction may not be in the best interests of the resulting child. It may be unethical to intentionally create fatherless children who may have to be taken care of by the public. For instance, after she uses her dead husband's sperm to conceive a woman may die in childbirth. Consequently, the resulting child would be born an orphan with no family to financially support him or her.[45] Even if the man leaves a sizeable estate, the child may not be entitled to inherit and/or the estate may be distributed prior to the child's birth. The outcome would be that tax payers have to support the child of a wealthy man. In additional to the economic impact of not having a father, the lack of a father may cause the child emotional problems. Donor and adopted children often attempt to reach out to their biological fathers to establish some type of relationship. Unfortunately, that option will not be available to the posthumously conceived child.

Death ends the marriage; therefore, the posthumously conceived child may be deemed to be legally illegitimate. Children born out of wedlock are no longer socially and legally stigmatized.[46] Nonetheless, with regards to the inheritance rights granted under the intestacy system, those children are not on par with marital children.[47] In some cases, the conception of posthumously conceived children may adversely affect the decedent's existing children. Consider the following scenario. A and his wife B have two children, C and D. A executes a will leaving his property to his children. When A dies, C and D expect to divide his estate between the two of them. If B obtains some of A's sperm with the intention of conceiving another child, his estate may have to be left open indefinitely to ensure that his potential children have the opportunity to inherit from his estate. In addition, instead of being divided into two parts, A's estate may have to be split into three or more portions. Is it fair to make C and D wait to receive their inheritance? Is it fair to clog up the probate court waiting for B to decide whether or not to conceive a child? Is it fair to give A's existing children less than A wanted them to inherit?

Children born as a result of parental requests for posthumous reproduction may face unique problems. The child may feel that he or she is a replacement for the person that died. A person who uses the sperm of his or her son to create a grandchild intends to parent that child. As a result, a child may end up with parents who are older. By the time the child turns eighteen his or her parents will be senior citizens. Like many people that age, the parents may suffer from declining physical and mental health. As a consequence, the child may be torn between taking college classes and taking care of his aging parents. For example, Missy Evans was forty-three years old when she got permission to harvest her son's sperm. Because Evans has to find an egg donor and a surrogate, the process could take years. Hence, Evans could be in her late forties or early fifties when the child is born. The fact that Evans hopes to have three grandchildren exacerbates the problem. If the grandparents die while the child is still a minor, the child may have to be placed in the foster care system unless there are other family members willing to step in and take the child. In the eyes of the law, none of the three people responsible for the child's conception would be obligated to financially support him or her. The child's father would be dead; the egg donor, the child's genetic mother, would be anonymous; and the gestational surrogate would be a stranger who engaged in a business transaction.

The person requesting the sperm

The person requesting the sperm will not come through the process unscathed. That person will pay a heavy price for the opportunity to conceive a child using posthumous reproduction. Those costs may be financial and/or emotional. Post-mortem sperm retrieval may cost thousands of dollars. Insurance companies do not pay for most assisted reproductive treatments, so the person trying to conceive the child will have to pay the total costs. Those expenses can be daunting for a person of modest means. After the sperm is retrieved, it costs more money to have it frozen and stored. Then, the woman has to pay for the cost of Intrauterine Insemination (IUI), in vitro fertilization (IVF) or intra-cytoplasmic sperm injection (ICSI). According to data listed on RESOLVE: The National Infertility Association's webpage, the average costs of those procedures are as follows: IUI cycle–$865, IVF cycle–$8,158, and ICSI procedure–$1,544. It is also likely that the woman will want to pay for the PGD procedure that costs about $3,550.[48] When the case involves a potential grandparent, that person has to pay extra money to purchase eggs from a donor. Even though the woman is referred to as a donor, she definitely does not give away her oocytes. In fact, an Ivy League-educated woman can ask a premium for her oocytes.[49] The potential grandparent will also have to pay about $20,000 to have the donor tested and treated. The costs do not stop there because the potential grandparent needs someone to gestate the donor eggs. Surrogacy is illegal, against public policy or inaccessible in most United States jurisdictions.[50] Therefore, it can cost as much as $80,000 to retain the services of a surrogate.[51]

Persons seeking posthumous reproduction are making life-changing decisions while they are grieving the loss of their love ones. They may have to temporarily postpone the grieving process while they try to navigate the court system and the health care system. As a result, for the person, it is an emotionally trying time. The person may suffer from survivor's guilt and regret. If the person later decides not to use the sperm, he or she has to make the difficult decision to have the sperm destroyed. That act may make them feel like they are losing their loved ones all over again. There is no guarantee that posthumous reproduction will result in a child. Sperm is often damaged during the retrieval, freezing and thawing processes. Thus, the woman may not have enough high quality sperm to conceive a child. The disappointment of not being able to conceive may further compound the woman's grief.

Conclusion

Posthumous reproduction is a controversial process. On the one hand, the existence of technology that permits a person to become a parent after death may give comfort to persons who are grieving the loss of their loved ones. This is especially true when the situation involves the death of a child. However, posthumous reproduction may be perceived as scientists crossing the line from assisting infertile persons to become parents to upsetting the natural balance. This perception is bolstered by cases like the one involving a sixty-year-old woman who wants to use her dead daughter's frozen eggs to give birth to her own grandchild. In 2011, the woman's twenty-eight-year-old daughter died of cancer. No fertility clinic in London will perform the procedure, so the woman asked the Human Fertilisation and Embryology Authority (HFEA) for permission to transfer the eggs to a clinic in New York. The HFEA denied the request because the daughter did not give her full written consent to the posthumous reproduction prior to her death. The woman successfully appealed the HFEA's decision to the High Court, so the case is still pending.[52] Some members of the public may be comfortable with the use of a dead man's frozen sperm as long as he gives some type of consent before he dies. For many people, the most troubling cases of posthumous reproduction involve the extraction of fresh sperm from dead men or men in vegetative states.[53]

Notes

1 Chris Weller, Sperm Retrieval After Death: What Are The Ethical Concerns? at www.medicaldaily.com/sperm-retrieval-after-death-what-are-ethical-concerns-246798 (June 13, 2013).
2 Question asked by Alexander M. Caron, professor of law and medicine and co-director of the Pacific Center for Health Policy and Ethics at the University of Southern California.
3 Beauchamp and Childress, Principles of Biomedical Ethics (Oxford University Press, 5th ed. 2001).
4 *Id.*
5 "I swear by Apollo Physician and Asciepius and Hygiea and Panaceia and all the gods and goddesses, making them my witnesses, that I will fulfil according to my ability and judgment this oath and this covenant: To hold him who has taught me this art as equal to my parents and to live my life in partnership with him, and if he is in need of money to give him a share of mine, and to regard his offspring as equal to my brothers in male lineage and to teach them this art–if they desire to learn it–without fee and covenant; to give a share of precepts and oral instruction and all the other learning to my sons and to the sons of him who has instructed me and to pupils who have signed the covenant and have taken an oath according to the medical law, but no one else." www.medicinenet.com (last accessed April 18, 2016). This is just one version of the oath. Most medical school graduates recite some version of the oath. All doctors are bound by the American Medical Association's Code of Medical Ethics: www.ama-assn.org (last accessed April 18, 2016).
6 Nancy J. Moore, Intent and Consent in the Tort of Battery: Confusion and Controversy, 61 Am. L. Rev. 1585, 1619–1620 (August 2012).
7 The informed consent doctrine obligates doctors to inform their patients about the risks, benefits and alternatives to planned procedures. Marc D. Ginsberg, Informed Consent: No Longer Just What the Doctor Ordered?: The "Contributions" of Medical Associations and Courts to A More Patient Friendly Doctrine, 15 Mich. St. U.J. Med. & L. 17, 20 (Winter 2010).
8 Mary Crossley, Becoming Visible: The ADA's Impact On Health Care For Persons With Disabilities, 52 Ala. L. Rev. 51 (Fall 2000).
9 Jo-Anne Herina Jeffreys, Advance Directives: Are They Worth The Paper They're Written On?, 190-APR N.J. Law 17, 18 (April 1998).
10 Kelly C. Mulholland, Protecting the Right to Die: The Patient Self-Determination Act of 1990, 28 Harv. J. on Legis. 609, 611 (Summer 1991).
11 Linda Choe, What, In the Name of Conception? A Comparative Analysis of the Inheritance Rights of Posthumously Conceived Children in the United States and the United Kingdom, 25 Syracuse Sci. & Tech. L. Rep. 53, 69–70 (Fall 2011).
12 Choe, supra note 11 at 72.
13 Alan Meisel, Barriers to Forgoing Nutrition and Hydration in Nursing Homes, 21 Am. J.L. & Med. 335, 353–354 (1995).
14 Shelly Sarig and Nili Tabak, An Unusual Petition For Posthumous Sperm Retrieval? What Does It Add to the Debate?, 27 Med. & L. 463, 467 (June 2008).
15 Richard F. Storrow, Parenthood By Pure Intention: Assisted Reproduction and the Functional Approach to Parentage, 53 Hasting L.J. 597, 607 (March 2002).
16 Daryl L. Gordon-Ceresky, Artificial Insemination: Its Effect On Paternity and Inheritance Rights, 9 Conn. Prob. L.J. 245, 256–257 (1995).
17 See Md. Code, Estates & Trusts § 1–206(b) ("**Child conceived by artificial insemination of married woman** (b) A child conceived by artificial insemination of a married woman with the consent of her husband is the legitimate child of

both of them for all purposes. Consent of the husband is *presumed*." *Id.* (emphasis added).

18 See *In re Baby Doe*, 353 S.E. 2d 877, 879 (S.C. 1987) ("Husband's consent to his wife's impregnation by artificial insemination may be expressed, or it may be implied from conduct which evidences knowledge of the procedure and failure to object.") *Id.*

19 Darren Boyle, Woman blames press innuendo as legal bid to harvest vegetative partner's sperm is dropped, www.pressgazette.co.uk (January 22, 2014).

20 Ludwig Edelsten, *The Hippocratic Oath: Text, Translation and Interpretation* (Baltimore: The Johns Hopkins Press, 1963).

21 Erin T. Alati, When a Spoonful of Sugar Doesn't Help the Medicine Go Down: Informed Consent, Mental Illness and Moral Agency, 6 Ind. Health L. Rev. 171, 195–199 (2009).

22 If the probate court is not able to locate any close relatives, the person's estate may go to distant relatives who are referred to as laughing heirs because they are so emotionally removed from the person that they may laugh at his or her demise. David V. DeRosa, Intestate Succession and the Laughing Heir: Who Do We Want To Get The Last Laugh?, 12 Quinnipac Prob. L.J. 153, 158 (1997). If no heirs are available, the person's estate will escheat to the state. See, e.g., A.R.S. § 12–881 (West 2016).

23 Marjorie Conner Makar, Domestic Violence: Why the Florida Legislature Must Do More To Protect the "Silent" Victims, 72-NOV Fla. B.J. 10, 17 (Nov. 1998).

24 Alati, supra note 52 at 199.

25 For a thorough analysis of posthumous harm, see James Stacey Taylor, *Death, Posthumous Harm, and Bioethics* (New York: Routledge, 2012).

26 Joel Feinberg, "Harm and Self-Interest" in *Law, Morality and Society: Essays in Honor of H.L.A. Hart*, ed. P.M.S. Hacker and J. Raz (Oxford: Clarendon Press, 1977), pp. 284–308.

27 Jessica Berg, Grave Secrets: Legal and Ethical Analysis of Postmortem Confidentiality, 34 Conn. L. Rev. 81, 90 (Fall, 2001).

28 Alexis Gregonian, Post-Mortem Pregnancy: A Proposed Methodology For the Resolution of Conflicts Over Whether A Brian Dead Pregnant Woman Should Be Maintained On Life-Sustaining Treatment, 19 Annals Health L. 401, 404–405 (Winter 2010).

29 Hilary Young, The Right to Posthumous Bodily Integrity and Implications of Whose Right It Is, 14 Marq. Elder's Advisor 197, 221–224 (Spring 2013).

30 Ernest Partridge, Posthumous Interests and Posthumous Respect, Ethics 91 (1981):243–64.

31 Some argue that there is a difference between persons and dead bodies. Since dead bodies are objects, they do not retain rights. Philippe Ducor, The Legal Status of Human Materials, 44 Drake L. Rev. 195, 212 (1996).

32 Barbara Baum Levenbook, Harming Someone after His Death, Ethics 94 No.3 (1984): 407–419.

33 *Hughes v New England Newspaper Publishing Company*, 43 N.E. 657, 658–659 (Mass. 1942) ("The general rule is that a libel upon the memory of a deceased person that does not directly cast any personal reflection upon his relatives does not give them any right of action, although they may have thereby suffered mental anguish or sustained an impairment of their social standing among a considerable class of respectable people of the community in which they live by the disclosure that they were related to the deceased." *Id.*

34 *Obstetrical and Gynecological Associates, P.A. v Hardin*, 2013 WL 6047595 (Ct. of App. TX. Houston (1st Dist.).

35 Chris Pleasance, Mother in court accused of stealing her ex-boyfriend's frozen sperm before using it to get pregnant to spite him for breaking up at www.daily mail.co.uk (August 11, 2015).

36 Niccol Kording, Nature v Nurture: Children Left Fatherless and Family-Less When Nature Prevails In Paternity Actions, 65 U. Pitt. L. Rev. 811, 845–846 (Summer 2004).
37 Clifton B. Kruse, Jr., My Basement Is Filled With Pornography! But You Don't Have A Basement, 73-NOV. Fla. B.J. 82, 83 (November 1999).
38 Alexander, Larry and Moore, Michael, "Deontological Ethics" in *The Stanford Encyclopedia of Philosophy* (Spring 2015 Edition), Edward N. Zalta (ed.) at http://plato.stanford.edu/archives/spr2015/entries/ethics-deontological/ (last accessed February 22, 2016).
39 Ethics Committee of the American Society for Reproductive Medicine, Posthumous collection and use of reproductive tissue: a committee opinion, 99 Fertility and Sterility 1842, 1844 (June 2013).
40 The public was outraged when Kenneth Douglas, a morgue attendant in Ohio, admitted to having sex with up to 100 corpses. His crime was discovered when his semen was found in a murder victim. Loulla-Mae Eleftheriou-Smith, Morgue worker admits to having sex with up to 100 dead women at www.independent.co.uk (August 18, 2014).
41 See, e.g., 13 M.R.S.A. § 1032 (West 2016).
42 See *Delio v Westchester County Medical Center*, 129 A.D. 2d 1, 13–14 (1987).
43 Anne Marie Tasse, The Return of Results of Deceased Research Participants, 39 J.L. Med. & Ethics 621, 627–628 (Winter 2011).
44 Lisa Hird Chung, Free Trade in Human Reproductive Cells: A Solution to Procreative Tourism and the Unregulated Internet, 15 Minn. J. Int'l L. 263, 269 (Winter 2006).
45 Charles Kindregan, Jr., Dead Dads: Thawing An Heir From The Freezer, 35 Wm. Mitchell L. Rev. 433, 443 (2009).
46 Nancy D. Polikoff, For the Sake of All Children: Opponents and Supporters of Same-Sex Marriages Both Miss the Mark, 8 N.Y. City L. Rev. 573, 586 (Fall 2005).
47 *Id.*
48 The Costs of Infertility Treatment at www.resolve.org/family-building-options (last accessed February 22, 2016).
49 Valarie K. Blake, Ovaries, Testicles, and Uteruses, Oh My!: Regulating Reproductive Tissue Transplants, 19 Wm. & Mary J. Women & L. 353, 387 (Winter 2013); Chung, supra note 75 at 279.
50 Sarah Mortozavi, It Takes A Village To Make A Child: Creating Guidelines For International Surrogacy, 100 Geo. L.J. 2249, 2258–2262 (August 2012).
51 Usha Rengachary Smerdon, Crossing Bodies, Crossing Borders: International Surrogacy Between the United States and India, 39 Cumb. L. Rev. 15, 32 (2008–2009).
52 Woman allowed to challenge dead daughter's egg use ruling at www.bbc.co.uk/news/health (February 24, 2016).
53 Sara Barton, Katharine F. Correia, Shirley Shalev, Stacey A. Missmer, Lisa Soleymani Lehmannn, Divya K. Shah, and Elizabeth S. Ginburg, Population-based study of attitudes toward posthumous reproduction, 98 Mental Health, Sexuality, and Ethics 735–740 (September 2012).

2 Legal regulations

Unlike other parts of the health care system, the assisted reproductive technology industry is not heavily regulated. Thus, it is not surprising that very few countries have specifically regulated the availability and use of posthumous reproduction. The regulations in place vary from complete proscription to liberal rules. When there is no applicable legislation in place, the issue may be governed by professional guidelines, self-regulation, or jurisprudence. This chapter analyzes those legal regulations.

Current regulations

Postmortem sperm retrieval and posthumous reproduction is statutorily prohibited in Germany, Sweden, and the Australian states of Victoria and Western Australia.[1] For example, a provision of Victoria's Infertility Treatment Act of 1995 makes it a criminal offense to use the gametes or embryos of dead people.[2] Hungarian law also does not permit the use of the gametes of dead persons for posthumous reproduction.[3] In France, after the *Parpalaix* case which will be discussed in Chapter 3, the Centre d'Etude et de Conservation du Sperme Humain (CECOS) enacted a policy prohibiting posthumous reproduction. The French courts upheld the policy and it was later codified.[4] The procedure is conditionally legal in the United Kingdom. In order for posthumous reproduction to take place in the United Kingdom, the gamete donor must give written consent.[5] Likewise, legal regulations enacted by the Canadian government ban posthumous reproduction without the written informed consent of the sperm donor.[6] Posthumous reproduction has conditional acceptance in the Netherlands and Greece as long as written consent is acquired before the sperm donor dies.[7]

Israel does not have any laws regulating posthumous reproduction. In 2003, the Israeli Attorney General's Office did publish guidelines for posthumous reproduction; however, those guidelines are not legally binding.[8] Persons can conceive using posthumous reproduction in Israel as long as they follow those guidelines. Under the guidelines, consent on the part of the dead man is presumed and next-of-kin consent is only permitted if it comes from the dead man's wife. The fact that procreation is so important in Israel may account for the country's opt-out system. The guidelines are applicable to cases involving men who die suddenly, but, the sperm of men who die as a result of a communicable disease or a disease known to adversely affect sperm cannot be used. The dead man's sperm must be harvested within 24 hours of his death and local sperm cryobanks must be available to accept the retrieved sperm. The guidelines recommend that the sperm be quarantined for one year to allow the wife to receive counseling and to allow doctors to screen the sperm for communicable diseases. The legal regulation of posthumous reproduction is evolving in countries like New Zealand.[9] Most other countries do not have any laws in place to regulate posthumous reproduction.

Few states in America have laws regulating the use of assisted reproductive technology. The laws that are in place deal with artificial insemination. None of the states have laws governing posthumous reproduction. In situations where the legislatures fail to act, the courts usually step in and create case law to help parties resolve their disputes. However, judicial involvement in posthumous reproduction has been limited to issuing orders for postmortem sperm retrieval, resolving disputes over embryos and addressing issues pertaining to posthumously conceived children. Because there is very little legal guidance in this area fertility clinics have to make tough decisions. To avoid liability, in most cases fertility clinics will only act in accordance with a court order. The following case is illustrative. While he was watching television, auto mechanic Johnny Quintana lost consciousness. Unfortunately Quintana could not be revived and he died at the age of thirty-one. Gisela Marrero, Quintana's long-time girlfriend, wanted sperm extracted from his dead body, so that she could conceive a child. The Jacobi Medical Center kept Quintana's body in cold storage and placed an ice bag on his testicles. Nonetheless, the Center refused to take any further action until Gisela was able to successfully obtain a court order. Gisela had to prove to the court that, based upon her relationship with Quintana, he would have wanted her to have his sperm.[10] There is no legal test or criteria a party has to satisfy in order to get a court's permission to have postmortem retrieval done. The courts handle the situations on a case-by-case basis. Most of the relevant law in this area comes from the courts' treatment of frozen embryos.

Guidance from the legal treatment of embryos and pre-embryos

Courts have used several different theories to resolve disputes over embryos and pre-embryos.[11] Most of those cases have involved disputes between the contributor of the sperm and the contributor of the eggs used to create the embryo. The disagreement usually occurs when the couple ends their relationship. In a typical case, one of the parties wants to use the embryo and the other one wants the fertility clinic to donate or destroy the embryo. None of the reported cases involves the death of one or both of the progenitors. Nonetheless, as the cases illustrate, embryos created while a couple is alive may be frozen for later use by them, but could be used to conceive a child after either the female or male partner or both have died. Therefore, analyzing the manner in which courts have decided these cases may assist in predicting the possible outcome of a case involving posthumous reproduction. The three main approaches courts have taken to determine who has the legal right to control the embryo are the following: (1) contractual, (2) contemporaneous mutual consent, and (3) balancing/equitable approach. Some courts have combined approach three with one of the first two listed approaches. No matter which approach a court adopted, it did not give one person the right to implant the embryos if an agreement existed mandating that both gamete donors had to consent to the use of the embryos. In attempting to resolve a dispute between a couple and a fertility clinic, one court used a property approach.[12] The property law approach never gained any traction.[13]

Contractual approach

Under the contractual approach, courts will enforce agreements governing the use of embryos that the parties enter into unless the terms of those contracts violate public policy. The contracts may be between the parties or between the parties and the fertility clinics. With regards to the disposition of embryos, the contract between the parties, even if it's oral, may supersede the provisions of the informed consent form the parties sign.[14] At least one court has explicitly rejected the contractual approach on the basis of public policy.[15] However, courts in five states[16] have endorsed the contract method.

A New York married couple decided to conceive using IVF after the wife could not get pregnant because she had been exposed to diethylstilbestrol.[17] Prior to the creation of their embryo, the couple signed a consent form stating that their frozen embryos could not be released for any purpose without their written mutual consent.[18] In addition, the couple signed a form agreeing that, if they decided not to use their embryos, the clinic could donate them to the IVF Program to determine if they were appropriate for research.[19] After the wife filed for divorce, she asked the court to award her sole custody of the embryos so she could use them to conceive a child. In response, the husband objected to the wife's request and sought to have the embryos disposed of in accordance with the consent agreements.[20] Ultimately, the New York Appellate Court ruled in favor of the husband. The judge writing for the Court stated: "[a]greements between progenitors, or gamete donors, regarding disposition of their pre-zygotes should generally be presumed valid and binding, and enforced in any dispute between them."[21] Thus, the Court ruled that, in accordance with the contracts signed by the couple, the embryos should be donated to the IVF program for research.[22]

Because the wife's malfunctioning fallopian tubes prevented her from conceiving a child, a New Jersey couple used IVF to create embryos.[23] Prior to undergoing the process, the couple did not sign a written contract indicating what they wanted to happen to any embryos they failed to use.[24] Unfortunately, the husband filed for a divorce before the embryos were used. The wife initially asked the Court for control of the embryos so that she could have them implanted into her own uterus, so she could get pregnant. Opposing his former wife's request, the husband requested that the Court order the clinic to store the embryos stored until he determined if he wanted to become a parent.[25] Since there was no contract involved in the case, the Tennessee Supreme Court decided the case by balancing the interests of the parties.[26] Nonetheless, the Court noted that it would have enforced any contract controlling the disposition of the embryos.[27]

A case in Oregon arose after a husband and wife tried to have a child using IVF.[28] The couple signed an agreement stating that the wife had the exclusive authority to determine the fate of the embryos.[29] Before the embryos could be transferred into the wife, the couple decided to divorce. They could not come to an agreement with regards to the unused embryos.[30] The Oregon Appellate Court concluded that the contract the couple executed made it clear that they intended for the wife to have the power to decide the manner in which the embryos were disposed.[31] In support of its decision, the Court reasoned: "Moreover, giving effect to a valid agreement evincing the parties' intent regarding disposition of embryos is consistent with our statutory and case law that give similar effect to prenuptial agreements and agreements made during a marriage."[32]

The contractual theory was also adopted by a Texas court in a case involving a dispute between a husband and a wife. Facts in that case showed that the couple decided to undergo IVF after they failed to conceive a child naturally and tried unsuccessfully several times to have a child using artificial insemination.[33] The informed consent form they signed contained a provision indicating that, if they divorced prior to transfer, the embryos should be discarded.[34] The Texas Appellate Court overturned the lower court decision awarding the embryos to the wife.[35] Instead, the Court relied on the terms of the consent form and ordered the clinic to throw out the embryos.[36]

A married couple wanted to conceive a child using IVF, so they had five embryos made from the man's sperm and donor eggs.[37] The implantation of three of the embryos into a surrogate resulted in the conception of a child. The remaining two embryos were stored at the clinic.[38] The written agreement between the couple and the clinic contained a provision requiring the couple to obtain instructions from a court if they could not agree on the disposition of the embryos.[39] In addition, in the contract, the couple agreed to have the embryos thawed and not implanted after they had been in storage for five years.[40] During the couple's divorce proceedings, they disagreed about what to do with the embryos. Contrary to the terms of the contract, the wife sought to have the embryos implanted into a surrogate. The husband wanted to put the embryos up for adoption.[41] The Court strictly enforced the contract and ruled that, since more than five years had passed, the embryos could not undergo further development.[42]

Contemporaneous mutual consent approach

Another theory a court may use to resolve embryos dispute is contemporaneous mutual consent. Courts utilizing this scheme determine the disposition of the embryo by relying on the contemporaneous mutual assent of the parties.[43] The contemporaneous mutual consent theory allows for flexibility and the possibility that the intentions of one or both parties might change. Therefore, under this approach, the terms of the contract the parties sign prior to the creation of the embryos do not control the disposition of the sperm if the parties agree on an alternate disposition. If either progenitor wants a different disposition than the one stated in the original contract, the court would give the person's current wishes preference over the ones expressed in the contract. However, if the other party does not agree with the new proposed disposition, the court would order the clinic to preserve the status quo by keeping the embryos in storage.[44]

Persons advocating for the use of this theory emphasize that it permits the parties to change their minds after they have signed the initial consent agreement. This theory can be categorized as a mutual modification of the contract. Courts implementing this approach may permit the parties' intention at the time of the disposition of the embryo to supersede the desire they expressed in the contract they signed prior to the creation of the embryos if both parties agree. If there is no agreement, the embryos would remain frozen until the parties reached a mutual understanding.

The only state that has explicitly implemented the contemporaneous mutual consent theory is Iowa. After the wife was unable to conceive a child naturally, an Iowa couple underwent IVF.[45] As a part of that process, the couple signed an informed consent form agreeing that the embryos could not be used or discarded without the signed approval of both parties.[46] Later, while the couple was in the process of obtaining a divorce, the wife requested custody of the embryos in order to have them implanted in her or a surrogate. The husband objected to the wife's request and asked the court to issue a permanent injunction requiring the clinic to abide by the terms of the contract.[47] The Iowa Supreme Court refused to strictly enforce the contract. The Court held that, even though the contract was enforceable and legally binding on the parties, it was "subject to the right of either party to change his or her mind about disposition up to the point of use or destruction of any stored embryo."[48] Relying on the contemporaneous mutual consent theory, the Court ruled that the embryos could not be used or discarded until the couple reached a settlement.[49]

Balancing approach

The balancing approach allows the court to consider the interests of the parties if there is no contract or if the contract is deemed unenforceable. Three states have adopted this method of solving embryo disputes.[50] As discussed earlier, the Court hearing the *Davis* case was inclined to enforce the contract. However, since the couple did not have a validly signed contract, the Court resolved the case by relying on the balancing test. As a part of the test, the Court considered the parties' relevant positions, the importance of their interests and the impact the Court's ruling would have on them. The primary interests the Court focused on were the wife's right to procreate and the husband's right to avoid procreation.[51] The Court decided that the husband's right to avoid procreation outweighed the wife's interest in giving the embryos to an infertile couple.[52] For the Court, it was a matter of equity. If the Court refused to permit the wife to donate the embryos, she would not be severely disadvantaged. On the other hand, if the Court granted the wife's request, the husband would be forced to become a parent without his consent. The Court was troubled by the emotional toll that might have taken on the man. The judge stated: "he would face a lifetime of either wondering about his parental status or knowing about his parental status but having no control over it."[53]

The New Jersey Supreme Court also adopted the balancing approach in a case involving a dispute over embryos. After the wife learned that she was unable to have a child, the couple decided to try IVF.[54] The consent form the couple signed contained a provision stating that, if the couple divorced, their legal ownership over the embryos would be extinguished and the embryos would belong to the IVF program unless a court ordered a different disposition.[55] During the couple's divorce action, the trial court gave the wife the right to discard the remaining embryos.[56] The husband appealed that decision because he claimed that the trial court should have enforced the contract between him and his former wife and had the embryos donated to infertile couples in the event he and his wife decided not to use them.[57] Eventually, the case made it to the New Jersey Supreme Court. That Court decided that the parties had not reached a definitive agreement pertaining to the disposition of the sperm because the signed consent form permitted the couple to obtain a court order governing the disposition of the embryos if they sought a divorce.[58] The lack of an applicable agreement prompted the Court to balance the interests of the parties. The Court concluded that the man would not lose his right to procreate if the Court did not allow him to use or donate the embryos because he already had children and had the ability to conceive more children naturally or with the assistance of IVF. On the other hand, the wife might lose her right to not procreate if the embryos containing her genetic material were used or donated.[59] The Court determined that it would be unethical to force the wife to become a genetic parent against her will.[60] Consequently, the Court refused to order the clinic to give the embryos to the husband so he could use or donate them.

A Superior Court in Pennsylvania also used a balancing approach to resolve a dispute.[61] That case contained facts similar to the above-discussed cases. Doctors diagnosed a woman with breast cancer and recommended appropriate treatment. Because the wife's treatment threatened her fertility she and her husband underwent IVF.[62] After the husband filed for divorce, the wife tried to get the embryos so that she could use them to conceive a child.[63] The Court did not apply the contractual theory because the couple had not signed the part of the consent form that dealt with the disposition of the embryos in the event that they got a divorce. Moreover, the Court found the contemporaneous mutual agreement approach to be unworkable due to the animosity between the parties.[64] In light of the facts of the case, the Court decided that the most appropriate approach was to balance the interests of the parties. The Court weighed the test in favor of the wife because she probably could not conceive a child without using the embryos.[65]

Conclusion

Posthumous reproduction is a process that occurs all over the world. By making numerous presentations on the topic, I have learned that everyone has an opinion about the practice. Even persons who have used assisted reproductive technology to conceive are wary about the use and availability of posthumous reproduction. Supporters of the use of posthumous reproduction agree that it should be regulated. Currently, fertility clinics are forced to handle demands for fresh sperm on a case-by-case basis. The law is slowly trying to catch up with the science that permits people to reproduce after their deaths.

Notes

1 Webb, S.M., Raising sperm from the dead, 17 J. Androl. 325–326 (1996).

2 §43 Infertility Treatment Act of 1995 ("A person must not: Inseminate a woman with sperm from a man known to be dead; or transfer to a woman a gamete from a person known to be dead. Transfer to a woman a zygote or embryo formed from a gamete from a person known to be dead; or Form a zygote with sperm from a man known to be dead; or Form a zygote, if the woman who produced the oocyte used to form the zygote is known to be dead. *Penalty*: 240 penalty units two years' imprisonment or both.")

3 Law No. 154, 1997, § 166, article No. 3; Dostal, J., Utrata, R., Loyka, S., Brezinova, J., Svobodova, M. and Shenfield, F., Post-mortem Sperm Retrieval in new European Union countries: Case report, 20 Human Reproduction 2359–2361 (2005).

4 Aziza-Shuster E., A child at all costs: Posthumous reproduction and the meaning of Parenthood, 9 Hum. Reprod. 2182–2185 (1994); see also Nicole Zwart-Hendrix, Chilling Aspects of Procreation, 21 Med. & L. 567, 569 (2002) (citing Art. L. 152–2 of the Code de La Sante Publique).

5 Human Fertilization and Embryology Act 2008 §39, Schedule 3 (the consent provisions). See also *The Queen (on the application of IM, MM) v Human Fertilisation and Embryology Authority*, 2015 WL 3630368 (June 15, 2015).

6 Assisted Human Reproduction (Section 8 Consent) Regulations SOR/2007–137; Webb, supra note 1 at 408.

7 Usha Ahluwalia and Maia Arora, Posthumous Reproduction and Its Legal Perspective, 2 International Journal of Fertility and Fetal Medicine, 9, 12 (January 2011) (citing Art. 7 Embryos Bill); Mavroforou, A., Koumantakis, E., Mavrophoros, D. and Michalodimitrakis, E., Medically assisted human reproduction: the Greek view, 26 Med. Law 339, 341 (2007) (citing Medically Assisted Human Reproduction Act 3089/02 which states: "Artificial insemination carried out after the death of the husband or the woman's partner, is allowed only by judicial permission and only under the following circumstances: a. The husband or the permanent partner of the woman suffers from a disease, which endangers his life or fertility b. The husband or the woman's partner has already given his consent before a notary for posthumous artificial insemination.").

8 Raziel, Arieh, Friedler, Shevach, Stassburger, Deborah, Kaufman, Sarit, Umansky, Ana, and Ron-El, Raphel, *Nationwide use of postmortem retrieved sperm in Israel: a follow-up report*, 95 Fertility and Sterility 2693, 2694 (June 30, 2011).

9 See Nicola Peart, Life Beyond Death: Regulating Posthumous Reproduction in New Zealand, 46 Vict. U. Wellington L. Rev. 725 (October, 2015).

10 See Dorian Block, Dead Man Johnny Quintana's Sperm Can't Impregnate Girlfriend, N.Y. Daily News (April 30, 2009) at www.nydailynews.com.

11 For consistency, I will use embryos to refer to cases involving either embryos or pre-embryos. Courts have discussed the difference between embryos and

pre-embryos and concluded that the distinctions are not legally relevant to the dispute. See *Davis v Davis*, 842 S.W. 2d 588, 593–594 (Tenn. 1992); John Robertson provides a brief discussion of the biologic difference between embryos and pre-embryos in In the Beginning: The Legal Status of Early Embryos, 76 Va. L. Rev. 437 (1990).

12 *York v Jones*, 717 F.Supp. 421, 425 (E.D. Va. 1989) (court treated the embryos as the couple's personal property and held that the cryopreservation agreement they signed was a bailment contract between them and the fertility clinic).

13 The property law approach will be discussed in detail in Chapter Four.

14 *Szafranski v Dunston*, 34 N.E.3d 1132 (2015).

15 See *A.Z. v B.Z.*, 725 N.E.2d 1051, 1057–1058 (Mass. 2000) (stating: "As a matter of public policy, we conclude that forced procreation is not an area amenable to judicial enforcement. It is well-established that courts will not enforce contracts that violate public policy.") *Id.*

16 Those states are New York, Oregon, Tennessee, Texas and Washington.

17 *Kass v Kass*, 696 N.E.2d 174, 176 (1998).

18 *Id.*

19 *Id.* at 176–177.

20 *Id.* at 177.

21 *Id.* at 180.

22 *Id.* at 181.

23 *Davis v Davis*, 842 S.W.2d 588, 591 (Tenn. 1992).

24 *Id.* at 589–590.

25 *Id.* at 589.

26 The Court stated: "In summary, we hold that disputes involving the disposition of preembryos produced by in vitro fertilization should be resolved, first, by looking to the preferences of the progenitors. If their wishes cannot be ascertained, or if there is dispute, then their prior agreement concerning disposition should be carried out. If no prior agreement exists, then the relative interests of the parties in using or not using the preembryos must be weighed." *Id.* at 604.

27 *Id.* at 597.

28 *In re Marriage of Dahl*, 194 P.3d 834 (Or. 2000).

29 *Id.* at 836.

30 *In re Marriage of Dahl*, 194 P.3d at 836.

31 *Id.* at 841.

32 *Id.* at 840.

33 *Roman v Roman*, 193 S.W.3d 40, 42 (2006).

34 *Id.*

35 *Id.* at 43.

36 *Roman*, 193 S.W. 3d at 54.

37 *In re Marriage of Litowitz*, 48 P.3d 261, 262 (2002), amended by 53 P.3d 516 (Wash. 2002).

38 *Id.* at 262–263.

39 *Id.* at 263.

40 *Id.* at 264.

41 *Id.*

42 *Id.* at 271.

43 *In re Marriage of Witten*, 672 N.W.2d 768 (Iowa 2003).

44 *Id.* at 778.

45 *Id.* at 772.

46 *Id.*

47 *Id.* at 772–773.

48 *Id.* at 782 (quoting *J.B. v. M.B.*, 783 A.2d 707, 719 (2001).

49 *Id.* at 783.

50 Those states are New Jersey, Pennsylvania and Tennessee.
51 *Davis*, 842 S.W. 2d at 598, 603.
52 *Id.* at 604.
53 *Davis*, 842 S.W. 2d at 604.
54 *J.B. v M.B.*, 783 A.2d 707, 709 (2000).
55 *Id.* at 713.
56 *Id.* at 710–711.
57 *Id.*
58 *Id.* at 713.
59 *J.B.*, 783 A. 2d at 717.
60 *Id.*
61 *Reber v Reiss*, 42 A.3d 1131 (Pa. Super. Ct. 2012).
62 *Id.* at 1132–1133.
63 *Id.* at 1133.
64 *Id.* at 1136.
65 *Id.* at 1142.

Part II

The sperm

Part II

The sperm

3 Frozen sperm (thaw it out or throw it out?)

The government has done very little to regulate the use of assisted reproductive technology (ART). Consequently, when health care providers are faced with ethical issues arising from the use of ART, they have no bright line rules to follow. Doctors are left struggling to make decisions on a case-by-case basis. The title of this section specifically mentions sperm because most posthumous reproduction cases involve the use of the frozen sperm of a man who is dead or in a vegetative state. However, in 2012, the American Society for Reproductive Medicine (ASRM) stated that human oocyte cryopreservation (the freezing of eggs) should no longer be considered to be experimental.[1] In addition, ASRM concluded that the procedure is relatively safe. The organization based its conclusion on the fact that studies have shown that children conceived using frozen oocytes do not have any more birth defects, developmental disorders or chromosomal abnormalities than children conceived through IVF using fresh eggs.[2]

As a result, fertility companies and some hospitals have started campaigns to encourage young women to have their oocytes frozen for later use. In some cases, those facilities are sponsoring "egg-freezing" parties.[3] This opens up the possibility that, if a woman dies after freezing her eggs, her husband or parents could seek to use those eggs to have a child conceived. In fact, in 2011, an Israeli court made history when it decided that the eggs of a dead female could be harvested and donated. The family of the seventeen-year-old accident victim planned to donate the eggs to the girl's infertile aunt.[4] Therefore, the principles and proposals discussed in this book are applicable to both women and men.

Men may choose to have their sperm frozen for several reasons. Traditionally, prior to going to fight for their countries, men had their sperm stored in hopes that they could use it to become fathers when they returned from combat.[5] That tradition has continued. Some soldiers who were deployed to Iraq and Afghanistan banked their sperm as an insurance policy.[6] Military men who are married or in long-term relationships may have their sperm frozen in compliance with requests from their partners. If a man is killed in combat, his spouse or significant other may be able to use the sperm to conceive his child.[7] Single military men and military men who are not in committed relationships may choose to bank their sperm because they are afraid that they may become sterile as a result of exposure to toxins and other environmental hazards.[8] California-based Cryobank is one of the fertility clinics that offers discounts to military men who want to have their sperm frozen and stored.[9] Men in dangerous professions, including police officers and firefighters, may decide to freeze their sperm in order to ensure that their bloodlines will continue if they are killed in the line of duty. Cryobank announced that it was expanding its discount program to include firemen, policemen, paramedics, and emergency medical technicians.[10]

Diseases and aging may cause a man to think about his mortality. Thinking about mortality may lead to a desire to procreate.[11] Therefore, a man who is diagnosed with a potentially terminal disease like cancer may decide to have his sperm stored prior to undergoing chemotherapy and/or radiation in case the medical treatment makes him infertile.[12] Medications used to treat chronic conditions like hypertension also pose a risk to a man's fertility. Hence, men suffering from those conditions may have some of their sperm banked at the start of the treatment.[13] Moreover, women are not the only ones with a biological clock. According to recent medical research, the potency of a man's sperm may decline as he ages. The man may also suffer from erectile dysfunction. Studies indicate that advanced paternal age increases the chances of disorders in the resulting offspring.[14] To keep the possibility of fatherhood open, a man may decide to store some of his sperm when he is young. Posthumous conception may also occur in cases where a man freezes some of his sperm because he and his wife are going through an assisted reproductive treatment like IVF. The man may die before his frozen sperm has been used to fertilize his wife's eggs.

Life happens and there is not always a happy ending. If a man dies before he can use his frozen sperm, the fertility clinic must decide what action to take with regards to the sperm. The man's spouse, significant other, parents or other next-of-kin may attempt to exercise decision-making authority over the sperm. That person may want the clinic to release the sperm so he or she can use it to conceive a child, donate it to an infertile couple, or discard it. The clinic faces a difficult decision. That decision is made easier if the man leaves instructions. Those instructions usually take the form of an agreement between the man and the fertility clinic. Nonetheless, any legal document that indicates the man's wishes is probably sufficient. In the event the man perishes without stating his preference with regards to his sperm, the wise clinic staff awaits instructions from its bioethics board or the court. In rare cases, a not so wise clinic staff may be influenced by emotion and release the sperm to the requesting party.

Acknowledging the wishes of the dead

The body has been buried, cremated or frozen. The only tangible part left of the deceased man is his frozen sperm. His spouse or significant other knows that the clinic has the sperm. He or she may have accompanied the man to the clinic when he made the deposit; he or she may have a relationship with the people at the clinic. In the midst of his or her grief, the person probably finds solace in the fact that he or she will be able to have a child for the man he or she loved and lost. The next step is for the person to have the fertility clinic thaw out the sperm, so he or she can use it to conceive. In response to the person's request, the fertility clinic searches its files and discovers the contract or consent form that the man signed. The agreement probably contains a provision detailing the instructions the man left pertaining to the use of his sperm if he died before it was used to fertilize an egg. The clinic staff has to decide whether or not to acknowledge the man's wishes in light of pressure from the dead man's spouse or significant other to take a different course of action. The man may want the sperm used so that he can become a father posthumously or he may want the sperm to be discarded. This chapter will discuss a case where a man did not want his sperm used to conceive a child after his death and one where the man strongly desired to become a father following his death.

Ethical considerations

From an ethical perspective, the clinic has a responsibility to comply with the dead man's request. At the time the man and the clinic entered into the agreement, the man was the doctor's patient. Thus, the doctor had an obligation to act in accordance with the man's dictates. It is unethical for a doctor to ignore that duty because the man is dead and unable to take actions to ensure that the clinic abides by the arrangements he made for the disposition of his sperm. During a man's lifetime, he has decision-making authority over his sperm and other body parts. That authority should not end just because he dies. On the other hand, it may be considered unethical to permit the dead man to control the actions of the living. If the man had his sperm frozen because he and his spouse were undergoing IVF, it is unethical to permit the wishes of the dead man to supersede the needs of the living.

If implementing the directions the dead man leaves with regards to the use of his sperm will result in negative consequences, it is unethical for the clinic to follow them. In some cases, executing the dead man's orders may adversely impact the woman involved in the case. For example, due to her age, the inability to use her dead husband's sperm may decrease the possibility that the woman will ever become a parent. However, it is not fair to use the man's sperm to create a child after he has explicitly indicated that he does not want to become a father after he dies. The decision to procreate is such a personal one that it is unethical for someone else to make that choice for a man even if he is no longer able to speak for himself. In cases where the man's desires are clearly stated, it is unethical to disregard them in order to satisfy another person. Courts have been hesitant to ignore the express wishes of the gamete provider. One court stated: "It is not the role of the judiciary to inhibit the use of reproductive technology when the Legislature has not seen fit to do so; any such effort would raise serious questions in light of the fundamental nature of the rights of procreation and privacy."[15] This sentiment is in line with the legal deference given to a decedent with regards to the disposition of his body. The expressed wishes of the dead with regards to the treatment of his remains prevail over the desires of his surviving next-of-kin.[16]

Contract law approach

There is no question that, if the man was living, the clinic would have to honor his instructions with regards to the disposition of his sperm. At least one court has held that an agreement to store reproductive tissue creates a contractual relationship between the donor and the fertility clinic.[17] Does the contract survive the man's death? Does the clinic's legal obligations to abide by the terms of the agreement ends when the man dies? The law has answered both of these questions in the affirmative. According to contract law principles, contractual commitments typically survive the death of the parties and are binding on their estates. In fact, there is a presumption that a contract will be enforced even after the death of one or both of the parties.[18] There are several contexts in which the law permits the contractual arrangements of a person to be carried out after the person dies. A real estate transaction is a good illustration of the contractual control given to a dead person.

Consider the following scenario. A signs a contract to buy B's house for $100,000. Prior to the closing, both parties to the contract die. If the $100,000 exists in A's estate, the person who inherits A's property is legally obligated to buy B's house. The person who inherits B's property has a legal duty to sell the house.[19] These duties arise because of the doctrine of equitable conversion. Under that theory, when the contract is signed, the buyer becomes the equitable owner and the seller retains the legal title of the property in trust for the buyer.[20] It does not matter who will be disadvantaged by the sale. If possible, the sale must go through in accordance with the terms of the contract. The reasoning is that the property involved, the house and the money, belonged to the original contracting parties, so they have a right to determine the manner in which it is disposed. This same rationale can be applied to the man who signs a contract stating what should happen to his sperm after his death. Other ways that the actions of a dead person may impact the living are by designating the beneficiary on a life insurance contract, executing a will or creating a testamentary trust. As discussed in Chapter Three, courts have indicated that contracts regarding the disposition of embryos may survive the death of the gamete contributors.

Law mandates that the clinic acts in accordance to the contract

In order to protect itself from liability, the fertility clinic has the man sign a consent form at the time that he deposits his sperm in the facility. Because of the frequency of divorce and the awareness of posthumous reproduction, clinics now include provisions in their consent forms permitting a man to indicate what he wants to happen to his sperm in the event of divorce or death. Once the man's wishes are clearly expressed in writing, the clinic is legally obligated to act in accordance with them. Nonetheless, as the embryo cases have shown, the existence of a contract may not deter a woman from filing a lawsuit to obtain her dead husband's sperm, so she can conceive a child. The *Kievernagel* case is an example of how courts will handle these types of cases. In that case, the court framed the issue as "[w]hether a widow has the right to use her late husband's frozen sperm to attempt to conceive a child where her late husband signed an agreement with the company storing the frozen sperm providing that the frozen sperm was to be discarded upon his death."[21]

Married couple Joseph and Iris Kievernagel signed a contract with the Northern California Fertility Medical Center, Inc. (Medical Center) to receive IVF treatments in order to help Iris conceive a child. As a part of the process, the Medical Center had Joseph deposit a back-up sperm sample. The sperm sample was frozen and was to be used only in the event that Joseph's fresh sperm could not be used on the day Iris was scheduled to be inseminated.[22] The Medical Center had the couple sign a document entitled *IVF Back-Up Sperm Storage and Consent Agreement* (the agreement). Joseph signed the agreement after Iris completed it. In the agreement, the sperm was classified as Joseph's "sole and separate property." Thus, Joseph was given sole decision-making authority with regards to the disposition of the sperm. Iris signed the form indicating her agreement to the fact that the sperm sample belonged exclusively to Joseph.[23] According to the agreement, the Medical Center would destroy the sperm sample if Joseph and Iris got divorced. Under the terms of the agreement, Joseph had to select what he wanted to happen to the sperm if he died or was incapacitated. Joseph's choices were to either have the Medical Center release the sperm to Iris or to have the Medical Center dispose of the sperm. Joseph selected the box indicating that he wanted to have the sperm discarded and placed his initials next to it.[24]

After Joseph was killed in a helicopter crash, Iris became the administrator of his estate. The Medical Center would not give Joseph's frozen sperm sample to Iris unless she presented it with a court order. Therefore, Iris filed a petition with the Probate Court asking it to order the sperm distributed as an asset of Joseph's estate. As interested parties, Joseph's parents opposed Iris' request. They argued that because the agreement he signed clearly showed that Joseph wanted his sperm sample to be discarded after he died it should not be released to Iris.[25] Joseph's parents also claimed that his selection on the agreement confirmed their belief that he would not want his sperm to be used to conceive a child after his death. The battle lines were drawn.

The Probate Court had to decide whether or not to order the Medical Center to thaw the sperm out so Iris could use it or to throw it out. At the evidentiary hearing, the Probate Court found out that Joseph never wanted children. He only agreed to the IVF because Iris desperately wanted to be a mother. Iris' yearning for children was so strong that Joseph felt that she would divorce him if he did not agree to participate in the fertility treatments. The Probate Court ruled against Iris and ordered the Medical Center to abide by the terms of the agreement and discard the sperm.[26] Iris asked the Probate Court to reconsider its decision. She claimed that Joseph wanted her to have his child and that he did not even read the agreement before he signed it. Finding that Iris had not proven that the agreement did not express Joseph's intent, the Probate Court denied her request. Consequently, the Probate Court refused to order the distribution of the sperm sample. The Probate Court judge reasoned that Joseph intended to have the fertility process ceased in the event of his death.[27]

Iris appealed the decision to the California Appellate Court (Appellate Court). On appeal, Iris argued that the Probate Court should not have strictly enforced the contract. She also claimed that, as the surviving spouse, the Probate Court should have considered her right to procreate and applied the balancing test adopted in *Davis.*[28] The Appellate Court concluded that the Probate Court had correctly analyzed the case. Since the agreement gave Joseph the exclusive decision-making authority over the sperm sample, his intent was the deciding factor.[29] The Probate Court's decision was consistent with the intent Joseph expressed in the contract. Consequently, the Probate Court did not commit a reversible error.[30]

The Appellate Court rejected Iris arguments based upon *Davis* because that case involved embryos and this case dealt with a sperm sample.[31] Since the woman in the *Davis* case contributed the egg used to create the embryo, she had an ownership interest in it. Therefore, it made sense for the court to balance her desire to procreate against her ex-husband's wish not to procreate. In this case, the sperm sample belonged solely to Joseph, so his right not to procreate takes precedence over any desire expressed by Iris. Iris' case was weakened by the fact that she signed the contract agreeing to give Joseph exclusive control over the disposition of the sperm sample. Nevertheless, Iris may have argued that it would be unfair to specifically enforce the contract.

Relying on equity

Kievernagel is the only reported case involving the application of contract law to a sperm dispute. Thus, the law in this area is still evolving. Because the area is so unregulated the existence of a contract between the dead man and the fertility clinic may not be the end of the dispute. The facts in *Kievernagel* are typical of posthumous reproduction cases, so the case analysis may offer some guidance, but it does not forego other approaches. Another court in a similar situation might exercise its discretion to come up with a more equitable outcome.

In *Kievernagel*, the couple may not have paid much attention to the language dealing with the death of the man because he was young and in good health. It is not uncommon for a person to sign a contract without reading and understanding every word of it. Most posthumous reproduction situations arise because the man is being treated for a life-threatening disease or contemplating the loss of his fertility. In light of that distinction, Iris may have been able to argue that, due to changed circumstances, it would be unconscionable for the court to enforce the contract.[32] At the time Iris agreed that Joseph could make the decision regarding the disposition of the back-up frozen sperm, she did not anticipate that she would need to use that sperm to conceive. Because the sperm sample was taken only as a back-up in case something prevented the use of Joseph's live sperm, it was not unreasonable for Iris to decide that she probably would not need to use the frozen sperm. The day the couple signed the contract, Joseph was ready, willing and able to make the necessary contribution.

The situation changed as a consequence of Joseph's tragic death. Because of those changed circumstances the only way Iris can conceive Joseph's child is to use the frozen sperm. Therefore, if the court specifically enforced the contract, Iris would be deprived of the opportunity to conceive Joseph's child. The facts of the case indicated that Joseph loved Iris and wanted to please her by helping her to have his child. Joseph was willing to make this sacrifice even though he did not really want children. Nothing in the record shows that sentiment changed before Joseph died. Joseph could have requested that the sperm sample be discarded after his death because he did not think Iris would need it to conceive a child. Moreover, the frozen sperm was meant to be back-up sperm in the event that Joseph's fresh sperm was unobtainable when it was time to inseminate Iris. Because Joseph's death has rendered him unavailable to contribute fresh sperm, so Iris can conceive, permitting Iris to use his frozen sperm would be true to the spirit of the agreement.

Ultimately, the court may reject an equity argument for several reasons. First, the evidence at trial indicated that Joseph's primary motivation was to save his marriage. When he signed the form, Joseph probably reasoned that, since his death would end the marriage, he did not want a child conceived with his sperm if he died before Iris. Because his main reason for agreeing to have the child would be gone Joseph's refusal to have a posthumously conceived child would be reasonable. Second, as a competent adult, Iris had a legal duty to read the contract or to have it read to her.[33] She should not be rewarded for failing to fulfill that obligation. Third, if the court did not enforce the contract, it would set a bad precedent. Clinics include contract clauses like the one discussed in the case in order to protect themselves from liability. Because state legislatures have not provided guidance in this area the clinics have to rely upon court rulings. Iris did not present any evidence to indicate that she signed the contract under duress. In fact, it appears that Joseph was the one pressured into having a child using IVF.

Probate law approach

Instead of putting his instructions in a contract, a man may make his intentions known by executing a will. A will speaks at death, so it is appropriate for disposing of property after the death of the owner. The probate system is in place to ensure that the reasonable wishes of deceased persons are honored. The Probate Court will carry out the dead man's intentions as long as the will is validly executed and the directives are not illegal, unconstitutional or against public policy. This approach protects the clinic because it would only act with an order from the Probate Court. In order for a will to be valid, it must be executed in the presence of a statutorily dictated number of disinterested witnesses. Therefore, the man's intentions with regards to the disposition of his sperm would be clearly expressed. The majority of people die without leaving a will. If a man takes the time out to have a will executed, it means that he has thought about his decision and it deserves to be respected. One scholar has opined that "it would be ironic indeed if the law were to protect pre-mortem wishes regarding the disposition of property, but ignore pre-mortem wishes concerning a matter as central to a person's identity as the desire not to create another human being."[34]

The only thing that can be disposed of in a will is property. Some persons are uncomfortable labelling a man's sperm as property. They would argue that it is unethical to permit sperm to be given away in the same manner as a boat or a car. The history of slavery in the United States may contribute to the reluctance to consider human tissue to be a piece of property. Nonetheless, at least one court has permitted a man to designate the owner of his sperm in his will.[35]

On September 24, 1991, William E. Kane signed an agreement to have his frozen sperm stored by California Cryobank, Inc. (the sperm bank). A provision in that agreement authorized the sperm bank to release his sperm to his girlfriend, Deborah Ellen Hecht, in the event of his death. Kane took two other steps to indicate that he wanted his sperm to go to Hecht. He also left the sperm to Hecht in his September 27, 1991 will.[36] Furthermore, in October of 1991, after he had deposited fifteen vials of his sperm into the sperm bank, Kane wrote to his existing children and his future children. In that October 21, 1991 letter, Kane communicated his hope that Hecht would use his sperm to conceive his children. Kane acknowledged that he would never know his prospective children, but he conveyed his love for them. Expressing his dissatisfaction with his life, on October 30, 1991, Kane committed suicide. On December 3, 1991, Kane's children by his previous marriage, William Kane, Jr. and Katherine Kane contested the will. [37]

Kane's children and Hecht reached an agreement to settle their differences over his property. After all the parties signed the settlement agreement, Hecht's attorney mailed a letter to the sperm bank asking it to release Kane's sperm to Hecht. The sperm bank denied the attorney's request and Kane's children refiled their challenges to his will. Hecht argued that the children's violation of the settlement agreement had rendered it unenforceable. She further claimed that Kane's sperm should not be governed by the terms of the settlement agreement because he had made a gift of the sperm to her prior to his death. In essence, Hecht was asking the Probate Court to treat the sperm as if it was non-probate property. Examples of non-probate property include life insurance, joint bank accounts and retirement accounts. When a person dies, these items automatically go to the person he or she has designated as beneficiaries. Hence, the Probate Court does not get involved with the distribution of the property. In response, Kane's children asserted that the settlement agreement was legally binding on the parties.[38]

The administrator of Kane's estate went to the Probate Court to get approval of a second settlement agreement entered into by the parties. Under the terms of that agreement, the estate agreed to assign its interest in the sperm to Hecht in exchange for her promise to release the estate from all potential causes of actions on behalf of any of Kane's future children.[39] Before the Probate Court could approve the second settlement agreement, an estate creditor filed an objection. In addition, Kane's children contended that the agreement never became binding because the estate administrator did not sign it. The estate administrator filed a petition on behalf of Kane's children asking the Probate Court for permission to either: (1) destroy the sperm on public policy grounds; or (2) give 100% or 80% of the sperm to Kane's children.[40] On January 4, 1993, the Probate Court ordered the sperm bank to destroy all of Kane's sperm. Hecht appealed that decision.[41]

The Appellate Court rejected Hecht's gift argument. In its analysis, the Appellate Court described sperm as reproductive material. Because that material had the potential to be used to create a person the Appellate Court classified it as "a unique type of property." Thus, it reasoned that it was not appropriate to apply the laws governing gifts of personal property to Kane's sperm. Since Kane could not make an inter vivos gift of his sperm to Hecht, at the time of his death, the sperm was a part of his probate estate. As a result, the Appellate Court determined that Kane maintained "an interest, in the nature of ownership, to the extent that he had decision-making authority as to the use of his sperm for reproduction." According to the Appellate Court, that interest fell within the Probate Code's definition of property.[42] After ruling that the artificial insemination of an unmarried woman was not against the public policy of the state, the Appellate Court turned to the issue of posthumous reproduction.[43]

Kane's children asked the Appellate Court to uphold the Probate Court's decision in order to prevent Hecht from using their dead father's sperm to conceive a child. The children made two key ethical arguments to support their case. First, they claimed that the Appellate Court should adopt a policy against posthumous reproduction in order to thwart the creation of orphaned children. The Appellate Court rejected that argument because it was not supported by legal precedent and the Court could not find a state interest that would rationalize intruding on a person's decision to become a parent using posthumous reproduction.[44] Second, the children maintained that Hecht would not be injured by the destruction of the sperm because she had other procreative options, but they would be harmed if Hecht was permitted to conceive siblings for them. They contended that, if Hecht gave birth to their dead father's children they would suffer financially and emotionally.[45] The Appellate Court opined that none of these arguments were relevant. The deciding factor was that Kane had clearly instructed the sperm bank to release his sperm to Hecht after he died. Because the sperm was Kane's property he was the only person who had the legal right to control the legal disposition of it. Consequently, the Probate Court abused its discretion when it ignored Kane's wishes and ordered the destruction of his sperm.[46]

Hecht stands for the proposition that a person has a property interest in his or her reproductive tissue even after the tissue is extracted from a person's body. This means that, like Kane, a man can dispose of his sperm in his will or other testamentary instrument. However, according to the reasoning in the *Hecht* case, a man cannot give his sperm as a gift. The Court justified the difference in treatment by examining the definition of property. The Court determined that the definition of property under the Probate Court was broad enough to encompass a man's right to control the treatment of his sperm after it was removed from his body. The Court seemed to indicate that the definition of property for gift purposes was not flexible enough to include a man's sperm.

Possible will challenge

A man who disposes of his sperm in his will has no guarantee that a court will carry out his wishes. No will is challenge-proof. The majority of jurisdictions have no-contest statutes in place. According to those laws, if a person challenges a will, he or she loses whatever bequest he or she would have received under the will.[47] Nonetheless, that does not prevent people from regularly challenging the validity of wills. I tell my students that there are two ways to attack the validity of a will. You can either question the competency of the testator or the legitimacy of the execution process. In these sperm cases, legal theories pertaining to the testator's state of mind at the time he executed the will are the most relevant. Because Kane committed suicide it is surprising that his children did not challenge his mental capacity. The legal theories that may have changed the outcome in the *Hecht* case are undue influence and insane delusion.

The law understands that the manner in which a person disposes of property in his or her will may be influenced by the actions of others.[48] For example, the fact that a woman leaves most of her estate to the grandchild who shows her the most kindness is acceptable. However, if that influence goes too far, the will is not valid. If the third party's control over the testator is so strong that it destroys his or her free will and substitutes that person's judgment for the testator's, a court may invalidate the will because it is a product of undue influence. The person contesting the will must prove the following: (1) the testator was susceptible to being unduly influenced; (2) a third party had the opportunity to influence the testator; (3) a third party was disposed to exercise influence over the testator; and (4) the will was exercised in a way that suggests it was the result of the third party's influence.[49] If the will is a product of undue influence, the court may invalidate the entire will or the provision that was a result of the improper acts.

The burden of proving undue influence is on the person who challenges the will. However, in some cases, the law presumes undue influence, and the proponent of the will must rebut that presumption. The presumption of undue influence may arise if evidence shows that a fiduciary or confidential relationship existed between the testator and the beneficiary. A confidential relationship is one based upon trust.[50] The typical confidential relationship is a legal one that arises when one party owes a fiduciary duty to the other. Examples of this type of confidential relationship include attorney–client and doctor–patient.[51] Relationships between family members and friends can be classified as confidential if one party exercises dominance and control over the other. The existence of a confidential relationship is not sufficient to create a presumption of undue influence unless suspicious circumstances are involved. Those circumstances may include the beneficiary actively participating in the preparation or procurement of the will; and receiving an unusually large portion of the estate.[52]

In order to avoid having the burden of proof, Kane's children could have argued that a confidential relationship existed between Kane and Hecht. However, they probably would not have prevailed on this argument. The person claiming the existence of a confidential relationship has the heavy burden of proving that fact by clear and convincing evidence.[53] Courts have not adhered to a strict legal definition of "confidential relationship." Instead, courts have evaluated the actions and capacities of the parties involved in the relationship to determine whether or not to categorize it as confidential.[54] Confidential relationships can come in many forms.[55] The fact that the relationship is sexual does not make it a confidential relationship.[56] The law requires one person to be dependent on the other person.[57] There has to be a "weakness on one side and strength on the other resulting in dependence or trust justifiably reposed in the stronger." One court listed factors that indicate the existence of a confidential relationship.[58] No facts in the record indicated that Hecht was the dominant one in the relationship. Hence, the children may not have been able to meet their burden of proof. That does not really matter because, even without the presumption, Kane's children may have been able to show that his will was a product of undue influence.

In light of his mental state, Kane was probably susceptible to being unduly influenced. The content of the letter Kane wrote less than a month after he executed his will was enough to show that he was having some type of emotional breakdown. That evidence coupled with the fact that Kane actually did commit suicide might lead a court to believe that he was in a vulnerable state. That vulnerability could have been exploited by someone who wanted to control the manner in which Kane disposed of his property. Hecht may have had the opportunity to influence Kane's actions. The couple lived together for five years and Kane was obsessed with Hecht enough to go to great lengths to ensure that she had the opportunity to conceive his children. In the October 21, 1991 letter, when discussing his desire for Hecht to have his children, Kane stated "I've been assiduously generating frozen sperm samples for that eventuality."[59] The manner in which she reacted to the will contest could lead a court to believe that she was willing to use her influence to control the disposition of Hecht's estate. In his will, in addition to his sperm, Kane left Hecht specific property and the residue of his estate. As a result, Hecht received the bulk of Kane's estate. Acknowledging that fact, Kane wrote: "I recognize that my children … are financially secure and therefore leave them nothing other than the land included in this bequest, subject to the conditions as set forth above."[60] The atypical manner in which Kane divided his estate may lead a court to believe that his actions were being controlled by Hecht.

Kane's children may attempt to have his will set aside on a theory of insane delusion. If the will is a product of an insane delusion on the part of the testator, the court may ignore the provisions of the will affected by the delusion. An insane delusion refers to a legal theory and not a psychological condition.[61] A delusion is legally insane if a rational person would not have drawn the same conclusion as the testator. It is different from a mistake. A person suffering from an insane delusion cannot be deterred from his belief even when confronted with reasonable evidence.[62] Consider the following example. A believes that rabbits can only come in colors of white, black and gray. B shows A a brown rabbit. If A reacts by saying: "I am glad you showed me a brown rabbit because I never knew they existed," A was suffering from a mistaken belief. However, if

A's response is: "Since the animal is brown, it cannot be a rabbit," A is suffering from an insane delusion. In order for a court to invalidate a will due to an insane delusion, the delusion has to impact the manner in which the testator disposed of his property in the will.[63] In the previous example, if A disinherits B because A believes that B tried to trick him into thinking that brown rabbits exist, A's will was a product of his insane delusion.

To make a case for insane delusion, Kane's children have to prove two things: (1) that Kane was suffering from an insane delusion; and (2) that insane delusion led Kane to dispose of his property in the manner that he did, including leaving his frozen sperm to Hecht.[64] They may be able to successfully show the first element. Kane's children may be able to use the language in the October 21, 1991 letter to try to persuade the court that he was delusional at the time he drafted his will. Kane explained his decision to commit suicide by stating: "[b]etrayal, over and over again, has made me tired." He also wrote about possible attacks by his enemies.[65] Kane's rantings in the letter may be enough to convince a court that he was delusional. They may argue that Kane's delusion led him to believe that he had to kill himself in order to avoid being defeated by his enemies. In the letter to his children, Kane wrote: "I would rather take my own life now than be ground into a mediocre existence by my enemies – who, because of my mistakes and bravado have gained the power to finish me."[66]

Those words may be enough for the court to rule in favor of Kane's children on the first issue. Nonetheless, they may not lead the court to determine that Kane's will was a product of an insane delusion. The delusion must materially impact the disposition made under the will.[67] To prove that, Kane's children had to show that he would not have left his sperm to Hecht if he were not suffering from the delusion. Kane's desire to have his sperm released to Hecht was consistent. He expressed it in his agreement with the sperm bank, in his will, and in the letter to his unborn child. Nothing in those documents indicated that his fear of his enemies contributed to Kane's dying wish to have Hecht conceive his child posthumously. Because posthumous reproduction is not illegal or against public policy the court would order the clinic to abide by Kane's instructions for the disposition of his frozen sperm. If the clinic refuses, there will be consequences.

Possible clinic liability

Because the contract between the man and the clinic probably survives the man's death the clinic is obligated to follow the mandates included in the contract. If the clinic disobeys the contract or releases the man's sperm without obtaining a court order, it may face legal liability. Likewise, when a man takes the time to execute a will indicating the manner in which he wants his sperm to be distributed, the clinic is legally bound to act accordingly. In *Moore*, the court found a hospital liable for breach of fiduciary duty and lack of informed consent for using some of a patient's spleen cells to make a cell line without his permission.[68] Thus, it would not be reasonable to think that a clinic would not be liable for the same tort if it permitted a man's sperm to be used to make a child without his consent.

The man would be dead, so the cause of action would fall to his heirs who object to the conception of the new child.

It is doubtful that the man's estate would be able to bring a successful breach of fiduciary duty claim against the fertility clinic. Courts have refused to recognize the tort because they have deemed it to be duplicative of a medical malpractice case.[69] Lack of informed consent would not be appropriate in this case because, at the time the clinic extracted and froze the man's sperm, it probably told him about the risks and benefits of the procedure.[70] Even if the clinic failed to meet the requirements of legal informed consent, it would not be relevant to the disposition of the man's sperm after his death.[71] The court rejected Moore's conversion action because it concluded that he did not have a property interest in the excised tissue once it was removed from his body.[72] Nonetheless, because sperm has been legally recognized as a man's personal property the outcome of a conversion action against a clinic that wrongly releases a man's sperm would probably be different. As a result, the man's estate may be able to bring a successful conversion action.

Conversion

In order for the man's estate to bring a conversion action, the man would have had to own his sperm.[73] A conversion occurs when a person "intentionally and without authority, assumes or exercises control over personal property belonging to someone else, interfering with that person's right of possession."[74] Property has been converted when a person who is not the owner exercises control over it. A conversion is different from a theft. For instance, if a person takes someone's laptop without permission, the laptop has been stolen. On the other hand, if the person turns the laptop into a super computer, the laptop has been converted. In order to prove that a conversion has occurred, the person must show the following: (1) his or her ownership or the right to possess the property at the time of the alleged conversion; (2) another person's conversion by an unlawful act or disposition of property rights; and (3) some type of harm. To satisfy the elements of conversion, the person does not have to present evidence that his or her property was manually taken. The complaining party only has to demonstrate that someone else either assumed control or ownership of the property or put the property to his or her own use.[75] For an examination of a relevant conversion cause of action, let us turn to *Moore*.

After John Moore was diagnosed with hairy-cell leukemia, he went to the University of California at Los Angeles (UCLA) Medical Center (Medical Center) for treatment. A doctor at the Medical Center told Moore that, to slow the process of the cancer, he need to have his spleen removed. Moore consented in writing to having the operation performed. Prior to the surgery, the doctors arranged to take parts of Moore's spleen to a research facility. Moore was not informed that the doctors planned to conduct research on his spleen cells. The research was not intended to benefit Moore.[76] Over the course of almost seven years, Moore went to the Medical Center because his doctor told him that the visits were important to his health. Each time Moore returned to the Medical Center, his doctor extracted samples of his blood and other bodily fluids and tissue, including his sperm. During that time, the doctors were secretly conducting research on Moore's cells in hope of using the cells for economic reasons. Moore was never informed that the procedures he was undergoing were non-therapeutic.[77]

As a consequence of their research on Moore's cells, the doctors created a cell line using his T-lymphocytes. When the Medical Center applied for a patent for the cell line, the application listed Moore's doctors as the inventors. With the assistance of the Medical Center, the doctors were able to negotiate several agreements for the commercial development of the cell line and other derivative products. The Medical Center and the doctors stood to make billions of dollars from the cell line created using Moore's cells. Moore filed suit asking the court to permit him to share in any royalties and profits that would be made from the misappropriation of his cells.[78] Moore put forth several causes of action. The one that is relevant here is the one seeking damages for conversion.[79]

Moore argued that he maintained the right to decide the disposition of his cells once they were excised from his body. He contended that he had that right because he still owned the cells. According to Moore, the conversion occurred when the doctors used his cells to make the cell line without his permission. In order to compensate him for his loss, Moore asked the court to give him a commercial interest in all products made from his cells or the patented cell line.[80] This was the first time the court was being asked to apply the tort of conversion to human cells.

The court noted that, in order to prevail on his conversion claim, Moore had to prove that he owned his cells after they were taken from his body.[81] Because only property can be converted the court would have to classify Moore's excised cells as property. The court ruled against Moore for several reasons. First, the court determined that the cause of action was not supported by legal precedent. The court opined that legislators never intended for courts to treat human cells like regular personal property. In order to avoid that possibility, there were special laws in place to regulate the use of dead bodies and other things derived from the human body.[82]

Second, the court reasoned that Moore's case was weakened by the fact that California's statutory law placed strict restrictions on the control a person had over cells once they were extracted from his or her body. The patient's ability to make decisions regarding the use of those cells was so statutorily limited that most of the rights included in the bundle of sticks that make up property ownership did not exist when it came to excised cells. The court concluded that, after the application of the statute, the only right the person had to control the use of the extracted cells could be protected by the availability of the doctrine of informed consent.[83]

The final reason why the court rejected Moore's conversion argument was that the patent line was the result of the doctors' labor. The court emphasized "the patented cell line is both factually and legally distinct from the cells taken from Moore's body."[84] In essence, the court determined that Moore's cells were just a small component of the resulting cell line. If A takes B's paperclip without B's permission and uses it as a spring for a clock, does B own the clock? Ultimately, the court concluded that it was not necessary to extend the tort of conversion to situations involving biological materials.[85]

The reasoning of *Moore* provides insight into the potential success of a conversion cause of action against a fertility clinic that ignores the wishes the man expresses in the contract. A conversion action can only be brought if the man retains ownership interests in his sperm after it has been extracted. *Moore* stands for the proposition that a person only maintains a limited right to control the use of excised cells. This leads to the belief that a person does not retain any ownership interest in the parts of his or her body that he or she voluntarily permits to be removed. Using that logic, once a man has his sperm retrieved and stored, his decision-making authority is somehow diminished. This would make it difficult for the dead man's estate to bring a successful conversion case.

Nonetheless, *Moore* is factually different from the case where a man's sperm is released without his permission. When Moore signed the informed consent form to have his sperm removed, he had no expectations of controlling what happened to it once it left his body. Moore's objective was to be cancer-free. The surgery helped him to achieve that goal. A man who has his sperm frozen and stored understands that the sperm may be thawed out and used to conceive a child. In light of the responsibilities that come with having a child, it is reasonable to presume that the man plans to control the use of his sperm. In fact, unlike the form that Moore signed, the agreement that a man signs with the clinic before his sperm is extracted specifically gives him the option of deciding the disposition of his sperm in the event of his death.

Another difference in the cases is the purpose of the forms involved. The purpose of the form that Moore signed was to protect him from unauthorized medical treatment. Whereas, the provision in the agreement that the sperm donor signs is designed to protect him from forced procreation. By subjecting Moore to unnecessary tests, the doctors violated the consent form. The remedy for that violation is the tort of lack of informed consent and not conversion. Therefore, denying Moore's conversion claim did not leave him without a remedy. On the other hand, there is no tort that is meant to cover situations where a dead man's sperm is used against his expressed intentions. Furthermore, once it was removed from his body, the genetic material at issue in the *Moore* case could only be discarded or used for research. The dead man's sperm can be used to create a child.

A conversion action may not be the appropriate cause of action in these types of situations. The man's estate would have to make the following conversion argument. First, the estate would have to show that the man still owned the sperm when the clinic released it. As discussed earlier in this chapter, the law has recognized sperm as personal property that a man can bequest in his will, so the estate will be able to prove this element. Then, the estate would have to prove that the clinic's unlawful act of releasing the sperm to the woman without the man's permission led to it being converted into an embryo. If the case is not brought in a timely manner, the sperm may have been converted into a child. The final element the estate would have to demonstrate is that the man was harmed by the conception of the child. This is a difficult argument to make. It is hard to see how a dead man would be harmed by having a child. Courts have been reluctant to find a live child to be a burden. Even jurisdictions that recognize a cause of action for wrongful pregnancy limit damages to pregnancy-related expenses, and do not award child-rearing expenses.[86] Courts have justified limiting damages in wrongful pregnancy cases by relying on public policy. One judge noted: "The extent of recoverable damages is limited by Ohio's public policy that the birth of a normal, healthy child cannot be an injury to her parents."[87] This public policy rationale will be even more compelling when the injured party has not suffered any discernible harm because he is dead and may not be obligated to provide financial support for the child. However, to avoid this potential cause of action, the fertility clinic should adhere to the dead man's clearly expressed wishes.

Bailment

The man's estate may have a bailment cause of action if the fertility clinic's release of the frozen sperm is contrary to the dead man's instructions. "A bailment is the delivery of property for some purpose upon a contract, express or implied, that after the purpose has been fulfilled, the property shall be redelivered to the bailor, or otherwise dealt with according to his directions, or kept until he reclaims it."[88] Bailments may be voluntary or involuntary. A voluntary bailment is created when a person willingly gives his or her property to someone.[89] For example, when a person goes to a restaurant and checks his or her coat, a voluntary bailment relationship is established. An involuntary bailment arises when a person loses his or her property and it is recovered by someone else.[90] In order to recover under a bailment theory, the man's estate would have to show the existence of an expressed or implied agreement to create the bailment; the delivery of the property in good condition; the acceptance of the property by the bailee; and the failure of the bailee to return the property or return of the property in a damaged condition.[91] After establishing the existence of the bailment relationship, the man's estate would have to prove that the bailee breached the bailment by failing to exercise reasonable care or violating the terms of the bailment agreement.[92]

Only property may be the subject of a bailment. Some may be uncomfortable with a man's sperm being treated like a piece of luggage that is left with a hotel bellman. However, there is precedent for this type of cause of action. In *York*, the court permitted an embryo to be treated as the subject of a bailment agreement.[93] An embryo is closer to being a person than a man's sperm. In order to become a fetus, an embryo only has to be implanted. On the contrary, a sperm that has not been used to fertilize an oocyte is just a component part at the beginning of the reproductive process. If a court is willing to treat an embryo as bailment property, a dead man's sperm can be likewise classified. Therefore, a review of the analysis of the *York* case is appropriate.

Steve and Risa York (the Yorks) underwent IVF at the Jones Institute (Institute) in Virginia, so they could conceive a child. During the course of the treatments, the Yorks relocated from New Jersey to California.[94] When the Yorks were down to their last embryo and still had not conceived, they asked the Institute to transfer that embryo to a clinic in California. In a letter, the head doctor at the Institute refused to approve the transfer. As a result, the Yorks sued for the return of their embryo.[95] The Court decided that the agreement the Yorks signed with the Institute established a bailor–bailee relationship between them and the Institute. As the bailee, the Institute only had limited control over the embryo. Thus, by refusing to follow the Yorks' instructions and transfer the embryo to the California clinic, the Institute breached the bailment contract.[96] The reasoning of *York* indicates that the fertility clinic has to follow the instructions that the man gives with regards to the disposition of his frozen sperm. Failure to obey the directions that the dead man leaves would expose the fertility clinic to a lawsuit for breaching the bailment agreement that it entered into with the man. The man's estate would be able to prove that a bailment existed because the man would have delivered his sperm to the clinic and the clinic would have accepted delivery of the sperm.

Ascertaining the wishes of the dead

Cases involving situations where a man leaves frozen sperm without disposition instructions are rare. However, when posthumous reproduction was a mere concept and not a reality, fertility clinics did not see the need to ask a man what he wanted done with his sperm in the event he died before it was used. Older agreements contained clauses pertaining to divorce, but not death. Sperm can remain frozen for at least ten years. Thus, there is a possibility that a situation can arise involving an older agreement that does not contain a provision setting out a man's preferences for his sperm if it was still frozen at his death. Under those circumstances, the clinic would turn to the court. In this section, I will discuss an older case where a woman sought to obtain her late husband's frozen sperm and the court had to try to ascertain his wishes.

Ethical concerns

The main ethical question is whether or not the man's silence should be presumed to be an objection or acquiescence to the use of his sperm to conceive a child after his death. When a man has his sperm frozen and dies without leaving instructions regarding the disposition of the sperm, should that sperm be governed by an opt-out system or an opt-in system? Persons who think that the main purpose of marriage is procreation would argue that it is unethical to deprive a man's wife of the opportunity to have his child if he has not objected to the possibility. Others would argue that the choice to procreate is a personal decision that should be explicitly made and not inferred. There is legal support for both viewpoints.

The organ donation system is an opt-in system. States have systems in place to ensure that a person has the opportunity to make his or her wishes with regards to organ donation known. For example, in most cases, if, at the time of death, the person has not signed an organ donor card, the health care provider assumes that the person did not want his or her organs removed. There are exceptions to this assumption that we will take up later in the book. But, for now, the focus is on the organ donation system as an opt-in system. On the other hand, some states legislatures have enacted statutes permitting medical examiners to remove corneal tissue from a dead person without the prior consent of the decedent or his next-of-kin.[97] Unlike the organ donation scenario, this is an opt-out system. Therefore, if a decedent fails to object during his lifetime or his next-of-kin does not explicitly oppose the extraction, the medical examiner can legally harvest the person's corneal tissue without worrying about reprisals.[98] The purpose of this opt-out system is to increase the amount of corneal tissue available for transplantation. A dead person's corneal tissue can be used to help other people gain their sight.[99] Should a dead man's sperm be treated like his kidney or his corneal tissue? The ethical answer is probably neither. A kidney can help someone live; corneal tissue can help someone see. However, sperm can help create an entirely new person. Conception is much more personal than transplantation. Hence, an opt-in system seems more appropriate. Thus, if a man does not direct his sperm to be used for procreation after his death, requests for the sperm should be denied. This is probably the position most courts would take today, but as the *Parpalaix* case indicates, that was not always true.

An early case

In an early French case, a woman fought for the opportunity to conceive a child using her dead husband's sperm.[100] Doctors arranged to treat Alain Parpalaix's testicular cancer with chemotherapy.[101] As a consequence of the treatment, Alain might have been unable to have children.[102] Therefore, prior to beginning treatment, Alain had his sperm retrieved and frozen. The frozen sperm was stored in a government-run sperm bank.[103] Alain did not sign any papers stating what he wanted to happen to his sperm in the event that he succumbed to his disease.[104] Unfortunately, Alain's treatment was unsuccessful and he died. Two days before his death, Alain married his long-time girlfriend, Corrine.[105] After Alain passed away, Corrine asked the sperm bank to release Alain's frozen sperm to her, so that she could conceive his child. Because Alain had not consented to the postmortem use of his sperm the sperm bank denied Corrine's request.[106] In response, Corrine sought a court order to force the clinic to give her the sperm. The court ruled in Corrine's favor and she obtained her dead husband's sperm.[107] The reason why the court granted Corrine's request is unclear. The judges may have assumed that Alain wanted to have children because he took steps to preserve his fertility. They may have also been moved by the fact that Alain married Corrine after he realized that his death was imminent. The outcome of the case would be different today because posthumous reproduction is illegal in France. Even in countries where the procedure is lawful, if a man dies without leaving instructions with regards to the disposal of his frozen sperm, his spouse or significant other will probably be unable to gain the right to use that sperm to procreate.

A matter of equity

Equitable estoppel

There may be some cases where it is unfair to permit the fertility clinic to discard a dead man's sperm if he fails to leave instructions. One situation is where a man and his wife's start the IVF process before he dies. In this type of situation, the man's sole purpose in having his sperm extracted and frozen may be so that an embryo can be created using his wife's oocytes. In the event that a man dies before the fertilization process can be completed, even if the man does not leave instructions, equity may dictate that the woman be permitted to use the sperm to conceive. This would be appropriate if the fertility clinic failed to ask the man about his wishes with regards to the disposition of his sperm. As a matter of fairness, a court may impose the doctrine of equitable estoppel to prevent the clinic from refusing to release the dead man's sperm without his consent.[108]

The elements of equitable estoppel are these: "(1) the party to be estopped must know the facts; (2) he must intend that his conduct shall be acted on or must so act that the party asserting estoppel has a right to believe the other party so intended; (3) the party asserting estoppel must be ignorant of the facts; (4) the party asserting estoppel must rely on the other's conduct to his detriment."[109] The woman who wants to use her dead husband's frozen sperm to continue the process they started while he was alive may be able to satisfy the elements of equitable estoppel. If so, the clinic would be estopped from claiming that it cannot give the sperm to the woman because her husband did not consent to the release.

It would be unfair for the clinic to deny the woman the right to use her dead husband's sperm for several reasons that coincide with the elements needed to prove equitable estoppel. First, the clinic knew that the man had his sperm retrieved and frozen so that his wife could use it to conceive his child. In light of the nature of their business, the clinic knew that the man could die before the process was completed. Therefore, the clinic should have planned for that eventuality. Second, the clinic acted as if it planned to help the woman to conceive that child. Because the clinic did not have the parties sign an agreement that indicated that the man's death would stop the process the couple reasonably assumed that the man's sperm would be used to fertilize the woman's oocytes. Third, the woman was ignorant of the fact that her husband's death would impact her ability to use his sperm. A representative for the clinic may argue that the man and his wife also knew that the premature death of one or both of them was a possibility. Nonetheless, the couple's desperation to have a child may have clouded their judgments. Moreover, if this was their first time engaging in this type of activity, the couple may have relied upon the clinic to work out all of the legalities. Finally, the woman relied on the clinic's conduct to her detriment because, if she is not permitted to use her dead husband's sperm, she will not be able to have his child. If the woman had known that she would not have the right to use the frozen sperm, she may have taken steps to have fresh sperm extracted from her dead husband's body. Courts have used this approach in cases dealing with children conceived using artificial insemination. Unless someone other than the fertility clinic objects a court may exercise its equitable powers to have a dead man's sperm released to his widow so that she can conceive posthumously.

Balancing the interests

The wife may ask the court to apply the balancing of interests approach taken in cases involving embryos when the couple does not sign an agreement. In those cases, courts balance the right to procreate against the right not to procreate. If that approach is used, the wife could argue that she would be disadvantaged if she is not permitted to use her dead husband's sperm. Factors like the woman's age and health may be relevant. The court may tip the scale in favor of a woman who is close to the end of her child-bearing years and/or in poor health. The woman's dead husband's sperm may provide her with the best opportunity to become a mother. On the other hand, the man's right to not procreate may not be impacted because he is no longer living. It is difficult to see how a dead man would be harmed by having a child, especially if he was in the process of trying to become a father at the time of his death.

It may not be appropriate for a court to use the balancing of interests test in a case involving sperm. Embryos are created using a man's sperm and a woman's oocyte. Because the embryo belongs to the man and the woman they both have interests that can be balanced. To the contrary, a man's sperm is the product of his body; therefore, he has sole decision-making authority over it. For example, the divorce courts treat marital property different from separate property. When dividing marital property, the court relies on the theory of equitable distribution.[110] Each party gets to retain ownership of his or her separate property. Applying that reasoning to the dead man's sperm, the sperm belongs to the dead man and not his wife. Therefore, if the man did not take steps to ensure that the wife could use it to conceive a child posthumously; the clinic is not legally obligated to release the sperm to the woman.

The gift of life

Hecht tried to get the Court to classify Kane's sperm as non-probate property by claiming that he had given it to her prior to his demise. The Court did not have to entertain Hecht's gift argument because the case could be resolved on other grounds. But, in dicta, the Court indicated that it would not have found that Kane gifted his sperm to Hecht. Nevertheless, that is not to say that a man cannot make a gift of his sperm to a woman. A woman may make this argument in cases where a man's wishes are not easily ascertained because a gift may be created orally. Therefore, a court will permit the woman to introduce extrinsic evidence to prove her case. There are two types of gifts – inter vivos gifts and gifts causa mortis.

The legal elements necessary to create an inter vivos gift are: (1) present of donative intent, (2) delivery, and (3) acceptance.[111] In order to satisfy the first requirement, the woman would have to show that the man meant for her to have an interest in his sperm while he was still alive. Let's consider these elements in terms of the *Hecht* case. Kane clearly stated that he wanted the sperm bank to retain possession of the sperm until after his death. The fact that nothing prevented Kane from giving Hecht a fresh sample of his sperm further indicates that he did not have a present intent to donate his sperm to Hecht. If Kane had died while he and Hecht were undergoing IVF, a court may have been willing to believe that he gifted the sperm to her at the time it was extracted. Under those circumstances, because Kane would have intended for his sperm to be used prior to his death Hecht might have been able to make a strong argument for present donative intent.

The delivery element is fulfilled when a person gives up dominion and control of the item that is the subject of the gift. The person can achieve that goal by placing the object in the hands of a third party.[112] When Kane had his extracted sperm frozen and stored in the sperm bank, he met the delivery requirement. In cases involving the disposition of frozen sperm, the man would have turned over the sperm to a medical facility for storage. Finally, if a gift is valuable, the law presumes acceptance on the part of the intended recipient.[113] Kane's sperm was important to Hecht because she obviously wanted to have his child. The fact that a woman is in court seeking to obtain her dead husband's sperm proves that she would have accepted it.

A stronger gift argument for a woman who seeks to gain possession of her dead husband's sperm may be that the man made a gift causa mortis. To successfully claim a gift causa mortis, the woman must show that: (1) the gift was made in anticipation of the man's death; (2) the gift was delivered; and (3) the man died in the manner anticipated.[114] It is easy to envisage a situation where a man who is being treated for a life-threatening disease expresses his desire to become a father. The possibility of having a child may give the man hope and help him to fight his disease. The woman would have to produce evidence showing that after the man accepted the fact that he would not survive, he told her to use his sperm to conceive his child. At that time, the man probably would have had his frozen sperm stored prior to undergoing the medical treatment, so the delivery requirement would be met. Once the man succumbed to his disease, the woman would be able to prove the final element.

The *Hecht* case presented facts that could have satisfied the elements of a gift causa mortis. First, Kane contemplated his death because he planned to commit suicide. Second, over the course of a few months, Kane delivered his sperm to the sperm bank for distribution. Finally, Kane died as a result of suicide. A gift causa mortis can only occur if the elements of an inter vivos gift are present. Hence, Hecht would have to show that Kane had a present donative intent. In the case of a gift causa mortis, the donor must intend for the gift to only take effect if the person dies in a particular way.[115] Consider the following example. A is scheduled to have heart surgery. A tells B: "If I don't survive, I want you to have my house." A gives the keys to the house to B and B accepts them. A comes through the surgery and makes a full recovery. A does not have to revoke the gift to B. The house never really belongs to B because the condition of A's death did not occur. In the *Hecht* case, Kane wanted Hecht to have his sperm even if he survived the suicide attempt. Therefore, he did not have the necessary donative intent to make a valid gift causa mortis.

Conclusion

Men may choose to have their sperm frozen for a variety of reasons. If the man dies before his sperm can be used to fertilize an oocyte, the storage facility has to decide the fate of that sperm. The clinic must acknowledge and carry out the man's wishes in regards to the disposition of his frozen sperm. In order to protect themselves from liability, most clinics have provisions in their agreements that require a man to indicate the manner in which he wants his sperm disposed in the event of his death. The man can choose to have the sperm destroyed, to have the sperm released to a designated person, or to have the sperm donated. The clinic is legally required to abide by the man's instructions or face a breach of contract action by the man's estate. In some cases, the man may make his wishes known in another legal document like a will. Under those circumstances, the clinic must follow the man's directions to avoid violating the court order that will probably be issued. In the rare cases where a man's wishes are unclear, the clinic must take steps to ascertain those wishes, so it can act accordingly.

Notes

1 Susan L. Crockin and Gary A. Debele, Ethical Issues in Assisted Reproduction: A Primer For Family Law Attorneys, 27 J. Am. Acad. Matrim. Law 289, 341 (2015).
2 Alicia J. Paller, A Chilling Experience: An Analysis of the Legal and Ethical Issues Surrounding Egg Freezing, And A Contractual Solution, 99 Minn. L. Rev. 1571, 1576–1577 (April 2015).
3 Charlotte Alter, Diane Tsai, and Francesca Triauni, What You Really Need To Know About Egg Freezing, www.time.com (July 16, 2015).
4 Mikaela Conley, Israeli Court Allows Family to Harvest Dead Daughter's Eggs at abcnews.go.com (August 11, 2011).
5 See John A. Gibbons, Comment, Who's Your Daddy?: A Constitutional Analysis of Post-Mortem Insemination, 14 J. Contemp. Health & Pol'y 187, 190 (1997) cited in Browne Lewis, Graveside Birthday Parties: The Legal Consequences of Forming Families Posthumously, 60 Case W. Res. L. Rev. 1159, 1169 (Summer 2010).
6 Frank Buckley, Insurance policy: Troops Freezing Sperm at www.cnn.com (January 30, 2003).
7 *Id.*
8 *Id.*
9 War-Bound Soldiers Urged to Bank Sperm Before Deployment at www.cryobank.com (November 3, 2008).
10 *Id.*
11 Wisman A. & Goldenberg J.L., From the grave to the cradle: evidence that mortality salience engenders a desire for offspring, J. Pers. Soc. Psychol. 2005 Jul; 89(1): 46–61.

12 Joseph H. Karlin, Daddy Can You Spare a Dime?: Intestate Heir Rights of Posthumously Conceived Children, 79 Temp. L. Rev. 1317, 1322 (Winter 2006).
13 *Id.*
14 William C. Hudson, Sperm Banks As A Strategy to Reduce Harms Associated With Advance Paternal Age, 70 Food & Drug L.J. 573, 573 (2015).
15 *Johnson v Calvert*, 851 P.2d 776 (1993).
16 *Alcor v Life Extension Foundation v Richardson*, 785 N.W. 2d 717 (Ct. App. Iowa 2010) (Man wanted his head to be frozen and his body to be cremated. His siblings had his remains embalmed and buried. Court ordered the siblings to sign a disinterment request so his body could be disposed in the manner that he dictated prior to his death.).
17 *Jeter v Mayo Clinic of Arizona*, 121 P.3d 1256, 1276 (2005).
18 *Cardwell v Sicola-Cardwell*, 978 S.W. 722, 726 (Ct. App. Tx 1998); *In re Cornell*, __P.3d.___ 159 Idaho 778 (Idaho, 2016), 2016 WL825003.
19 *Shay v Penrose*, 185 N.E. 2d 218, 220, 221 (Ill. 1962).
20 *Cassidy v Pavlonnis*, 205 P3d 58, 61–62 (2008).
21 *In re Estate of Kievernagel*, 166 Cal. App. 4th 1024, 1025 (2008).
22 *Id.* at 1026.
23 *Id.*
24 *Id.*
25 *Kievernagel*, 166 Cal. App. 4th at 1026.
26 *Id.* 1027.
27 *Id.*
28 *Id.*
29 *Kievernagel*, 166 Cal. App. 4th at 1031.
30 *Id.* at 1032.
31 *Id.*
32 Unforeseen change in circumstances may sometimes render a contract unconscionable even if that was not the case when the parties entered into the contract. ("Subsequent events or a change in conditions which the parties cannot reasonably be supposed to have had in mind when the contract was made, and which work a hardship on defendant, have frequently furnished a sufficient reason for refusing specific performance." *Link's Estate v Wirtz*, 638 P.2d 985, 991 (Kan. App. 2d 1982)).
33 *McDonald v Miners & Merchants Bank, Inc.*, 310 N.W. 2d 591, 593–594 (S.D. 1981).
34 Anne Reichman Schiff, Arising from the Dead: Challenges of Posthumous Procreation, 75 North Carolina L. Rev. 901, 943 (1997).
35 *Hecht v Superior Court*, 16 Cal. App. 4th 836 (1993).
36 *Id.* at 840.
37 *Id.* at 841.
38 *Id.* at 842.
39 *Id.*
40 *Hecht*, 16 Cal. App. 4th at 843.
41 *Id.* at 845.
42 *Id.* at 850.
43 *Id.* at 845.
44 *Hecht*, 16 Cal. App. 4th at 858.
45 *Id.* at 858–859.
46 *Id.* at 861.
47 *Townsend v Townsend*, 89 Cal. Rptr. 3d 760, 762 (Cal. App. 4th 2009).
48 *Estate of Ziegelmeier*, 585 P2d 973, 974 (1978).
49 *In re Estate of Clinger*, 872 N.W.2d 37, 48 (2015).
50 *Orwick v Moldawer*, 822 A.2d 506, 511 (Md. App. 2003).

51 *In re Estate of Brevard*, 213 S.W. 3d 298, 302–303 (Tenn. 2006).
52 *Dean v Jordan*, 79 P.2d 331 (1938), cited in *In re Estate of Barnes*, 2016 WL 348057 (January 28, 2016).
53 *Foster v Ross*, 804 So. 2d 1018, 1023 (Miss. 2002).
54 *Egr v Egr*, 131 P.2d 1908 (1942).
55 *Robinson v Robinson*, 517 S.W. 2d 202, 206 (Tenn. Ct. App. 1974).
56 See *In re Caspelich*, 22 So.3d 1199, 1207 (2009) (Under facts similar to the ones in *Hecht*, the court refused to find a confidential relationship based upon an intimate relationship). See also *Matter of Estate of Beal*, 769 P.2d 150, 151 (1989) (The court found that a confidential relationship existed between an older man and a younger woman because he was completely dependent on her).
57 *Kelly v Allen*, 558 S.W.2d 845, 847 (Tenn. 1977); *Iacometti v Frasinelli*, 494 S.W.2d 496, 499 (Tenn. Ct. App. 1973).
58 "The factors courts use to determine whether a confidential relationship exists are as follows: (1) whether one person has to be taken care of by others, (2) whether one person maintains a close relationship with another, (3) whether one person is provided transportation and has their medical care provided for by another, (4) whether one person maintains joint accounts with another, (5) whether one is physically or mentally weak, (6) whether one is of advanced age or poor health, and (7) whether there exists a power of attorney between the one and another.": *In re Estate of Dabney v Hataway*, 740 So. 2d 915, 919 (Miss. 1999).
59 *Hecht*, 16 Cal. App. 4th at 841.
60 *Id.* at 840–841.
61 *Dougherty v Rubenstein*, 914 A.2d 184, 193–194 (Md. 2007).
62 *In re Millar's Estate*, 207 P.2d 483, 487 (Kan. 1949).
63 *Matter of Estate of Raney*, 799 P2d 986, 993 (Kan. 1990); *In re Quam's Will*, 102 N.W.2d 217, 220 (1960).
64 *Breeden v Stone*, 992 P.2d 1167, 1171 (2000).
65 *Hecht*, 16 Cal. App. 4th at 841.
66 *Id.*
67 *In re Klein's Estate*, 183 P.2d 518, 526 (Wash. 1947).
68 *Moore v Regents of University of California*, 730 P2d 479, 485–486 (Cal. 1990).
69 *Neade v Portes*, 739 N.E. 2d 496, 500–501 (Ill. 2000).
70 *Brown v Dibble*, 582 N.W. 2d 134, 136–137 (Wis. 1998) (discussing the purpose of the informed consent requirement).
71 *Id.*
72 *Moore*, 730 P.2d at 488–489.
73 See *Terry v Witherspoon*. 255 S.W. 471 (Tex. Civ. App.-Amarillo 1923), aff'd. 267 S.W.2d 973 (1925) cited in *Branham v Prewitt*, 636 S.W.2d 507, 512 (Tex. Civ. App.-San Antonio 1982) ("Ownership of the property at the time of the conversion is material as bearing on the issue of conversion.")
74 *C & B Enterprises U.S.A., L.L.C. v Koegel*, ___N.Y.S. 3d____ (2016) WL717877, quoting *Colavito v New York Organ Donor Network, Inc.* 860 N.E. 2d 713, 717 (2006).
75 *Spates v Dameron Hosp. Assn.*, 7 Cal. Rptr. 3d 597, 608 (2003).
76 *Moore*, 730 P.2d at 480–481.
77 *Id.* at 481.
78 *Id* at 482.
79 *Id.* at 483.
80 *Moore*, 730 P.2d at 487.
81 *Id.* at 488.
82 *Id.* at 490.
83 *Id.* at 491–492.
84 *Moore*, 730 P.2d at 492.

85 *Id.* at 493.
86 *Fulton-Dekalb Hosp. Authority v Graves*, 314 S.E.2d 653 (1984); *Pressil v Gordon*, 477 S.W.3d 402, 409 (Houston (14th Dist.) (2015).
87 *Johnson v University Hospitals of Cleveland*, 540 N.E. 2d 1370, 1370 (1989).
88 *Kirby v Chicago City Bank & Trust Co.*, 403 N.E.2d 720, 723 (Ill. App. 1980).
89 *S/M Industries, Inv. v Hapag-Lloyd, A.G.*, 586 So. 2d 876, 882 (Ala. 1991).
90 *Moore v Moore*, 835 P.2d 1148, 1153 (1992); *Hoblyn v Johnson*, 55 P.3d 1219, 1229 (2002).
91 *Robinson v St. Clair County*, 493 N.E. 2d 1154, 1156 (Ill. App. 3d 1986).
92 *Garofoli v Whiskey Island Partners*, Ltd., 25 N.E.3d 400. 405–40 (Ohio 2014).
93 *York v Jones*, 717 F. Supp. 421 (Va. 1989).
94 *Id.* at 423.
95 *Id.* at 424.
96 *Id.* at 427.
97 *Korndorffer v Baker*, 976 S.W.2d 696, 701 (Houston (1st Dist. 1997).
98 *Georgia Lion's Eye Bank, Inc. v Lavant*, 335 S.E. 2d 127, 127 (1985).
99 *Id.* at 128 ("The record indicates that before the passage, approximately 2 corneal transplants were performed each year. In 1984, however, more than 1,000 persons regained their sight through transplants.").
100 See *Parpalaix v CECOS*, Tribunal de grande instance [T.G.I.] [ordinary court of original jurisdiction] Creteil, Aug. 1, 1984, Gaz. Pal. [1984], 2, pan. jurisp., 560; see also E. Donald Shapiro & Benedene Sonnenblick, The Widow and the Sperm: The Law of Post-Mortem Insemination, 1 J.L. & HEALTH 229, 229–33 (1986) (discussing *Parpalaix*, which was the first case in France to deal with the issue of postmortem insemination in 1984). Most of the discussion of this case comes for Shapiro & Sonnenblick.
101 Shapiro & Sonnenblick, supra note 100 at 229.
102 *Id.*
103 *Id.*
104 *Id.* at 229–30.
105 *Id.* at 230.
106 *Id.*
107 *Id.* at 233. Unfortunately for Corinne, her subsequent attempts at artificial insemination proved unsuccessful and she never carried Alain's child. *Id.*
108 *Laura G. v Peter G.*, 830 N.Y.S.2d 496, 502 (2007) (man equitably estopped from denying his paternity to a child his wife conceived after being artificially inseminated with donor sperm without his written consent.)
109 *Brown v Brown*, 125 S.W. 3d 840, 843 (2003).
110 *Cohen-McLaughlin v McLaughlin*, 18 N.Y.S.3d 634 (2015).
111 *Matter of Saathoff's Estate*, 295 N.W. 2d 290, 296 (Neb. 1980).
112 *Howell v Howell*, 197 S.W.3d 505, 508–509 (Ken. 2006).
113 *In re Estate of Soupcoff*, 477 A.2d 1388, 1390 (Pa. 1984).
114 *McCarton v Estate of Watson*, 693 P.2d 192, 194 (Ct. App. Wash. Div. 1 1984).
115 *Flint v Varney*, 264 N.W. 277, 279 (Iowa 1935).

4 Fresh sperm (extract and release?)

It is slowly becoming more common for persons to try to have the sperm harvested from dead men and men in vegetative states. Prior to complying with these types of requests doctors are requiring court orders. These requests are mainly made by wives and girlfriends. However, occasionally a parent seeks to become a grandparent using the sperm or eggs of his or her dead child. This chapter examines the ethical and legal issues that occur when doctors are called upon to retrieve fresh sperm from the body of a man who is unable to contribute it naturally. When frozen sperm is involved, the issues focus upon his consent and/or intent. In situations where someone requests fresh sperm, the doctors have to decide whether or not to extract the sperm and to whom to release the sperm. The three main methods that can be used to extract sperm from the body of a man who is dead or in a vegetative state are stimulated or electro ejaculation[1], microsurgical epididymis sperm aspiration (MESA)[2] and testicular sperm extraction (TSE).[3]

The military wife

On Valentine's Day of 2007, Kynesha and Dayne Dhanoolal got married. Afterwards, Dayne, a sergeant in the United States Army, was deployed to Iraq. The newlyweds planned to start a family when Dayne returned home. In preparation, Kynesha had surgery to have her uterine fibroid tumors removed, so she would increase her chances of conceiving Dayne's child. Unfortunately, Dayne was killed on March 31, 2008 when an improvised explosive device (IED) hit his vehicle. The Army had Dayne's body transferred to Dover Airforce Base. Kynesha refused to allow Dayne's death to end her dream of having his child, so she asked the Army to have some of Dayne's sperm extracted. In response, the Army informed her that, if she obtained a temporary restraining order, it would postpone embalming his body, so she could have his sperm retrieved. The embalming process would have damaged the sperm.

Kynesha was appointed administrator of Dayne's estate because he died without executing a will. In that capacity, she had the authority to control his remains. However, in anticipation of his deployment, Dayne designated his mother, Monica Mary Brown, as the person to handle the disposition of his remains. He only authorized his wife, Kynesha, to receive his financial benefits. Monica and Kynesha could not agree on the extraction of Dayne's sperm, so Kynesha sought a court order. In support of her motion for a temporary restraining order to prevent the Army from embalming Dayne's body, Kynesha made several arguments. She contended that, as the surviving spouse, she had a quasi-property right regarding the disposition of Dayne's remains. In addition, Kynesha claimed that Monica would not be harmed by the extraction of Dayne's sperm. Kynesha also made a public policy argument. She maintained that it would be in the public's interest to preserve the sanctity of marriage and the right of procreation. After the court permitted sperm to be retrieved from Dayne's dead body, Monica and the rest of his family stopped objecting to the possibility of Kynesha having Dayne's child posthumously.[4]

The devastated fiancée

Stephanie Lucas was looking forward to marrying Cameron Robinett and having his children. Before the marriage could take place, Cameron died three days after he was injured in a motorcycle accident. After doctors declared Cameron brain dead, Stephanie started a "Go Fund Me" campaign online to raise the $6,000 that she needed to pay upfront to have Cameron's sperm extracted. If Stephanie did not raise the money quickly, Cameron's sperm would not be viable. In her online plea, Stephanie stated: "In lieu of flowers or gifts to honor Cameron, we're asking you to make a donation to actually bring a part of Cameron, the amazing, handsome, silly, guy that I loved with my whole heart, back to life."[5] In just one day Stephanie was able to raise more than $11,000. Cameron's sperm was retrieved and placed in cold storage.[6] Stephanie planned to wait at least a year before attempting to conceive.

The comatose man

Diane and Stephen Blood were in the process of trying to conceive a child when he contracted meningitis. While Stephen was in a coma, Diane asked his doctors to harvest some of his sperm. The doctors were surprised by Diane's request. However, they removed two samples of Stephen sperm using electro-ejaculation. After Stephen was declared dead, Diane sought to have his sperm released, so that she could use it to conceive a child. The Human Fertilisation and Embryology Authority (HFEA) challenged Diane's right to have Stephen's sperm because it had been harvested without his prior written consent. Therefore, the doctors retrieved the sperm in violation of the Human Fertilisation and Embryology Act 1990. Diane understood that she would not be allowed to use Stephen's sperm in the United Kingdom, so she sought permission to have the sperm exported to Belgium. The HFEA refused to grant Diane's request to transport the sperm. Eventually, Diane was able to successfully appeal the HFEA's decision to the Court of Appeal. As a result, the HFEA, in compliance with the Court of Appeal's ruling, permitted Diane to take Stephen's sperm to another country for use. The

Court made it clear that the decision was not intended to serve as a legal precedent for these types of cases. Consequently, because the law currently prohibits a man's sperm from being stored without his written consent a woman in Diane's situation would not be able to obtain similar relief from the Court. Diane, who conceived two children using her dead husband's sperm, has no regrets.[7]

The first live birth

Gaby Vernoff was heartbroken when her husband, Bruce Vernoff, died suddenly as the result of an allergic reaction. At the time, Dr. Cappy Rothman was the director of the Center for Reproductive Medicine at Century City Hospital. He and his team went to the coroner's office and retrieved sperm from Bruce's epididymis. The epididymides are the coiled tubes located at the back of each testis, the place where sperm produced in the testicles mature. Rothman opined that extracting fresh sperm from the epididymis where sperm is stored is the best technique to use. Bruce's sperm was extracted thirty hours after he died. This was cutting it close because sperm can only survive between twelve and thirty hours in a dead body. After the sperm had been frozen for fifteen months, Gaby used it to conceive and gave birth to a baby girl.[8]

The hypothetical case

Malcolm Denton fell off of his horse and suffered severe spinal injuries. While undergoing emergency surgery, Malcolm died of his injuries. Katherine Blanchard, a nurse at the hospital where Malcolm died, was a friend of Sandra Davis, Malcolm's girlfriend. Katherine called Sandra and told her about Malcolm's death. As a consequence, Sandra rushed over to the hospital. Malcolm's body was still warm when Sandra arrived at the hospital. Once Dr. Greg Abbott confirmed that Malcolm was deceased, Sandra begged him to extract some of Malcolm's sperm, so she could use it to conceive his child. Sandra showed the doctor letters from Malcolm stating that he wanted her to be the mother of his children. The sympathetic doctor complied with Sandra's request, and she left the hospital with a little piece of Malcolm. Sandra looked forward to holding Malcolm's child in her arms one day. The doctor was glad that something good had come out of the tragedy. The doctor's happiness lasted until Malcolm's wife arrived and demanded to see her husband.

To extract or not extract

When the frozen sperm of a dead man is involved, the person has to go to a fertility clinic in order to request the release of the sperm. In turn, the fertility clinic acts in accordance with the agreement that it had with the man or follows the dictates of a court order. The process is orderly enough because there is no sense of urgency. If the woman is not satisfied with the actions that the clinic takes, she has the opportunity to present her case in court. The situations involving the postmortem retrieval of fresh sperm are more chaotic. These circumstances typically occur when a man is killed or dies suddenly. In order to maintain the viability of the sperm, the extraction has to be made within hours of his death. Because a man in a vegetative state may be physically deteriorating doctors may be forced to retrieve his sperm as soon as it is feasible. Due to the emergency nature of these types of cases, the parties usually do not have time to pause and breathe. The doctor has to make the decision to extract or not to extract quickly. As a result of the pace of the process, the dead or vegetative man's sperm may be harvested even before there is a definite recipient. People may be troubled by the fact that a doctor who may have no prior relationship with the man is called upon to remove sperm from his dead or dying body. There will definitely be ethical concerns.

Ethics considerations

After a tree dies, it may be chopped down to use as firewood. The process may take place little by little. A person may chop away at the tree until there is nothing left but the stump. That action is acceptable because a tree starts off as an object and ends up as an object. It is unethical to treat a dead man like a piece of property by cutting away the parts that represent the essence of who he is. Even though the options available to extract sperm are not overly invasive, some may consider using needles and knives on a dead man to extract his sperm to be the mutilation of a dead body. As a society, we tend to respect the dead. That reverence may stem from the fact that we are all just one heartbeat away from death. Therefore, we can put ourselves in the position of the dead person, and imagine the manner in which we would want to be treated. Further, some may be moved by the fact that a dead person is unable to protect himself or herself from abuse. The perceived helplessness of the dead person may bring out the protective instinct in people. For some people, dying is a process; for others, it is almost instantaneous. It only takes a moment for a man to be transformed from an autonomous person to something resembling an object. The average person needs more than a moment to view a loved one as a corpse. Therefore, some members of the dead man's family may object to the extraction of his sperm.

Ethical concerns are magnified when the request involves retrieving sperm from the body of a man who is in a vegetative state without having the man's consent. It may be seen as dehumanizing the man by treating him as nothing more than a source of sperm. If the man was not incapacitated, doctors would not even think about manipulating his body to artificially release his sperm unless he had given his written consent. It seems unfair to treat a man who has been rendered helpless by injury or disease as if he no longer has the right to autonomy. Persons may frown on the requesting party's actions. Instead of focusing upon the medical needs of the man, that person is putting his or her energy and resources into obtaining his sperm so he or she can have a child in the future. It is as if the person has given up on the incompetent man and is planning to create a replacement person to love. Doctors should not be complicit in the requesting person's unethical conduct.

Given the time constraints, doctors may extract the sperm and wait on the court to tell them to whom to release the sperm. Sperm is usually retrieved by an urologist who may not be associated with a sperm bank or a fertility clinic. After the sperm is retrieved, it must be frozen and stored in an appropriate facility. Several potentialities may result in the facility being stuck with the sperm. For instance, the court may decide that the person who requested the sperm is not entitled to use it to conceive the man's child. In addition, once the requesting person has had time to grieve, he or she may decide that posthumous reproduction is not a good idea. In fact, a wife may feel pressured to conceive her dead husband's child. Pamela Maresca's story is illustrative.

Pamela Maresca lost her husband as the result of an automobile accident after they had been married for a mere sixteen days. At that time, Pamela was a twenty-two-year-old college student. While surgeons were harvesting Manny's organs, Leslie Maresca, Manny's mother, suggested that they have his sperm extracted and frozen, so Pamela could have his child. The doctor removed Manny's epididymis gland and extracted his living sperm cells. Because she was on birth control the doctors told Pamela that she had to wait to try to conceive. It seemed that Leslie was more desperate for a grandchild than Pamela was to have a child. For example, Leslie said: "If for some medical reason it turns out that Pam could not carry Manny's baby, then he has got a sister who would be happy to do it or I could even carry the child."[9] Eventually, Pamela decided that she did not want to use Manny's sperm to conceive a child. Nonetheless, Leslie still expressed her interest in having a grandchild.[10]

A few other ethical concerns must be mentioned. One is the fact that, in a rush to retrieve the sperm while it is still viable, the doctors may not have enough time to screen the dead man's sperm for genetic abnormalities and other risks to the resulting child. If the sperm is tested after extraction and doctors uncover a problem, the woman will probably be devastated. It would be like she is losing her husband for a second time. It is unethical to expose the woman to that kind of pain at a time when she is especially vulnerable. Along those same lines, extracting the man's sperm may give the woman false hope. The sperm may be of low quality prior to retrieval or it may become damaged during the extraction process. For example, Gisela Marrero was unable to conceive using sperm extracted from her dead boyfriend because the sample was insufficient.[11] Finally, by extracting the sperm, the clinic may be the catalyst of disagreements among the dead man's remaining family members. Once the dead man's sperm is retrieved and frozen, the court may have to get involved if someone objects to the sperm being released to his spouse or another requesting party. For example, the litigation in Diane Blood's case arose because the clinic extracted her comatose husband's sperm in violation of the law.

Legal perspectives

Most of the published lawsuits involve women going to court to obtain the right to use their dead husband's frozen sperm. With regards to the retrieval of fresh sperm, the majority of the reported cases that required judicial intervention appear to be those involving requests from parents and girlfriends. The cases described at the beginning of this chapter demonstrate that, as long as wives and intended wives can afford to pay for the process and receive family support, doctors are likely to comply with the request to extract sperm from a dead man's body. The case involving the military wife was probably treated differently because the deceased soldier had designated his mother as the person with the authority to handle his remains. If the mother had supported the wife's request for postmortem sperm retrieval, the restraining order may not have been necessary. The Army was trying to protect itself from potential litigation. Because they are given very little guidance on the appropriate way to handle requests for postmortem sperm harvesting the clinic's response depends upon the opinion of the doctor that happens to be on duty at the time that the request is made. Until there is a uniform regulatory scheme for posthumous reproduction, fertility clinics have to rely upon other areas of law for guidance.

Probate law approach–the surviving spouse inherits the sperm

The man's surviving spouse may argue that he or she has a right to have his sperm extracted because like other personal property sperm is inheritable. The estate of a man who dies without executing a valid will is distributed in accordance with the state's intestacy system. When a man dies intestate, his surviving spouse has the legal right to receive a portion of his estate before it is distributed to anyone else. After the surviving spouse receives a share, the man's estate is divided among his descendants if he has any. If the man is not survived by descendants, depending on the jurisdiction, the surviving spouse might take the entire estate or it might go to the man's parents. Probate law is in place to govern the disposition of the property of the dead. In order for probate law to be applicable, a man's sperm must be classified as personal property. In the *Hecht* case, the court permitted Kane to dispose of his sperm in his will just like any other piece of property that he owned. If a man's sperm can be bequeathed in his will, it should be able to become a part of his probate estate. Once the sperm is placed under the jurisdiction of the Probate Court, it can be distributed to the next-of-kin in the manner dictated by the intestacy scheme. An analogy is a bank account that is the husband's separate property. If the husband does not designate a beneficiary, the bank account becomes a part of his intestate estate. The man's surviving spouse is legally eligible to receive all or a portion of the contents of the account. Likewise, since a man's sperm is probate property, his surviving spouse should be entitled to have his sperm extracted so that he or she can use it to conceive.

Unfortunately, for the surviving spouse an argument based upon the intestacy system is flawed. A situation involving fresh sperm is factually different from the *Hecht* case. In *Hecht*, the man went to great lengths to have his sperm extracted and frozen, so that it would be available to his girlfriend. There was no question about the fact that he wanted sperm retrieved from his body because he permitted it to happen while he was still alive. Fresh sperm inside of a man's body is different from frozen sperm outside of a man's body.[12] A probate court may be reluctant to classify the former as property. It would be too much like labeling a living person as property. Because of the history of slavery in America and the rest of the world people are uncomfortable thinking of a person as a piece of property. Furthermore, in the *Hecht* case, the man gave his written permission for his extracted sperm to be given to his girlfriend. The case turned on the fact that the man consented to the use of his sperm.

The purpose of the intestacy system is to carry out the presumed intent of the decedent.[13] The law presumes that the man would want his property to be distributed to his surviving spouse and next-of-kin. This presumption makes sense because if the property does not go to the man's survivors, it may end up being claimed by the state. The inheritance system was established on the premise that a man wants the property that he spends a life-time acquiring to be inherited by his relatives. There is no similar logical reason to assume that a man would want his sperm harvested so that it can be given to his surviving spouse or next-of-kin. The average person expects his or her dead body to remain intact. If the probate argument fails, the surviving spouse may claim that he or she has a property interest in the body.

Property law approach–the surviving spouse has a property interest in the body

Property ownership is made up of a bundle of sticks that represents a collection of individual rights.[14] Those rights include the right to include, the right to exclude, the right to convey, and the right to dispose.[15] The number of sticks in the bundle varies. State law dictates the sticks that are in the person's bundle.[16] The law determines how many of the rights the person has to possess in order to take the action he or she contemplates.[17] Relying on the "bundle of sticks" concept, the surviving spouse may be able to argue that he or she has a property interest in the man's dead body. A man's surviving spouse can exercise the right to include by permitting the man's body to be invaded in order to have his organs harvested.[18] In addition, the surviving spouse's right to exclude may be illustrated by his or her ability to prevent unauthorized autopsies[19] and his or her authority to prevent a doctor from excising the man's corneal tissue.[20] Further, the surviving spouse's right to convey may be evidenced by the power that he or she has to donate the man's body to science and/or his organs for transplantation.[21] Finally, the man's surviving spouse has the legal right to determine the disposition of his body. He or she may decide to have the man buried, cremated or frozen.[22] If the surviving spouse is able to successfully argue that he or she owns the man's dead body, he or she may be able to convince a court that she should be able to authorize the extraction of his sperm.

The right to include

The law permits a surviving spouse to donate his or her husband's organs. In 1968, the National Conference of Commissioners on Uniform State Laws

(NCCUSL) approved the Uniform Anatomical Gift Act (UAGA) to encourage persons to donate their organs in order to increase the number of organs available for research and transplantation. It also sought to clarify the persons who could consent to the organ donation.[23] All fifty states and the District of Columbia have enacted some version of the UAGA. In an attempt to make it easier for people to donate and to ensure that the donor's wishes are carried out, the NCCUSL revised the UAGA in 1987. About half of the states adopted the 1987 revisions.[24] Even after the 1987 amendments, health care providers sought approval from family members before following the instructions left by the dead donor. To resolve that problem, in 2006, the NCCUSL revised the UAGA for a second time. The drafters included language in the revised version of the UAGA indicating that when a donor's intentions are clear, "there is no reason to seek consent from the family as they have no right to give it legally." The drafters emphasized that the donor's decision should take precedence over the wishes of the surviving family members. However, if a person has not made a gift or expressed opposition to the donation of his or her organs, family members have the authority to consent to the donation of the person's organs.[25] If the person is survived by a spouse, the spouse is the person who is legally authorized to give or deny permission to invade the person's body to remove the organs for donation. Nothing prohibits the surviving spouse from designating himself or herself as the recipient of the dead man's kidney if he or she needs one.

The question becomes whether this right to include gives the surviving spouse enough of an ownership interest in his or her dead husband's body to allow him or her to have his sperm extracted. If he or she can consent to have the dead man's organs removed, should he or she be able to consent to have his sperm harvested? Courts would probably answer this question in the negative. Because organs and sperm serve different purposes the law should not treat the disposition of them in the same manner. When the UAGA was promulgated, it does not appear that the drafters intended for it to apply to sperm. The USGA permits a man's organs to be donated for transplantation, therapy, research and education. Procreation, the primary purpose for which sperm is used, does not fit into any of the enumerated categories. To ensure that there is a consistent supply of organs, if a man does not consent to the donation of his organs, the law permits his next-of-kin to take over the task as long as he has not indicated his opposition to being an organ donor. There is no such process in place for sperm donations.

In jurisdictions where there are regulations, only the man can legally consent to the extraction of his sperm. These regulations seek to protect a man's autonomy. Organ donation and sperm donation also have different consequences. As a result of an organ donation, an independent third party may receive the gift of better health. The main consequence of the donation and use of sperm is the conception of a dependent third party. From a public policy perspective, the former result is more desirable than the latter. Due to the shortage of viable donor organs, there is a need for more organ donations. Given the current overcrowding in the world, one would be hard pressed to argue that there is a need for more children. Even though a surviving spouse has the right to permit a doctor to enter his or her dead husband's body to remove his organs, it is doubtful that a court would find that he or she has the authority to have the man's sperm extracted.

The right to exclude

The right to exclude is considered to be the most important stick in the bundle.[26] That exclusivity permits the possessor of the right to prevent others from using or possessing the property.[27] After a man dies, his surviving spouse has the right to stop a medical examiner from conducting an unauthorized autopsy and to prevent a doctor from entering his body to remove his corneal tissue. With regards to a dead body, the right to exclude does not give a surviving spouse absolute ownership of his or her dead husband's body. In an early case, a New York Court ruled in favor of a widow who filed suit after an autopsy was performed on her husband without her consent.[28] The Court noted that a person's right to possess a dead body for burial included the right to receive the body in the same condition it was in when the person died. Therefore, if that right was violated, the person had a valid cause of action for damages.[29] The Court emphasized that the person did not have a property right in the dead body. The person's legal interest was limited to the right to possess the body for the purpose of a decent burial.[30] This right can be superseded by a statute that permits a medical examiner to conduct an autopsy with or without the surviving spouse's consent.[31]

The moment the man dies his surviving spouse has the right to legally possess his body. In most cases, the surviving spouse's quasi-property right in the dead body gives him or her the authority to prevent a doctor from mutilating the body by performing an autopsy.[32] The surviving spouse has a corresponding right to ask that his or her husband's body be autopsied. Therefore, it appears that the surviving spouse has the power to control the manner in which a man's body is treated once he dies. In light of that dominance, a surviving spouse may argue that he or she should have the legal authority to control the handling of all parts of the dead man's body, including his sperm. Because the surviving spouse is able to request that a procedure as invasive as an autopsy be performed on his or her dead husband's body he or she should be able to ask for postmortem sperm retrieval. Courts will probably not find this argument to be persuasive.

One of the main reasons why the law prohibits unauthorized autopsies is to ensure that the next-of-kin is able to give the deceased a proper burial ceremony. For some cultures, decorum dictates that a public viewing of the corpse be held, so the condition of the body is very important. Other persons object to autopsies on religious grounds. None of these reasons support permitting a surviving spouse to have his or her dead husband's sperm harvested without his consent. If the sperm remains inside of the man's dead body, it will not adversely impact his ability to receive a proper interment. In order to determine cause of death, the law typically mandates that an autopsy be performed in situations where the person dies young, suddenly or under suspicious circumstances.[33] The purpose of the autopsy is not to retain the man's organs and other tissues. In fact, some or all of these items may be discarded during and after the autopsy. On the other hand, a surviving spouse who asks that sperm be extracted from his or her dead husband's body probably has only one goal in mind – procreation.

In almost half of the states, a medical examiner can remove the cornea or corneal tissue from a dead body unless he or she knows that the surviving relatives have objected to the removal.[34] Unlike organ harvesting, the statutory framework governing corneal extraction has created an opt-out system.[35] The legislative decision to make it easier for medical examiners to remove corneas and corneal tissue was motivated by the desire to increase the supply available to persons suffering from vision impairments. Corneal extraction has the potential to modify the outer appearance of the dead. Therefore, the law gives the next-of-kin the opportunity to object to the removal. If the surviving relatives do not oppose the procedure in a timely manner, the medical examiner does not need permission to extract the corneas and corneal tissue. Nonetheless, the surviving spouse has the legal right to prevent the medical examiner from removing his or her dead husband's corneas. Corneal tissue is so different from sperm that a court is unlikely to be convinced that a surviving spouse's right to control the removal of his or her dead husband's corneas should lead to a similar right to decide whether his sperm should be extracted. A surviving spouse's right to exclude a third party from entering her dead husband's body to remove organs or corneal tissue is probably not expansive enough to give him or her the authority to have the dead man's sperm harvested without his prior consent.

The right to convey

The right to convey refers to the ability to transfer ownership of a piece of property to another person. The conveyance may be in exchange for consideration or gratuitous. This legal right is usually meant to encompass transfers of real property. The term "sale" is reserved for situations involving personal property. In this case, I am using conveyance and sale interchangeably. A person has the legal right to donate his or her body for scientific research. Once the gift is accepted, the donee has the right to control the final disposition of the body.[36] If a person does not exercise his or her right to convey his or her body, that right falls to the surviving spouse. It seems unfair to deny a surviving spouse who is selfless enough to donate his or her dead husband's body to possibly improve the lives of others the opportunity to keep some of his sperm. Courts may not be moved by this equity argument because the natures of the gifts are so different. On the one hand, the gift of the body to scientists may lead to discoveries that save the lives of countless people. On the other hand, if the surviving spouse retains the sperm for himself or herself, that gift could result in the creation of children without the man's consent. Neither the man nor society will be adversely impacted if his body is donated to science. However, the self-donation of the man's sperm to his surviving spouse has the potential to go against his wishes and to place a financial burden on society. Proving that he or she has a right to convey the dead man's body may not help the surviving spouse to achieve his or her goal of getting the right to have some of the dead man's sperm retrieved.

The right to dispose

The right to dispose of property is an inherent aspect of property ownership.[37] For example, an owner has the right to sell his property, to gift it, to bequeath it and to destroy it. Courts have held that a body is not property in the ordinary commercial sense. Nonetheless, the law acknowledges that the right to the possession of a dead body for the purposes of a decent burial belongs to the surviving spouse.[38] That right gives the surviving spouse the authority to arrange the final disposition of the body.[39] In essence, the surviving spouse has the legal right to decide whether to bury, cremate or freeze his or her dead husband's body. The surviving spouse's authority over the body does not end until the body has been buried.[40] However, the court has the power to limit the actions a person can take with regards to a dead body.[41] For instance, most states have statutes making it a crime to desecrate a dead body.[42]

None of those statutes exempt a surviving spouse from prosecution. Therefore, a man or woman would probably not be permitted to mutilate his or her dead husband's body. A surviving spouse might argue that until he or she buries his or her husband he or she has the legal right to control what happens to the body. Therefore, he or she should have the authority to have some of the man's sperm retrieved prior to his burial. Some courts refer to the surviving spouse's interest in his or her dead husband's body as a quasi-property right. However, with regards to the right to dispose, the surviving spouse's interest in the body is classified as a duty and not a right. As his surviving spouse, the person is obligated to ensure that the man is given a proper burial. The surviving spouse's qualified right to dispose of his or her husband's body is limited to his or her ability to control the treatment of his body before and after burial. Authorizing the harvesting of the dead man's sperm likely exceeds the scope of power that the right to dispose gives to the surviving spouse.

The law has acknowledged that a surviving spouse has some interest in his or her dead husband's body that resembles ownership. However, that quasi-property law interest is probably not sufficient for the person to successfully ask a court for permission to harvest the dead man's sperm. In cases involving men in vegetative states[43] it would not be appropriate for the spouse to make arguments based upon either probate law or property law. Before a health care provider or a court complies with a man or woman's request to harvest sperm from his or her incompetent husband, it will try to ascertain the husband's wishes. That inquiry may be helped by the adoption of a medical ethics approach.

Medical law approach–the surviving spouse gets the sperm if the dead man so desires

The decision of whether or not to permit the extraction of sperm from a man in a vegetative state may be informed by the manner in which the law treats vegetative patients in general. Patients in vegetative states usually have the ability to survive for years. A court gets involved in the case when relatives ask the health care provider to withhold nutrition and hydration from the vegetative patient. Like any other patient, a patient in a vegetative state has a right to refuse medical treatment even if that refusal will result in death.[44] At the core of that right is the patient's right to self-determination.[45] Because a patient in a vegetative cannot verbalize his or her wishes with regards to maintaining or ending life-sustaining treatment the court has to take steps to ascertain the decision the patient would make. If the patient has executed a living will or other type of advance directive, the court's decision is made easy. In cases where the patient's wishes have not been expressed in writing, the person's next-of-kin has the legal right to exercise the patient's right to refuse medical treatment. However, that right must be exercised in a way that reflects the wishes of the patient. The decision-maker's opinions cannot supersede the views of the patient.

Courts rely on three different tests (subjective, limited objective, and pure objective) in order to determine whether or not to order the cessation of life-sustaining treatment. The level of evidence that is available to show the incompetent patient's wishes determines the test that is utilized. If there is clear and convincing evidence of what the patient would want, the subjective test is applied to permit the medical decision-maker to substitute his or her voice to ensure that the health care provider acts accordingly.[46] For example, if the evidence shows that the incompetent patient would not want to continue receiving life-sustaining treatment, the medical decision-maker can ask the hospital to stop the treatment. If some trustworthy evidence of the incompetent patient's intent can be found, but not enough to fully determine subjective intent, the court may use the limited objective test. Under that test, the court will only allow life-sustaining treatment to be terminated if it concludes that action would be in the patient's best interests.[47] When there is no reliable evidence indicating the patient's wishes, courts employ the pure objective test. This test allows life-sustaining treatment to be withdrawn in cases where the "effect of administering life-sustaining treatment would be inhumane due to severe recurring and unavoidable pain."[48]

A man in a vegetative state cannot consent to the extraction of his sperm. However, that may not end the inquiry. The spouse is usually the one who gets to determine whether or not to withdraw life-sustaining treatment from a patient who is in a persistent or permanent vegetative state. Therefore, the spouse of a man in a vegetative state has the legal authority to request that he be deprived of nutrition and hydration. If a man or woman is permitted to make medical decisions that result in his or her husband's death, why should he or she not be allowed to make choices that may cause the man's bloodline to continue? From a medical ethics perspective, in order to get the right to have sperm extracted from his or her vegetative husband, the spouse must present evidence showing that the man would have wanted to have a child conceived using his sperm or that the sperm retrieval is in the man's best interests.

Subjective test

If the spouse successfully meets the requirements of the subjective test, he or she may be granted permission to have the man's sperm extracted. As the decision-maker, the spouse has a duty to determine subjectively the course of action the man would have taken if he were competent. The decision regarding the man's sperm should focus upon the man's wishes and not the spouse's desires. In order to get the court to apply the subjective test, the spouse has to show by clear and convincing evidence, that the incompetent man would want his sperm retrieved. This is a heavy burden for the person to carry. Clear and convincing evidence dictates a high standard of proof. It requires the introduction of evidence that "should produce in the mind of the trier of fact a firm belief or conviction as to the truth of the allegations sought to be established."[49] The spouse's ability to meet her burden of proof may depend upon the stage where the couple is in the reproductive process.

In one scenario, a happily married couple talks about having children in the future. Then, before they can attempt to conceive, the man ends up in a vegetative state. Typically, when the spouse tries to convince a health care provider to retrieve sperm from the incompetent husband's body, the spouse claims that the couple had agreed that they wanted children. Therefore, the spouse would probably try that same tactic with a court. The spouse's self-serving testimony about conversations that he or she had with the man about children may not be persuasive to the court. Because the man is in a vegetative state he is unable to verify or contradict the statements that the surviving spouse makes with regards to their communications on the subject of children. Furthermore, the court may not consider the content of those conversations to be relevant. Even a man who wants to be a father may change his mind if he knows that he will never be able to interact with the child. Therefore, evidence of the man's views on fatherhood prior to his incapacitation probably would not be enough to satisfy the clear and convincing evidence burden.

In another scenario, before the man becomes incapacitated, the couple may be trying to conceive using assisted reproductive technology. The woman may need fresh sperm from the man's body because his previously frozen sperm samples are insufficient to help her achieve a pregnancy. The woman may be able to present a copy of the signed agreement between the man and the sperm bank showing that the man indicated that, in the event of his death, he wanted his frozen sperm released to his wife. A court may conclude that the provision in the agreement is enough to show clear and convincing evidence that the man wanted to conceive a child with his wife even if he died before the conception. Based upon that conclusion, the court may reason that, since the man did not have a problem becoming a father posthumously, he would want his wife to conceive his child even if he is incapacitated. That supposition may be enough for the court to permit the woman to speak for her incompetent husband.

Best interests test

The objective tests are both about deciding what is in the best interests of the patient. With regards to maintaining or removing life-sustaining treatment, the court evaluates the benefits and the burdens of the treatment to determine what is in the incompetent patient's best interests.[50] If the treatment only prolongs the patient's pain and suffering and provides no opportunity for improvement, the court is likely to permit it to be terminated. Situations involving postmortem sperm retrieval are different from those dealing with the withdrawal of medical treatment. The spouse is asking the court to decide if the man's best interests will be served by the extraction of his sperm. This is a difficult question to answer because it is unclear whether or not the man will benefit or suffer because of the extraction of his sperm. I am not discussing the possible conception of a child from the sperm. I am talking about the retrieval process. The procedure itself will probably not increase the man's level of pain and suffering. The main benefit is that it leaves open the possibility that the man may become a father in the future. In a case like this, the court will probably determine that anything that goes against a man's right to self-determination is not in his best interests. Therefore, it all boils down to consent. If the spouse is not able to prove that the man would have wanted his sperm retrieved posthumously, the court will probably not grant her request.

The medical ethics approach may not be appropriate in cases dealing with posthumous reproduction. The right to refuse medical treatment and the right to not procreate are both fundamental rights. In the event that a person is not able to exercise those rights, should someone else be able to exercise them on the person's behalf? Courts have answered this question in the affirmative in the context of withdrawing life-sustaining treatment. The question with regards to the right to procreate has not been directly posed. However, case law indicates that the right to procreate is a personal decision that cannot be made by a substitute decision-maker. Therefore, if a spouse cannot present proof that the man wanted to reproduce posthumously, the court will probably not give permission to have sperm extracted from the man's body.

Possible health care provider liability

A health care provider who extracts fresh sperm from the body of a man who is dead or in a vegetative state may have to defend that action in court. Cases involving the man's spouse are unlikely to expose the doctor to the threat of litigation. Doctors should be concerned about situations involving significant others and parents. Because neither a significant other nor an engaged person is legally recognized as a man's next-of-kin a health care provider should not harvest his sperm in response to that person's request. The wise course of action is for the health care provider to insist on a court order approving the process. A health care provider who complies with the request may be sued by the man's next-of-kin. If the health care provider fulfills the request of one parent, he or she may be sued by the other parent. The lawsuit will be based upon the unauthorized extraction of the man's sperm. I will discuss a couple of the possible causes of action.

Man in vegetative state (medical battery)

When a doctor performs a procedure without the patient's consent, he exposes himself to two possible tort actions – medical battery and lack of informed consent.[51] I will not discuss the tort of lack of informed consent because medical battery is a more appropriate cause of action.[52] A battery refers to the unsanctioned touching of the person of another.[53] Unlike in the case of a traditional battery case, the plaintiff pleading a medical battery does not have to show that the defendant meant to cause harm or offensive contact.[54] To establish a medical battery, the plaintiff must prove "a total lack of consent to the procedure performed, that the treatment was contrary to the patient's will, or that the treatment was at substantial variance with the consent granted."[55] Because a medical battery is an intentional tort to avoid liability the doctor must prove that the patient consented to the touching at issue.[56]

The first thing the person who challenges the extraction of the man's sperm will have to prove is that the man did not consent to the procedure. In most of the cases involving requests for fresh sperm, there has been no prior written consent on the part of the man. The purpose of the consent requirement is to prevent doctors from performing procedures on patients without their informed consent. The only times doctors can act without consent is in emergency situations.[57] In an attempt to overcome this requirement, the doctor may ask the court to apply a broad interpretation of consent. For example, the doctor may argue that the man's consent should be presumed if, prior to his incapacitation, he indicated that he wanted to father children with the person who requested the sperm extraction. No court has recognized presumed or implied consent in the context of medical battery. However, cases involving retrieving sperm from men in vegetative states are so unique that a court may be willing to think outside of the box. Unlike men who die suddenly, a man in a vegetative state usually has a relationship with the doctor who harvests his sperm. Despite the emotional appeal that the person makes, the doctor must remember that the man is his patient. Consequently, the doctor should respect the autonomy of the man by not extracting his sperm without his prior consent. A doctor who fails to obtain his patient's consent before retrieving his sperm has taken the first step towards committing a medical battery.

The second thing the plaintiff has to prove is that the sperm extraction was contrary to the vegetative man's will. Even if a man has taken the time to execute an advanced directive, there is probably not any evidence of his position on the issue of sperm extraction. Those types of topics are not covered by a living will or a health care power of attorney. Consequences, the parties will have to speculate about the man's wishes. The plaintiff would have to present extrinsic evidence to support an argument that the incapacitated man would not have wanted his sperm harvested. This type of evidence will be difficult to find because sperm extraction is not usually a topic that men sit around and discuss. Even men who are participating in IVF may be reluctant to talk with their friends about the process. The doctor would have to rely on testimony from the person requesting the sperm to show that the extraction was not contrary to the man's wishes. That person would make arguments to convince the doctor to extract the sperm. The primary argument would be that the man wanted to have children. However, proof of that fact may not lead a court to conclude that a man would want his sperm extracted once he slips into a vegetative state. If neither side is able to present compelling evidence about the man's wishes, the court may rule in favor of the person opposing the extraction. In these types of cases, time is not of the essence, so a doctor should refrain from harvesting his patient's sperm without a court order.

Dead man (modified tortious interference with an expectancy (TIWE))

There is a relatively new tort that is sometimes alleged by disappointed heirs.[58] Instead of contesting the will, the person claims that a third party interfered with his or her ability to receive the inheritance that the person anticipated.[59] In some situations, the amount that one person inherits is dependent upon the number of other persons who have the right to receive a portion of the estate. The extraction and use of a dead man's sperm may increase the number of his heirs. For instance, if a man dies intestate with two surviving children, after the surviving spouse receives a portion, the estate will be divided between the children. Therefore, each child will be entitled to receive a half of the estate. That distribution may change if the man's surviving spouse conceives more of his children after his death. This reduction in inheritance can occur whether or not the man dies intestate or executes a valid will leaving his estate to his "children." A unique cause of action that may be available to a person whose inheritance is diminished by the conception of a posthumously conceived child is a modified form of TIWE. The claim would be different from a regular cause of action because the alleged wrongdoing would not be directly connected to the testamentary process. The health care provider would be sued for indirectly interfering with the receipt of the expected inheritance.

To bring a successful TIWE cause of action, the plaintiff must prove the following: "(1) the existence of an expectancy; (2) defendant's intentional interference with the expectancy; (3) conduct that is tortious in itself, such as fraud, duress, or undue influence; (4) reasonable certainty the expectancy would have been realized but for the interference; and (5) damages."[60] The person claiming the expectancy has to show that the expectation of inheriting is reasonable. To satisfy this requirement the plaintiff only has to prove that he is a "natural recipient of his parents' bounty."[61] As long as the complaining party has the right relationship to the deceased man, the first element of the tort will be fulfilled. However, the remaining elements are subject to dispute.

The second thing that the person has to show is that the health care provider intentionally interfered with his or her ability to receive the anticipated inheritance. In lay nomenclature, a person's "intention" refers to something a person means to do on purpose. It would be difficult for the plaintiff to convince the court that the doctor extracted the dead man's sperm with the intention of reducing the plaintiff's inheritance. Nonetheless, in legal terminology with regards to intentional torts, "intent" has two possible meanings. The tortfeasor must act with either the intent to cause harm to another or the belief that the harm is "substantially certain" to occur.[62]

The tort requires the plaintiff to establish that the doctor acted with the purpose of injuring the plaintiff's expectancy. Therefore, the plaintiff must persuade the court that, at the time he retrieved the dead man's sperm, the doctor intended two actions. First, the doctor expected the sperm to be used to conceive the dead man's children. Second, the doctor could have anticipated that the existence of the posthumously conceived children would adversely impact the inheritance rights of the dead man's existing children. The plaintiff will likely fail to satisfy this element of the tort. A doctor who harvests sperm from a dead man's body is not motivated by the desire to harm his existing children. The doctor may not even know that the man has children. The doctor respond to a request made by a distraught person. The doctor does not intend to injure the plaintiff and has no reason to believe that the alleged harm will occur. From a public policy perspective, courts will be reluctant to place the burden on doctors to know the intricacies of probate law. The discussion in this paragraph is also relevant to the fourth element of the tort. Therefore, it is doubtful that the plaintiff will be able to successfully plead that aspect of the tort.

The third element of the tort mandates that the plaintiff presents evidence showing that the doctor engaged in tortious or wrongful conduct.[63] This element requires the plaintiff to prove the elements of an independent tort. When describing the tort, courts refer to torts like undue influence and fraud that impact the execution of the will. However, the list of possible tortious action is not meant to be exhaustive. In cases dealing with postmortem sperm retrieval the plaintiff had several possible tort causes of action. I will briefly discuss two torts that arise when a dead body is mistreated in some way. The man's surviving spouse has the right to possession and control of his body.[64] Therefore, the causes of action I am going to describe are only relevant if the dead man is not survived by a spouse. I am thinking of situations where a man's significant other asks to have his sperm harvested.

Most states have adopted some version of the Restatement of Torts cause of action for the intentional interference with a dead body. The Restatement (Second) of Torts §868 provides: "One who intentionally, reckless or negligently removes, withholds, mutilates or operates upon the body of a dead person or prevents its proper interment or cremation is subject to liability to a member of the family of the deceased who is entitled to the disposition of the body."[65] This tort would be applicable to situations involving the extraction of a dead man's sperm without the proper consent. A doctor would not be able to successfully argue that postmortem sperm extraction was not an operation. The doctor's strongest argument would be that he received consent to perform the procedure. However, the law does not place the wishes of a girlfriend or significant other over those of the dead man's next-of-kin.

Some jurisdictions like New York still permit a person to bring a common law action for loss of sepulcher.[66] Based upon the right of sepulcher, a dead man's next-of-kin has the absolute right to the "immediate possession" of his remains, so they can arrange for a proper interment. A person who illegally interferes with that right or inappropriately handles the body of the deceased is liable for damages.[67] The purpose of the damages is to compensate the dead man's relatives for their emotional suffering and mental anguish. The plaintiff does not have to prove emotional distress. To recover damages, he or she has to prove that the emotional trauma was "the natural and proximate consequence of some wrongful act or neglect on the part of the one sought to be charged."[68] The plaintiff can show a loss of sepulcher by proving that the sperm retrieved was done without the proper consent. These are just two of the potential torts the plaintiffs can claim in order to satisfy the third element of TIWE.

The final element the plaintiff has to prove is damages. In tort cases, the most common types of damages are monetary and emotional. The plaintiffs will probably be able to prove compensatory damages if they can show that the amount of inheritance that they received was less than they would have received if the dead man's sperm had not been used to conceive more heirs.

To whom to release

As the examples presented at the beginning of the chapter indicate, the request to a physician to harvest the sperm of a man who is dead or in a vegetative state may be made by the man's spouse, parents, girlfriend or fiancée. In an increasing number of cases, physicians are not requiring that the requesting party obtain a court order. Because this area is really not regulated the physician has to decide which requests to honor. Who should be permitted to use the sperm of a man who is dead or in a vegetative state? In this section, I will briefly examine the possible answer to this question.

SPOUSES

It may be easier for the clinic to decide to release a man's sperm to his spouse. Marriage has a special status in society. Once a person gets married, he and his spouse are considered to be a unit. People are comfortable with the health care provider releasing the man's sperm to his spouse for several reasons. First, one assumes that, given a choice, a man would want his spouse to be the co-parent of his child. Unless there is evidence to the contrary, that assumption may be enough for a court to order the clinic to release the sperm to the man's surviving spouse. In the cases dealing with frozen sperm, the wife was only denied access to her husband's sperm if he specifically indicated that he did not want her to use it to conceive a child. Second, even though his or her testimony about the man's wishes may be self-serving, the spouse is probably in the best situation to know what the man would have wanted to happen to his sperm. During a marriage, couples often discuss intimate matters. That is one of the reasons why spouses may not be permitted to testify against one another or to disclose the content of confidential conversations they have with one another.[69] A third reason why it may be acceptable to release the sperm to the spouse is that the parties in a marriage are presumed to act in one another's best interest. That is the reason why the spouse is the one who is allowed to make health care decisions on behalf of an incompetent patient. Lastly, the law recognizes the special relationship between a man and his spouse by making it difficult for a man to disinherit his spouse. In fact, it is easier for a man to disinherit his minor child than it is for him to disinherit his spouse.[70] From a practical perspective, the clinic is probably safe from liability if it releases the sperm to the man's spouse because there usually is no one else who has legal standing to object.

PARENTS

If the dead or vegetative man is unmarried and the parents agree, courts have allowed the man's parents to obtain his fresh sperm. There is a legal framework that supports releasing the sperm to the man's parents. Under the parental rights doctrine, courts have presumed that parents act in the best interests of their children.[71] Therefore, unless they voluntarily terminate their rights, parents have the rights to rear their children without undue government interference.[72] The government will only intercede when there is some type of abuse. Parents have a right to make medical decisions on behalf of their children. That right does not end just because the child becomes an adult. Moreover, under the intestacy system, if an unmarried man dies intestate without surviving children, his parents are the first in line to inherit his property. This is the case even if the man is in a long-term relationship. Significant others do not have the right to supersede the rights of the parents. For instance, prior to the legalization of same-sex marriage, health care providers would often recognize the parents, and not the partner, as the medical decision-makers. Similar to cases involving surviving spouses, the clinic can release the man's sperm to his parents without the fear of litigation.

From an ethical and public policy perspective, it may not be a good idea for the clinic to release the sperm to the man's parents. Cases where the parents obtain the sperm of their dead son are especially troubling. Once the parents have the sperm, in order to make their dreams of becoming grandparents come true, they will have to buy donor eggs and hire a surrogate to gestate the embryo. In the United States, surrogacy is illegal in some jurisdictions and has been deemed to be against public policy in others. Therefore, the parents may have to go outside of the country to find a surrogate. Reproductive tourism opens up a set of other problems that may not be in the best interests of the parents, the surrogate or the posthumously conceived child. Even if the parents manage to obtain a surrogate problems may still arise. What happens if the surrogate refuses to surrender custody, of the child? Surrogate custody dispute cases will be discussed in Chapter Five.

In some cases, the dead man's mother may buy donor eggs and decide to gestate the child. This would result in a situation of a woman giving birth to her own grandchild. From a medical perspective, based upon the age or health of the woman, it may be unethical for a doctor to implant the embryo into the dead man's mother. In addition, a lot of people may be uncomfortable with that scenario. Parents who want to use the sperm of their dead son to create a child usually plan to raise the child. At the height of the A.I.D.S. and crack epidemics, grandparents were forced to step in and raised their grandchildren. Those situations were necessary, but not ideal. As previously discussed, it may not be in the child's best interests to be raised by grandparents. The possibility that a teenager will be forced to be a caregiver is too high.

Girlfriends and significant others

In cases where the request does not come from a spouse or parent, the health care provider should act with caution. Requests by girlfriends and significant others may be challenging for several reasons. First, in some circumstances, the man's dating life may be very active. Therefore, a health care provider may have a tough time determining to whom to release the sperm. It would be unwise for the health care provider to adopt a first-come, first serve policy. Besides, neither health care providers nor courts want to undertake the job of deciding with which woman the man would want to conceive a child. It would be against public policy and unethical for the health care provider to release the sperm to more than one woman. Second, it may be next to impossible for the health care provider to confirm the presence of a relationship if the couple is not legally married when the request is made. The health care provider usually has to make the decision to extract the sperm fairly quickly, so there may not be time to verify the veracity of the person's contention. Third, as previously discussed, society typically assumes that a man wants to procreate with his spouse. That assumption is evident by the law's presumption that a man is the father of children born to his wife during their marriage.[73] No such presumption exists in non-marital situations.

The world is changing. The number of persons who are choosing to live together without the benefit of marriage is increasing.[74] Likewise, the number of children born as a consequence of non-marital relationships continues to expand.[75] Therefore, it may be time for the law to recognize the relationships that people value. If a man is engaged to marry a woman or a man dies before the deed is done, is that relationship less important than one involving a couple who has been married for five years? In the past, the law has recognized less formal relationships. For instance, some states still give legitimacy to common law marriages.[76] The solution to the above-raised concerns is not to disregard relationships that have not been formalized through marriage. Instead, the law can place a heavy burden on the girlfriend or significant other to prove that the dead man had contemplated having children with him or her. When evaluating these non-marital relationships, the court should consider whether or not the couple had established a husband-spouse type relationship. In making that determination, some factors the courts might deem relevant include how long the couple had been together, if the couple lived together, if the couple already had children together and any other evidence indicating that the couple intended to have a long-term relationship.

Conclusion

Most people do not plan for accidental death or sudden illness. This is especially true among young men. A man's loved ones are usually devastated when tragedy strikes. Erma Bombeck said: "children make your life important." It may be that sentiment that drives a person to want to insure that the dead man has children so that his life will have significance. Instead of idly mourning, a spouse, a parent, a girlfriend or a significant other may ask a health care provider to extract fresh sperm from the dead man's body. In some cases, the health care provider will not act without a court order. At other times, influenced by the fact that time is of the essence, the health care provider may comply with the request. In both situations, the health care provider opens itself up to liability if one of the man's loved ones objects to the procedure. If the sperm is released to a spouse or a parent, the chance of litigation is small. However, a health care provider who gives the man's sperm to a girlfriend or significant other may have to go to court to justify that decision. Currently, non-marital relationships are not on par with marital ones. Thus, the health care provider may be unable to defend its actions.

Notes

1 To obtain sperm using electro ejaculation, the doctor uses a rectal probe to deliver electricity through the rectal wall, inducing seminal emission. If the man's cardiac activity has stopped, doctors may not be able to retrieve his sperm using electro ejaculation. In that case, doctors may be forced to surgically extract the sperm. Dana A. Ohl, John Park, Carl Cohen, Karen Goodman, Alan C. Mengi, Procreation after death or mental incompetence: medical advance or technology gone awry?, 66 Fertility & Sterility 889, 891 (December 1996).

2 Microsurgical epididymal sperm aspiration (MESA) is done as follows. The doctor makes a small cut in the skin of the scrotum. Then, the doctor uses a microscope to aspirate fluid directly from the opening in the epididymal tubule with a micropipette. The fluid sample is examined to see if sperm is present. The doctor continues the process until he is able to obtain a sufficient amount of sperm. Sherman J. Silber, Zsolt P. Nagy, Jiaen Liu, Hugo Godoy, Paul Devroey and Andre C. van Steirteghem, Conventional in-vitro fertilization versus intracytoplasmic sperm injection for patients requiring microsurgical sperm aspiration, 9 Human Reproduction 1705, 1706 (1994).

3 Testicular sperm extraction involves the doctor removing a small piece of tissue from the testicle and extracting sperm from it. This is referred to as a surgical biopsy of the testis. Jacob Rajfer, TESA or TESE: Which is Better for Sperm Extraction?, Rev. Urol. 2006 Summer, 8(3): 171.

4 *Kyneshia Dhanoola v United States Department of Army, Emergency Motion for Temporary Restraining Order*, Case 4:08-CV-42-CDL (04/04/08). It is unclear whether or not Kyneshia conceived a child using her dead husband's sperm. According to her Facebook page, she got engaged to Wendell Dowers on February 28, 2016.

5 A baby with my deceased fiancé, www.gofundme.com/gp6egw (November 3, 2014).

6 Lizzie Parry, Woman has her fiance's sperm extracted just hours after his death thanks to generous strangers who donated $11,000 for the procedure at www.dailymail.co.uk (November 8, 2014).

7 Emma Brockes, Blood Lines, Interview: Diane Blood at www.theguardian.com/science (October 18, 2004).

8 Baby Is Born Using Sperm From Dead Father, www.articles.latimes.com (March 27, 1999).

9 Widow Hopes Sperm Allows Husband To "Live On" at http://articles.chicagotribune.com/1994-06-03/news/9406030273_1_pam-maresca-manny-maresca-leslie-maresca (June 3, 1994).
10 Susan Kerr, Post-Mortem Sperm Procurement: Is It Legal?, 3 Depaul J. Health Care L. 39, 42 (1999–2000).
11 Browne Lewis, *Graveside Birthday Parties: The Legal Consequences of Forming Families Posthumously,* 60 Case W. Res. L. Rev. 1159, 1179 (Summer 2010).
12 The law has recognized that sperm extracted from a man's body is property. No court has said the same about sperm that remains inside of the body. See *Kurchner v State Farm Fire and Cas. Co.*, 858 So.2d 1220, 1221 (2003) ("Florida Statutes that govern the donation and disposition of sperm recognizes that sperm removed from the body become property").
13 *Estate of Britel*, 236 Cal. App. 4th 127, 138 (2015).
14 *Schweihs v Chase Home Finance L.L.C.*, 41 N.E.3d 1011, 1021 (2015).
15 *Id.*
16 *United States v Craft*, 535 U.S. 274, 278 (2002).
17 *Mitchell Aero, Inc. v City of Michigan*, 168 N.W.2d 183, 185–186 (1969).
18 *Kelly-Nevils v Detroit Receiving Hosp.*, 526 N.W. 2d 15, 18 (Mich. App. 1995).
19 *Kelly v Brigham & Women Hosp.*, 745 N.E. 2d 969, 973 (Mass. 2001).
20 *Sattler v Northwest Tissue Center*, 42 P. 3d 440, 442 (Wash. 2002).
21 *Brown v Delaware Valley Transplant Program*, 615 A.2d 1379, 1381 (Pa. 1994).
22 *Crawford v J. Avery Bryan Funeral Home, Inc.*, 253 S.W. 3d 149, 157 (Tenn. 2007).
23 Unif. Anatomical Gift Act (1968) Prefatory Note, 8A U.L.A. 64–65 (1993). See also *Perry v Saint Francis Hospital & Med. Ctr.*, 886 F.Supp 1551, 1557 (D.Kan. 1995).
24 Gloria Banks, Legal and Ethical Safeguards: Protection of Society's Most Vulnerable Participants in a Commercialized Organ Transplantation System, 21 Am. J.L. & Med. 45, 67 (1995).
25 Unif. Anatomical Gift Act § 3(a).
26 *Keyzer v Amerilink*, Ltd., 618 S.E. 2d 768, 773 (N.C. 2005).
27 *Petition of Borough of Bryertown*, 466 A.2d 239, 245 (1983) citing *Loretto v Teleprompter Manhattan CATV Corp.*, 458 U.S. 419 (1982) and *Kaiser Aetna v United States*, 444 U.S. 164 (1979).
28 *Foley v Phelps*, 1 A.D. 531, 37 N.Y.S. 471 [1st Dept. 1896].
29 *Id.*
30 *Whitehair v Highland Memory Gardens, Inc.*, 327 S.E. 2d 438, 441 (1985).
31 See, i.e. M.C.A. § 46–4–103(1) (West 2016).
32 *Darcy v The Presbyterian Hospital in the City of New York*, 95 N.E. 695 (1911).
33 *Kellogg v Office of Chief Medical Examiner of City of New York*, 735 N.Y.S.2d 350, 359 (Sup. Ct. 2001).
34 R. Alta Charo, Skin and Bones: Post-Mortem Markets in Human Tissue, 26 Nova L. Rev. 421, 431 (Winter 2002).
35 See K.S.R. § 311.1961(1)(a)–(c) (West 2016) ("(1) In any case in which a patient is in need of a cornea or corneal tissue for a transplant, the coroner, medical examiner, or his appropriately qualified designee with training in ophthalmologic techniques may, upon the request of any person authorized ***, provide or authorize the removal of the cornea or corneal tissue by a qualified physician under the following conditions: (a) The decedent has been defined as a "coroner's case" ***, an autopsy has been ordered ***, and the cornea or corneal tissue are suitable for transplant; (b) No objection by the next of kin is *known* by the coroner or medical examiner; and (c) The removal of the cornea or corneal tissue will not interfere with the subsequent course of an investigation or autopsy or alter the postmortem facial appearance" (emphasis added)) *Id.*

36 *Regents of University of California v Superior Court*, 107 Cal. Rptr. 3d 637. 646–647 (2010).
37 *Congdon v Congdon*, 200 N.W. 76, 83 (Minn. 1924).
38 One of the first cases in the United States to recognize a cause of action for unlawful autopsy was *Larson v Chase*, 50 N.W. 238, 239 (Minn. 1891) ("The right to the possession of a dead body for the purposes of preservation and burial belongs, in the absence of any testamentary disposition, to the surviving husband or wife or next of kin, and the right of the surviving wife (if living with her husband at the time of his death) is paramount to that of the next of kin.").
39 See M.D. Code, Health-General § 5–509(c)(1) (West 2016).
40 *Dougherty v Mercantile-Safe Deposit & Trust Co.*, 387 A.2d 244, 246 (1978).
41 *Spanich v Reichelderfer*, 628 N.E.2d 102, 104 (1943).
42 See M.C.L.A. § 750.160 (West 2016). See also 21 Okl. St. Ann. § 1161.1 D (West 2016) (D. For purposes of this section, "desecration of a human corpse" means any act committed after the death of a human being including, but not limited to, dismemberment, disfigurement, mutilation, burning, or any act committed to cause the dead body to be devoured, scattered or dissipated; except, those procedures performed by a state agency or licensed authority in due course of its duties and responsibilities for forensic examination, gathering or removing crime scene evidence, presentation or preservation of evidence, dead body identification, cause of death, autopsy, cremation or burial, organ donation, use of a cadaver for medical educational purposes, or other necessary procedures to identify, remove or dispose of a dead body by the proper authority"). *Id.*
43 According to Dr. Fred Plum: "Vegetative state describes a body which is functioning entirely in terms of its internal controls. It maintains temperature. It maintains heart beat and pulmonary ventilation. It maintains digestive activity. It maintains reflex activity of muscles and nerves for low level conditioned responses. But there is no behavioral evidence of either self-awareness or awareness of the surroundings in a learned manner." *Matter of Jobes*, 529 A.2d 434, 438 (1987).
44 *Matter of Conroy*, 486 A.2d 1209, 1225 (N.J. 1985).
45 *Matter of Roche*, 687 A.2d 349, 351 (1996).
46 *Conroy*, 486 A.2d at 1231.
47 *Id.*
48 *Id.* at 1232.
49 *Liberty Mut. Ins. Co. v Land*, 892 A.2d 1240, 1244 (N.J. 2006).
50 *Matter of Clark*, 510 A.2d 136, 145 (1986).
51 *Blanchard v Kellum*, 975 S.W.2d 522, 524 (Tenn. 1998).
52 "[T]o recover on a claim of lack of informed consent, a plaintiff must prove that there was an undisclosed risk that was material; that the risk materialized, injuring plaintiff; and that plaintiff would not have consented to the procedure if she had been informed of the risk. A material risk is a risk which a reasonable person would consider significant in deciding whether to undergo a particular medical treatment": *Miller-McGee v Washington Hosp. Ctr.*, 920 A.2d 430, 440 (D.C.2007) (quoting *Abbey v Jackson*, 483 A.2d 330, 332 (D.C.1984)).
53 *Conte v Girard Orthopaedic Surgeons Medical Group, Inc.*, 132 Cal. Rptr. 2d 85, 859 (2003).
54 *Carter v Pain Center of Arizona, P.C.*, 2016 WL386791.
55 *Fiala v Bickfords Sr. Living Group, L.L.C.*, 43 N.E.3d 1234, 1240 (IL. App. 2015).
56 *Prince v Esposito*, 628 S.E. 2d 601, 602 (2006).
57 *Curtis v Jaskey*, 759 N.E. 2d 962, 965 (2001).
58 *All Children's Hosp., Inc. v Owens*, 754 So.2d 802, 806 (2000).
59 The claim is only available if there is no remedy available in probate court. *Garruto v Cannici*, 936 A.2d 1015, 1022 (2007).

60 *Bjork v O'Meare*, 986 N.E. 2d 626, 631 (2013) *citing In re Estate of Ellis*, 923 N.E. 2d 237 (2009).
61 *Morrill v Morrill*, 679 A2d 519, 521 (1996).
62 *Wedge Products, Inc. v Hartford Equity Sales Co.*, 509 N.E. 2d 74, 75 (Ohio 1987).
63 *Commerce Bank, N.A., v Blasdel*, 141 S.W.3d 434, 456 (2004).
64 *Estes Woodlawn Memorial Park, Inc.* 780 S.W. 759, 762 (Tenn. Ct. App. 1989).
65 See *Crawford v J. Avery Bryan Funeral Home, Inc.*, 253 S.W.3d 149, 157–158 (Tenn. 2007); *Weiley v Albert Einstein Medical Center*, 51 A.3d 202, 209 (Pa. Super. 2012).
66 *Shepherd v Whitestar Development Corp.*, 113 A.D. 3d 1078 (N.Y.S. 2d 2014).
67 *Mack v Brown*, 82 A.D. 3d 133, 137–138 (N.Y.S. 2d 2011).
68 *Id.*
69 *Bolin v State*, 642 So.2d 540, 540–41 (Fla. 1994).
70 Louisiana is the only state that prohibits a parent from disinheriting a child. Ralph C. Brashier, Disinheritance and the Modern Family, 45 Case W. Res. L. Rev. 83, 118 (Fall 1994).
71 *Troxel v Granville*, 120 S.Ct. 2054, 2057, 530 U.S. 57, 66 (2000).
72 *Von Eiff v Azicri*, 720 So.2d 510, 513 (1998).
73 *Ex parte Presse*, 554 So.2d 406, 408–409 (1989).
74 Lois M. Collins, U.S. marriage rate hits new low and may continue to decline at national.deseretnews.com (May 20, 2015).
75 Vanessa S. Browne-Barbour, "Mama's Baby, Papa's Maybe": Disestablishment of Paternity, 48 Akron L. Rev. 263, 269 (2015).
76 Jennifer Thomas, Common Law Marriage, 22 J. Am. Acad. Matrim. Law 151, 151–152 (2009).

Part III

The child

5 Posthumously conceived children (adjudicating the parents)

There are no reported cases of a court denying the request of a spouse to have sperm extracted from a dead or vegetative man. In cases where the man has not expressed a contrary intent, spouses have been permitted to use the frozen sperm of a dead or vegetative man to conceive "his" child. I placed quotations around the word "his" because it is not a foregone conclusion that the dead or vegetative man will be adjudicated as the father of the posthumously conceived child. Diane Blood won the right to conceive children using sperm that was extracted from her comatose husband's body. However, that was not the end of Diane's battle. When Diane gave birth to her first son, she was not permitted to put her late husband's name on the birth certificate. She faced that same obstacle with the arrival of her second son. In both cases, the law mandated that Diane leave the children's paternal details blank. Stephen was not legally recognized as the father of the children until the passage of the Human Fertilisation and Embryology (Deceased) Fathers Act 2003 that allowed Diane to re-register the births of her sons, so she could list her late husband as their father.[1]

A parent–child relationship refers to the legal relationship that exists between a parent and a child. That relationship may be created by biology, adoption, law or equity.[2] The parent–child relationship brings burdens to parents and benefits to children. There are numerous reasons why children need parents. The primary ones are economic, medical, and emotional. Children are dependent on their parents for economic support. If the parent is in the home, he or she helps to provide adequate food, clothes and shelter for the child. Non-custodian parents are legally required to pay child support.[3] Children of deceased parents have the opportunity to inherit and to receive benefits under the Social Security Program.[4] Children who live in single-family homes tend to live in poverty.[5] Those children who have no parents are probably even more financially disadvantaged. Chapter Six will tackle the financial issues that posthumously conceived children may encounter.

Parents are an important source of genetic information. Thus, it is important for a child to know the medical histories of both sides of his or her family tree. Posthumously conceived children may be deprived of this information if the deceased parent's family avoids contact because they do not approve of the manner in which the child was conceived. In those cases, the child is not just denied access to essential data. In the event the child has a chronic illness, the child also loses the chance to ask for assistance in the form of things like bone marrow and organs. From an emotional perspective, most children have an inherent desire to bond with their parents. That is why adopted children[6] and children conceived using donor gametes are seeking ways to connect with their biological parents.[7]

This chapter discusses what happens after the posthumously conceived child is born. Specifically, it examines the approaches that the law may take when adjudicating parents for the child. The first part discusses a few theories that may be used to legally recognize the dead man as the father of the posthumously conceived child. Advances in assisted reproductive technology have added uncertainty to the determination of maternity. Therefore, the chapter will conclude with an analysis of the theories that have been used to identify the legal mother of a child who is conceived as a result of a surrogacy arrangement. I will explore approaches the court can take to adjudicate a dead man or woman as the parent of a posthumously conceived child. But, first, I will briefly discuss the legal treatment of different classes of children.

When it comes to the law, all children are not treated equally. There appears to be a three-tier system. The tier in which a child is placed depends upon the manner in which the child is conceived. The children who are the most protected are first-tier children. These children only have to be born in order to receive the right to be financially supported during the lifetime of their parents and to inherit upon the death of their parents. The children that are usually classified as first-tier children are marital and adopted children. Children born during the marriage are given special treatment because society seeks to promote and protect the act of marriage.[8] During the debate over same-sex marriage, opponents emphasized that the primary purpose of marriage was procreation. They reasoned that because same-sex couples could not conceive children without assistance they were not intended to participate in the institution of marriage.[9] Adopted children are also in the first tier. They obtain that status because society wants to encourage people to adopt abandoned, neglected and abused children. Part of that encouragement is monetary. For instance, in most states, adoptive parents are eligible to receive a stipend or subsidy.[10]

Second-tier children usually come into existence because their parents engage in behavior that society deems to be inappropriate or unacceptable. That tier consists of non-marital children and stepchildren. Non-marital children are children who are conceived without the benefit of marriage. Their conception is the result of fornication[11] or adultery.[12] In the not too distant past, both of those acts were criminal offenses.[13] Stepchildren are created by death or failed marriages. To receive the same benefits as marital children, non-marital children have to overcome a few hurdles. The law has chosen to marginalize the relationships between stepparents and stepchildren. In most jurisdictions, without an adoption, there can never be a legal parent–child relationship between stepparent and a stepchild. It does not matter the age that the child is at the time the relationship develops. My sister was about eight months pregnant with another man's child when she met a nice man. After the baby was born, they started living together.

It does not matter that my sister named my nephew after her boyfriend; that my nephew calls the man "dad" or that my sister's boyfriend financially supports the child. Because my sister was not married to her boyfriend when the child was born, the boyfriend did not adopt the child; and as the boyfriend and the child are not genetically related a legal parent–child relationship does not exist between my nephew and my sister's boyfriend. Therefore, my sister is not legally entitled to ask her boyfriend to pay child support. Moreover, if something happens to my sister's boyfriend, my nephew would not be eligible for any type of surviving child benefits.

Children conceived using assisted reproductive technology occupy the third tier. These children are only recognized as legal children if their parents take the actions mandated by the applicable statutes. For instance, a legal parent–child relationship between the woman's husband and a child she conceives using donor sperm only exists if the man consents in advance to the process. The law surrounding children conceived through surrogacy arrangements is uncertain. As a result, those children are often disadvantaged. Posthumously conceived children would probably be placed at the bottom of this third tier. There conception is neither widely understood nor accepted. The inheritance rights of posthumously conceived children will be discussed in Chapter Six. Nonetheless, legal theories exist that can impact the tier in which these children are placed.

Designating a dad

The marital child approach

If the wife is the person that uses the man's sperm to conceive a child, the law should recognize the child as a child of the marriage. Under at least two scenarios, a man may be recognized as the legal father of a marital child "born" after his death. One instance involves the posthumously born child. This situation occurs when a woman is pregnant at the time of the man's death and the child is not born until after the man dies. The posthumously born child is treated on par with marital children who are born before the man's death. In order to acquire that status, the child just has to be born within a certain period of time after the man dies. Courts adopt a rebuttable presumption that the generally accepted gestation period is 280 days.[14] Therefore, as long as the child is born within the 280 day time frame, the child is presumed to be a child of the marriage.

The drafters of the Uniform Parentage Act (UPA) argued for the recognition of a more expansive gestation period. Under the provisions of the UPA, a child born to a woman within 300 days after the death of her husband is a marital child.[15] The UPA approach has been embraced by the majority of American jurisdictions. The second possible situation involves the legal "birth" of a child through adoption. Adoption can be a long and arduous process. As a result, there is always the possibility that a man may die before the adoption is finalized by the court. The fact that the man is dead by the time that the child is officially adopted will not adversely impact the child's position as a marital child. There appears to be no good reason to treat a child who is conceived posthumously using a man's sperm differently from children who are born under the above-described circumstances.

Despite the lack of a genetic connection, a man may be deemed the legal father of a child conceived during his marriage. That possibility exists if the man's wife receives another man's sperm through sexual intercourse or by artificial insemination. A man is presumed to be the legal father of all children born to his wife during their marriage. Similarly, a man should be presumed to be the legal father of a child born to his wife as a result of posthumous reproduction. A man who consents to the artificial insemination of his wife with donor sperm is the legal father of the resulting child. Likewise, a man who consents to his wife using his sperm to conceive a child should be recognized as the legal father of the posthumously conceived child. Arguments based on one or both of these principles may be utilized to have a dead man legally adjudicated as the father of his posthumously conceived child.

Marital presumption of paternity (traditional and best interests)

One of the strongest presumptions in the law is that a husband is presumed to be the father of a child conceived or born during his marriage.[16] This is a longstanding legal principle. The presumption is based upon Lord Mansfield's common law rule.[17] Historically, because of the existence of the presumption parties were not permitted to dispute the paternity of a child born to a married woman. The reasons why courts enforced the presumption were two-fold. The law sought to protect intact marriages and to promote the best interests of children.[18] Judges doubted that a couple would remain married if a third party was allowed to question the paternity of the woman's child. Courts believed that allegations of infidelity on the part of the woman would irreparably harm a marriage. In additional, courts wanted to ensure that families did not fall prey to dishonest accusations. Because the technology needed to conduct genetic paternity tests was not available courts had to solve cases relying on "he said, she said" evidence. For example, if A asserted that he was the father of a child B's wife had given birth to and B's wife denied his claim, the court had no definite way to determine which party was telling the truth.[19] As a result, courts applied the marital presumption to discourage third parties from challenging the paternity of a pregnant woman's husband. The presumption also served to protect marital children from the stigma of illegitimacy.[20] One court stated: "The presumption of legitimacy arising from birth during wedlock 'is not lightly to be repelled.' "[21]

Traditionally, although the presumption was supposed to be rebuttable, courts applied strict evidentiary requirements that made it difficult to overcome.[22] The presumption could only be rebutted by a showing that it was not possible for the woman's husband to be the father of her child. To prove that implausibility, the person had to demonstrate that the man did not have access to his wife during the time the child was conceived. It was not enough to prove that the husband and his wife were alienated and not having sexual intercourse. The person trying to contest the husband's paternity had to show that the man did not have contact with his wife because he was "beyond the four seas" (outside of the jurisdiction of the King of England).[23] Presently, the presumption can be rebutted by clear and convincing evidence that the woman's husband is not the child's biological father.[24] That task can be accomplished through the use of blood tests and other DNA testing if the court deems that to be appropriate.[25]

Courts still apply the marital presumption of paternity. If fact, the legal principle has been codified in the majority of American jurisdictions.[26] However, over the years, courts relaxed the evidentiary rules and made it easier for the presumption to be rebutted. Courts were motivated by the fact that the main reasons for the presumption had been diluted. For example, an increase in the frequency of divorce frustrated one of the primary purposes of the marital presumption of paternity. Concealing the actions of an unfaithful wife is no longer necessary to preserve a marriage. If a woman had an affair that resulted in the conception of a child, that woman was likely to file for divorce, so she could start a life with the biological father of her child. She had that choice because the law removed most of the obstacles to obtaining a divorce. Therefore, a woman no longer had to remain in the marriage and hope that her husband would forgive her and accept the child.[27] Currently, the presumption is only applicable in cases where the marriage is intact at the time that someone tries to challenge the husband's paternity.[28] In those circumstances, the presumption cannot be rebutted by a third party seeking to assert his own paternity against that of the woman's husband.[29]

Moreover, a strict application of the marital presumption was not necessary to protect the child from poverty and the stigma of illegitimacy. The advances in DNA technology made it possible for social service agencies to identify the biological father of the child. Consequently, even if the man was not married to the child's mother, he was legally obligated to pay child support. As a result, the woman's husband was not viewed as a necessary safety net for the child. Additionally, as more and more women gave birth to children without the benefit of marriage, society became more accepting of children who were born out-of-wedlock. In response, the law changed to treat non-marital children on par with marital children with regards to child support and other financial benefits. Because of existing technology, it is relatively easy to determine the identity of the child's biological father. Nevertheless, a court will not order blood or genetic tests to rebut the husband's paternity if that action is not considered to be in the best interests of the child.[30]

Artificial insemination approach

Despite the lack of regulation in the assisted reproductive technology area, the majority of states have statutes in place to govern the use of artificial insemination. Under those statutory schemes, a man is the father of a child his wife conceives using donor sperm if he *consents* to the artificial insemination.[31] It does not matter that the man does not have a biological connection to the child. His paternity is based upon his consent. The form that the consent obligation must take varies. Nonetheless, if the woman is able to show that her husband consented in some manner to her being artificially inseminated, he will be legally recognized as the father of the artificially conceived child.

Expressed consent

Preference is given to written consent.[32] For example, under the Connecticut statute, the woman's husband must give written consent to be legally adjudicated as the father of the artificially conceived child.[33] Connecticut is not alone in its treatment of artificially conceived children. A number of other states also mandate that the husband consent in writing to the artificial insemination of his wife in order for the resulting child to be deemed his legal child. Using slightly different language, the Minnesota statute declares the husband of the inseminated woman to be the *biological* father of the children that his wife conceives with his written consent.[34] The classification as biological children places the artificially conceived children on par with the other marital children.

In *Lane v Lane*, a New Mexico court gave the state's artificial insemination statute a broad reading.[35] The following facts brought the case before the court. In December of 1984, the husband and wife got married. The wife wanted children, but the husband refused to have his vasectomy reversed. To placate the wife, the husband agreed with her plan to be artificially inseminated with sperm from an anonymous donor. Even though he never signed the consent form, the husband actively participated in the process. In addition to driving his wife to her medical appointments and attending birthing classes, the man was present for the birth of the child. The couple made sure that the husband's name was placed on the child's birth certificate and told their family and friends that he was the biological father.[36]

A few years after the birth of the child, the husband filed for divorce. He listed the child as a child of the marriage in his petition. The wife responded by requesting sole legal and physical custody of the child. To bolster her claim, the wife filed an amended answer claiming that her estranged husband was not the biological or legal father of the artificially conceived child.[37] At the district court level, the husband and wife were given joint custody of the child, and the wife filed a timely appeal. She argued that because he had not given written consent to the artificial insemination he should not be recognized as the child's legal father. The wife asked the court to treat the man as a stranger to the child and deny him joint custody.[38] The Appellate Court determined that the man had not given written consent in compliance with the statutory mandates. But, the court concluded that strict compliance with the language of the statute was not obligatory as long as the statutory mandates were followed closely enough to satisfy the legislature's intent and to accomplish the statutory objectives.[39]

According to the court, the legislature required written consent to have definitive proof that the husband had consented to the procedure. In the event that there was uncertainty, the writing could be introduced to end any disputes.[40] The court also opined that by consenting to the artificial insemination, the woman's husband would expose himself to numerous parental obligations with regards to the resulting child. Therefore, the legislature wanted to ensure that the husband took time to think before agreeing to be a parent to the artificially conceived child. The writing requirement gave the husband more time to contemplate the consequences of putting his signature on the agreement.[41] As a consequence, the court concluded that to comply with the spirit of the statute, there had to be some type of writing.[42]

The court found that the statute did not specify the timing of the consent or the content of the writing. Consequently, the court opined that the purposes of the statute could be fulfilled if the writing indicated: "(1) the husband knows of the conception by artificial insemination, (2) the husband agrees that the husband will be treated as the lawful father of the child so conceived, and (3) the wife agrees that the husband will be treated as the lawful father of the child."[43] The court also decided that the consent could be given before the procedure, after the procedure, or after the birth of the child. Relying upon the aforementioned factors, the court held that the husband had substantially complied with the statute.[44] The court reasoned that the pleadings filed in the divorce action satisfied the writing requirement. In his signed petition, the husband claimed responsibility for the child, and in her signed answer, the wife agreed. The husband's willingness to be a parent to the artificially conceived child indicated his consent to the procedure.[45] In this case, a broad reading of the written consent requirement benefitted the child. Other states have achieved similar results by removing the requirement that the man's consent be in writing.

In order for the child to be recognized as legitimate, most states require that the husband's consent to the artificial insemination of his wife be in writing; however, a few states have taken a different approach. For instance, the Maryland statute contains a presumption that the husband consented to the insemination of his wife.[46] Since the husband is presumed to have consented to the procedure, the resulting child is his legal child. In Utah, the lack of the husband's written consent does not eliminate the possibility that he will be considered the legal father of a child born to his inseminated wife. If, after the birth of the child, the husband acts like a father by openly treating the child as his own, he will be determined to be the legal father.[47] Several state statutes mandate that a husband consent to the artificial insemination of his wife to be considered the legal parent of the resulting child without specifically stating that the consent has to be in writing. Courts have to decide what steps the husband must take to comply with those statutes. That approach gives the courts a great deal of flexibility. On the other hand, some statutory schemes give the courts no discretion because the husband's paternity is established by presumption or implication.

Presumed consent

In some states, legislatures have put in place a different system to determine a man's paternity when his wife conceives using artificial insemination. Instead of declaring the husband to be the child's legal father, laws in those jurisdictions make it impossible or extremely arduous for the husband of an artificially inseminated woman to contest his paternity.[48] As a result, the man is legally recognized as the child's legal father by operation of law. The drafters of the Uniform Status of Children of Assisted Conception Act advocated for the approach.[49] The presumption of paternity may be rebuttable or irrebuttable.

For example, in Florida, the husband of an artificially inseminated woman is not allowed to challenge his paternity once he consents to the procedure. Under Florida's artificial insemination law, if a married woman is artificially inseminated with her husband's written consent, the law irrebuttably presumes that man to be the father of any resulting child.[50] The Georgia statute has language that is similar. Because the child is presumed to be a marital child and the husband cannot challenge that fact, he is deemed to be the child's legal father.[51]

Some jurisdictions that have resolved the issue in this way have not completely precluded the woman's husband from objecting to being named the father of the artificially conceived child. For example, Delaware allows, but restricts, attempts by husbands of women who conceive using artificial insemination to disavow their paternity. According to Delaware law, a man who wants to dispute his paternity must file suit within two years of finding out that the child has been born. For the man to have a valid cause of action, a court must conclude that he did not agree to the artificial insemination before or after the child was born.[52] The law in Texas is comparable, but the man has four years to file his case. The time restrictions are removed if the court decides that the man has proven the following facts: (1) his wife was inseminated with another man's sperm without the husband's consent; (2) he did not reside with the woman between the probable time she was inseminated and the time he filed suit; and (3) he did not openly hold the child out as his child.[53] The UPA's approach is a hybrid of the Texas and Delaware statutes.[54]

In Louisiana, a man who consents to the artificial insemination of his wife is presumed to be the legal father of the child she conceives. Therefore, he is not permitted to legally disclaim the child. However, if the man did not agree to the insemination he can file an action to have his paternity disavowed. The man must bring the case within one year after he knows or should know that his wife gave birth to a child conceived using artificial insemination. If the man and his wife did not reside together during the three hundred days before the child was born, the statute of limitations for the filing of the disavowal action does not start to run until the husband is notified in writing that an interested party has claimed that he is the father of the artificially conceived child.[55]

New Hampshire legally acknowledges a man as the presumptive father of a child who is born under any of the following situations: (1) while the man is married; (2) within 300 days after a court dissolves the man's marriage; or (3) within 300 days after a competent court finds that the man and his wife are legally separated. As a result of the presumption, the man's name can be legally placed on the child's birth certificate.[56] A party seeking to refute the presumption must do so by presenting clear and convincing evidence.[57] The legislature did not place any language in the statute indicating that it was not meant to apply to children conceived using assisted reproduction. On the contrary, the statute provides that a person cannot rebut the presumption by simply showing that the child was conceived through the use of assisted reproduction so long as the husband agreed to his wife's artificial insemination. In cases where the man is unable to successfully rebut the presumption of paternity, a legal father–child relationship is created between him and the child.[58]

It is hard for a man to rebut the presumption of a father–child relationship between himself and a child his wife has using artificial insemination. As a consequence of the presumption, the man has many legal obligations towards the artificially conceived child. In recognition of that fact, New Hampshire's legislature put a statutory scheme in place that contains several mechanisms designed to protect the rights of the husband of an artificially inseminated woman. The legislature wanted to ensure that the man provided informed consent to his wife's artificial insemination.[59] To that end, the law mandates that, before the woman undergoes artificial insemination, she and her husband must participate in counseling.[60] Moreover, distinct from most jurisdictions, the husband's written consent is not enough to make him the legal father of an artificially conceived child. To be responsible for the child, the husband has to give his written agreement to accept the "legal rights and responsibilities of parenthood."[61] That agreement represents the man's willingness to be legally obligated to provide for any children that result from his wife's artificial insemination with another man's sperm.[62] Even if the procedure is performed in the absence of the mandated counseling or the husband's consent, the man may still be presumed to have assented to the insemination if he fails to make a timely objection. To satisfy this requirement, the man must file an action contesting his paternity within thirty days after he discovers or should have discovered that the child has been born.[63]

Conclusion

Both of these principles would have to be modified to apply to situations involving posthumously conceived children. The marital presumption only applies if the child is *conceived or born during the marriage*. Therefore, the posthumously conceived child is only a child of the marriage if the marriage survives the death of the husband. Before he dies, a man might agree to permit his wife to be artificially inseminated with his sperm after his death. If a man is legally adjudicated the father of another man's child because of his consent, his agreement should be enough to have him named the father of his *own* biological child. However, the artificial insemination statutes are only relevant if a man consents to the insemination of *his wife*. The woman is only legally recognized as the man's wife if the marriage survives the death of the husband. Consequently, the legal question becomes whether marriage should survive the death of one of the parties.

Marriage is much more than the relationship between the two parties who exchange vows. It is a legal status that confers numerous benefits on the parties. Some aspects of the marital relationship may be said to continue after death. For example, the surviving spouse has the right to receive a portion of the dead person's property and certain government benefits. Nonetheless, it is doubtful that a court would accept the argument that the actual marriage lasts after one of the participants dies. There are several good reasons to conclude that death should mark the end of a marriage. From an emotional perspective, after the man dies, his surviving spouse needs to have closure. As a part of the closure process, the survivor must release his or her role as "spouse" and embrace his or her new status as "surviving spouse." Letting go of the past will enable the man or woman to move on with his or her life. There are some practical problems that may arise if marriage is recognized after the death of one of the spouses. Because the law only permits a person to have one legal spouse, before a person can remarry, he or she must sever the relationship with the existing spouse. Living persons can cut their marital ties by filing for divorce. Once a man dies, the only way that the surviving spouse would be free to obtain another husband is if death legally ends a marriage. A posthumously conceived child is not eligible to receive the same treatment as a marital child because the child's parents are no longer married after one of them dies.

Non-marital child approach

Based upon the fact that death legally ends the marriage of the child's parents, another approach is to classify the posthumously conceived child as a non-marital child. Those children are not treated as well as marital children, but they are entitled to some benefits from their fathers. However, that was not always the case. Currently, only a few states have statutes and cases specifically governing the inheritance rights of posthumously conceived children. Therefore, the possibility that those children may be treated like non-marital children still exists. Because a man will be dead when his posthumously conceived children are born the cases dealing with the inheritance rights of non-marital children may be the most relevant, so this section will mostly focus on the law in that area. Here, I will give a brief summary of the journey children born to unmarried people made from being referred to as "bastards" or illegitimate to being recognized as out-of-wedlock or non-marital children. The change in the names reflected society's opinion about those children and the legal rights afforded to them.

Historically, a man was not acknowledged as the legal father of a child that he conceived with an unmarried woman. The child of that relationship was considered to be legally fatherless. In a famous quote, Blackstone said: "[T]he incapacity of a bastard consists principally in this, that he cannot be heir to any one neither can he have heirs, but of his own body; for being nullius filuis,[64] he is therefore of kin to nobody, and has no ancestor from whom any inheritance blood can be derived."[65] Legally, the non-marital child was initially treated as nobody. Consequently, the child did not have the right to receive financial support from either of his or her living parents. For example, in England, the streets and government orphanages were filled with the children abandoned by their wealthy fathers. That trend continued in America. It took years of litigation, but the stigma of illegitimacy was finally removed from the non-marital child.

Beginning in 1968, quite a few cases concerning the legal rights of non-marital children came before the United States Supreme Court. Those cases related to a diversity of legal issues, involving immigration,[66] financial support,[67] civil procedure,[68] tort, workers'[69] compensation,[70] probate,[71] and social security.[72] A growing recognition of the legal relationship between parents and their non-marital children arose out of those cases. Consequently, state legislatures and courts created laws that afforded non-marital children access to some of the benefits possessed by marital children.

Originally, non-marital children had to fight to get the law to acknowledge the relationships that existed between them and their mothers. For instance, in 1968, the United States Supreme Court heard two cases pertaining to the tort recovery rights non-marital children had in cases in which their mothers were victims.[73] Both cases challenged the constitutionality of Louisiana's wrongful death statute that prevented non-marital children from receiving damages. The Supreme Court ruled that the statute violated the United States Constitution because it discriminated against non-marital children by making them ineligible to recover for the wrongful death of their mothers,[74] and that it discriminated against the mothers of non-marital children by not letting them recover for the wrongful death of their non-marital children.[75] The decisions of these two cases permitted non-marital children to have the same rights with regards to the relationships with their mothers as marital children. Even though the cases involved tort claims, the outcomes of the cases changed the legal landscape for non-marital children in other areas of the law.

After several cases before the United States Supreme Court, non-marital children were placed on an equal footing with marital children when it came to financial support from their living parents. However, non-marital children still have to overcome some hurdles to be eligible to inherit from their fathers. I will briefly analyze three cases that improved the plight of non-marital children. The first case deals with the man's obligation to provide financial support for his children while he is still alive. The second one examines the inheritance rights of non-marital children.

In *Gomez v Perez*[76] the Supreme Court determined the financial obligations that a man owed to his non-marital children. The Court had to decide if affording non-marital children fewer legal rights than marital children violated the Equal Protection Clause of the United States Constitution. The litigation arose because the unmarried mother of a non-marital child wanted the genetic father to pay child support.[77] The trial court acknowledged that the man was the child's biological father, but refused to grant the mother's request for a child support order. The court based its decision on the conclusion that a man was not legally required to financially support his non-marital children.[78]

The woman filed a timely appeal. She pointed out that the state's common and statutory laws required a man to financially support his marital children.[79] In light of that fact, the woman contended that the state's denial of child support to non-marital children deprived her daughter of equal protection under the law.[80] The Supreme Court opined that "a State may not invidiously discriminate against illegitimate children by denying them substantial benefits accorded children generally."[81] As a result, because the state obligated a man to financially support his marital children it had to mandate that he do the same for his non-marital children.[82] The opinion failed to discuss the ability of non-marital children to inherit from their fathers under the intestacy system or their eligibility for government benefits that were provided to marital children. Those issues were left for another case.

The Supreme Court decisions indicated that a state could not deny non-marital children legal rights to dissuade women from having children out of wedlock. As a result, the Court consistently invalidated laws that prevented non-marital children from inheriting from their fathers wholly because of the manner in which they had been conceived.[83] Yet, the Justices conceded that state legislatures had the authority to control the regulation of probate systems.[84] Therefore, the Court gave deference to state statutes that required non-marital children to follow specific procedures before they could inherit from their fathers.[85] In the 1970s, the Court evaluated the validity of two state inheritance statutes.

In 1977, the United States Supreme Court heard a case challenging the legality of a provision of the Illinois Probate Act (Probate Act).[86] At the time he died, Sherman Gordon was paying court-ordered child support to his live-in girlfriend, Jessie Trimble, for Deta Trimble, his non-marital child.[87] Gordon died intestate leaving an estate that only consisted of a car. The Probate Division of the Circuit Court did not recognized Deta as one of Gordon's legal heirs because she had not met the requirements of the Probate Act.[88] Under the provisions of the statute, a non-marital child could only inherit from his or her father if the following two stipulations were satisfied: (1) the child's parents had to marry each other; and (2) the child's father had to acknowledge the child.[89] If Deta had been a marital child, she would have inherited her father's whole estate without being required to meet any standards. Therefore, Trimble challenged the Probate Court's decision in the Illinois Supreme Court arguing that the statute violated the Equal Protection Clause because it discriminated on the basis of illegitimacy and gender.[90] The Illinois Supreme upheld the statute because it was necessary for the state to encourage family relationships[91] and to maintain "an accurate and efficient method of disposing of property at death."[92]

After losing in the state supreme court, Trimble took her case to the United States Supreme Court. The Court ruled in favor of Trimble. The Court decided that the constraints put on the inheritance of non-marital children were not the best way to discourage persons from having children without the benefit of marriage. The Justices emphasized that the non-marital child did not have any control over the decision her parents made with regard to marriage. Hence, the child should not have to suffer any legal consequences that may result from her parents' decision not to marry each other.[93]

The Court did not believe that the Act was necessary for the state to protect the probate system from false paternity claims. In fact, the Court concluded that the statute was overinclusive since it prevented non-marital children with lawful paternity claims from inheriting.[94] For example, Deta could not inherit under the statute despite the fact that she possessed a valid paternity order and a child support order from a competent court.[95] The Court was also concerned about the undue burden that the Act placed on non-marital children. Even if the father acknowledged the child, the child could not inherit unless he married the child's mother. The Court felt that this two-step requirement made it practically impossible for a non-marital child to inherit. Essentially, the state was prohibiting non-marital children from inheriting from their fathers. Because the Court had denounced that practice in earlier cases, it concluded that the statute violated the Equal Protection Clause.[96]

In a case decided a year after *Trimble*, the Court was again asked to evaluate a statute that placed limitations on the inheritance rights of non-marital children.[97] After Mario Lalli died intestate, his widow, Rosamond Lalli, argued that his two non-marital children should be denied the opportunity to inherit from his estate. Rosamond based her argument on the fact that the non-marital children had not complied with the requirements of the state's paternity statute.[98] Robert, the non-marital son, claimed that the probate statute was unconstitutional because it discriminated against non-marital children by requiring them to submit additional proof of paternity.[99] The Court ruled that the statute did not violate the United States Constitution.[100] The Court thought that the process mandated by the statute fostered significant state interests without placing an unnecessary burden on non-marital children. Distinct from the statute in *Trimble*, the statute challenged in *Lalli* epitomized a middle position that the Justices deemed to be fair. Under the statute, non-marital children were not prevented from inheriting from their fathers if they followed the procedure set forth therein.[101]

According to the Court, the statute survived the constitutional challenge because the procedure set forth in the statute protected the interests of the probate courts,[102] the non-marital children,[103] and the supposed father.[104] The statutory procedure could potentially reduce the number of fabricated claims filed before the court. Because the father would be alive to challenge the claims, persons might be disinclined to file fraudulent claims. Persons making false paternity allegations would undoubtedly be less likely to file those claims in court if they knew they had to face the purported father. Conversely, if the father was not around to defend himself from such claims, the floodgates could open and the courts would be swamped. This could cause the probate process to become even more expensive and inefficient.[105] The statute gave non-marital children more inheritance rights than they had before it was enacted.[106]

As the above cases indicate, in order for a state inheritance statute to survive a constitutional challenge, it must provide non-marital children with the opportunity to inherit from their fathers. The Supreme Court has given states considerable latitude in probate matters. Nonetheless, any statutory scheme that explicitly or implicitly precludes non-marital children from forming a father–child relationship for inheritance purposes would likely be nullified. Still, states do not have to give non-marital children the precise same inheritance rights as marital children. Non-marital children have a different legal status than marital children. Therefore, the key is to provide equal opportunity, not strict equality.[107] In response to Supreme Court precedents, states have been careful to take the middle ground. Thus, statutes in most states give non-marital children the opportunity to inherit from their fathers as long as they take the steps necessary to prove paternity.

Conclusion

If the law categorizes a posthumously conceived child as a non-marital child, that child will benefit by having the opportunity to establish a legal father–child relationship with the deceased man. This would give the child second-tier status and not the first-tier status that is afforded other children who are the result of a marital union. Because the child will be conceived after the marriage of his or her parents ends it would not be unreasonable to call the posthumously conceived child a non-marital child. However, it does not seem fair to ignore the fact that, if the man had survived, the child probably would have been born during the marriage. Persons who have children outside of the context of marriage usually make a conscious choice to procreate in that manner. Therefore, they should not expect their children to have all of the legal rights of marital children. Most adults know the numerous benefits that marriage offers. As some of the cases discussed in Chapter Six indicate, when a woman conceives a child using a dead husband's sperm, she assumes that the law will acknowledge the biological father of the child as the legal father. Once the law permits a woman to conceive a child using posthumous reproduction, the child should not be labelled as a non-marital child. That classification disregards the vows that the couple took before the man died. Because the idea of a woman being married to a dead man makes people uncomfortable a better approach may be to treat the dead man like a sperm donor.

The sperm donor approach

When a man and his wife conceive a child through sexual intercourse, the man is considered to be more than a sperm donor. Situations involving posthumous reproduction do not involve intimate contact between the man and the woman. Therefore, it may not be farfetched to classify the dead man as a sperm donor. In cases involving frozen sperm, the man's sperm is usually obtained by having him ejaculate into a cup or vial. This is no different from the college student who goes to a local sperm bank to make a donation. Fresh sperm is extracted from the body of a man who is dead or vegetative by surgery or artificial ejaculation. The man is not aware that he is making the contribution, but he is still a sperm donor. If the dead man is categorized as a sperm donor, he may or may not be adjudicated the legal father of the posthumously conceived child. As previously stated, the man's death ends the marriage, so he may be considered to be a non-spousal sperm donor. Therefore, it may be helpful to examine the legal relationship between sperm donors and the children that they help to conceive.

States have taken varied approaches with regards to the legal responsibility that a non-spousal sperm donor has to a child who is conceived as the result of artificial insemination. The approach taken by the UPA[108] and most states is to proclaim that the sperm donor should not be adjudicated as the child's father.[109] Some jurisdictions have attempted to resolve the problem by disregarding the parental rights of the sperm donor. Under the laws in those states, because the sperm donor is not recognized as the resulting child's biological father he is not obligated to financially support the child.[110] Other states have tried to handle the paternity issue by focusing on the rights of the child in relation to the sperm donor. In those situations, an artificially conceived child has no legal right to be supported by the sperm donor.[111] In a few states, the non-spousal sperm donor may have some legal rights with regards to the artificially conceived child.[112] Finally, some states do not have a statute explicitly addressing the parental status of a sperm donor.[113]

Though the man may be the biological father of the child conceived with his sperm, legislatures in several states have passed laws depriving him of that status. By not legally recognizing the sperm donor as the male parent of the child, the laws discharge him of any parental responsibilities to the child.[114] Florida law deals with the parental status of a sperm donor in a unique way. The statute concedes that the sperm donor has some parental rights. Nonetheless, the law demands that the donor relinquish all rights to the child created as a result of his donation.[115] To increase the number of sperm donations, states must take steps to make sure that a man is not legally responsible for a child conceived using his sperm.[116] To that end, state legislatures have made it clear that donating sperm does not make a man an instant father. The Wisconsin legislature included the following language in its statute: "The donor of semen provided to a licensed physician for use in artificial insemination of a woman other than the donor's wife is not the natural father of a child conceived, bears no liability for the support of the child and has no parental rights with regard to the child."[117] As this statutory language indicates, a non-spouse who donates sperm to inseminate a woman does not have a legal obligation to financially support the artificially conceived child.[118] That lack of responsibility applies to cases involving the insemination of married and unmarried women. In addition to discharging the sperm donor's financial obligations towards the child, state statutory schemes sever any relationship between the sperm donor and the child.[119]

Under the laws of some jurisdictions, it is possible for the sperm donor to become financially responsible for the artificially conceived child. For instance, in New Hampshire, a sperm donor can consent in writing to provide financial support.[120] If a licensed physician facilitates the process, statutes in Kansas and the New Mexico eliminate possible parental obligations a non-spousal sperm donor may owe to the artificially conceived child. Nevertheless, the parties may sign a written agreement indicating that the non-spousal sperm donor will act as the biological father of any children that are conceived as a result of artificial insemination.[121] The language in the New Jersey statute is similar to that included in the Kansas and New Mexico statutes.[122]

As indicated above, to receive the protections provided by the artificial insemination statutes in several states, sperm donors must deposit their sperm with a licensed physician.[123] Therefore, if the woman conceives as a consequence of self-insemination, the sperm donor may be acknowledged as the child's legal father.[124] No particular medical expertise is needed to perform artificial insemination, so it is not hard to envision a case where a woman is inseminated at home using a turkey baster.[125] In that situation, the woman will probably know the donor, and a licensed physician will not be involved in the procedure. In almost half of the states with such statutes, because the sperm donor is the biological father and he did not obey the statutory mandates, he may be deemed to be legally responsible for paying child support.[126] This situation may be the most applicable to cases involving women using the sperm of their dead husbands to conceive a child.

A number of states have not passed laws regulating the parental status of sperm donors. In those states, the courts have dealt with the issue on a case-by-case basis, relying on common law principles and family law statutes. For example, Pennsylvania has not adopted the UPA and it does not have a statute that governs the legal rights and duties of a non-spousal sperm donor.[127] As a result, the courts are not given guidance when deciding cases involving the parental rights of sperm donors.[128] Such a case arose when two women decided to create a family. Jennifer L. Schultz and Jodilynn Jacob attempted to solidify their relationship by both partaking in a commitment ceremony and establishing a civil union. When the women decided to start a family, Jennifer asked her friend Carl Frampton to donate sperm to be used to inseminate Jodilynn. Jodilynn conceived two children using Carl's sperm. When the women ended their relationship, the court awarded Jodilynn physical custody of the two children. At that time, Jennifer received partial physical custody and Carl was awarded partial physical custody of the children for one weekend each month.[129] Jodilynn filed a successful child support action against Jennifer. Jennifer argued that Carl should be obligated to pay child support. Thus, she tried unsuccessfully to join Carl as an indispensable party. The trial court reasoned that, as a sperm donor, Carl was not legally obligated to pay child support and therefor was not an indispensable party.[130] Jennifer appealed the trial court's denial of her request.[131]

The Appellate Court applied the doctrine of equitable estoppel and decided that fairness dictated that Carl pay child support because he was their biological father.[132] The court's decision to obligate Carl to pay child support was influenced by the fact that Carl acted like a parent. The court considered the following actions to be legally relevant: (1) Carl voluntarily provided financial support for the children; (2) Carl was present when at least one of the children was born; (3) Carl was awarded partial physical custody of the children; and (4) Carl permitted the children to call him "Papa."[133] The court reasoned that, because Carl acted as if he were a parent, he should be estopped from denying his parental responsibilities, including the obligation to pay child support.[134]

Conclusion

While he is in college, a man may make several anonymous sperm donations. Given the length of time that sperm can remain frozen, the man may be dead by the time that his donated sperm is used to conceive a child. The man's lack of a legal connection to the child is not based on the fact that he is dead. The man is not recognized as the legal father of the child because he is an unknown non-spousal sperm donor. At the time he donated his sperm, the man probably signed away his parental rights. The man's death would not negate the fact that he is the child's biological father. In some jurisdictions, if the man is a known sperm donor, he may be legally adjudicated as the child's father. Likewise, there is a strong argument to be made that the dead man has "donated" his sperm to his widow, so that she can conceive his child. That donation may be voluntary or involuntary. If the law permits the sperm to be used without the man's consent, that should not impact his ability to be recognized as the legal father of the resulting child. Because, when he dies, a man is no longer married to the woman, the best approach may be for the law to treat the man as a non-spousal sperm donor. Once the man is labelled as such, the applicable law will determine whether the child will be permitted to have a legal father. In some cases, the courts may be called upon to designate a legal mother for a posthumously conceived child.

Making a mom

Most of this chapter has focused on men and sperm because the majority of the requests come from women. However, there are at least four scenarios where the involvement of a surrogate[135] may be required.

Scenario One: A woman who gets permission to use her dead or vegetative husband's sperm to conceive a child may not be physically able to gestate the child because she has fibroid tumors or has had a hysterectomy. In that case, the woman will have to seek the services of a gestational surrogate. The surrogate may be a friend, a family member or a stranger who is paid for her services.

Scenario Two: After the death of his wife or girlfriend, a man may want to conceive a child using her eggs. Because most men do not have the necessary equipment, the dead woman's husband may require the services of a gestational surrogate.

Scenario Three: I have discussed one case where a dead man's mother was considering gestating an embryo created using his sperm and donor eggs. In another case, a dead woman's mother is trying to get permission to gestate an embryo made up of her eggs and donor sperm. These cases are probably atypical. In the event that a parent is allowed to harvest the eggs of his or her dead child, that person will probably employ a surrogate to gestate the embryo. If the parent decides to buy donor eggs or sperm, he or she will hire a gestational surrogate. In some rare cases, the parent may decide to obtain the services of a traditional surrogate who would supply the eggs and the womb. After the *Baby M* case, persons have been reluctant to acquire the services of a traditional surrogate.

Scenario Four: A man may receive permission to use his dead husband's sperm to have a child conceived. In order to achieve that goal, the man will have to use either a traditional or gestational surrogate. There is no uniform law pertaining to the legal maternity of a surrogate. I will examine the three tests and one proposed test that may be used to determine the legal mother of a child who is conceived as the result of a surrogacy arrangement. One court relied on a multiple factor test to adjudicate the legal mother in a surrogacy custody dispute.[136]

The legal mother is the woman who supplies the genetic material used to conceive the child

In some jurisdictions, the woman who supplies the genetic material is deemed to be the legal mother of the child conceived as the result of a surrogacy arrangement. For example, paternity tests are used to make sure that the man acknowledged as the child's legal father is biologically related to the child.[137] Additionally, to lose custody or be denied visitation, the biological parent must be found unfit.[138] Society values blood relationships. The law reflects that respect for blood connections by giving preference to blood relatives in several frameworks. For example, a biological parent must give consent before his or her child can be legally adopted. This is true even in cases where the biological parent has no contact with the child. As a result of the fascination with blood ties, in most jurisdictions, stepchildren are not permitted to inherit from stepparents under the intestacy system (unless the children have been adopted).[139] The reason behind that exclusion is the assumption that a person would want preference given to his or her biological children. The following case demonstrates the genetics approach to maternity.

Belsito v Clark[140]

After she was diagnosed with cervical cancer, doctors removed Shelly Belsito's uterus but left her ovaries intact, so she was capable of producing eggs.[141] When Shelly and Anthony Belsito got married, they agreed that they wanted to have children.[142] Carol S. Clark, Shelly's sister, agreed to act as a surrogate for the couple. Doctors implanted two of the embryos that were created by fertilizing Shelly's eggs with Anthony's sperm into Carol's uterus. A couple of weeks later, a test confirmed Carol's pregnancy.[143] When she was getting ready for the impending birth of the child, Shelly spoke with the hospital personnel about the child's birth certificate. At that time, hospital personnel informed her that because Carol was giving birth to the child, Carol, not Shelly, would be listed on the birth certificate as the child's legal mother. Shelly also learned that the child would be classified as a non-marital child because the legal parents, Carol and Anthony, were not married to each other. Shelly and Anthony responded by going to court to obtain a declaration that, because they were the child's legal parents, they did not need to adopt the child. In addition, they requested a court order requiring the hospital to list the child as their marital child on the birth certificate and to identify them as the legal parents on the birth certificate.[144]

The court had to determine whom to adjudicate as the child's legal and natural parents. To make that decision, the court had to determine what makes a person a natural parent. Once it reviewed the applicable case law, the court found that, to be recognized as a natural parent, a person had to be connected to the child by genetics. That genetic connection could be established by evidence showing that the adult and the child were genetically connected by DNA.[145] The court ruled that "the test to identify the natural parents should be, 'Who are the genetic parents?' "[146]

The court gave several reasons why it adopted the genetics test. First, the court opined that a genetic test was more consistent with the public policy of not permitting a woman to sell her parental rights. The court rationalized that, because she did not supply the genetic material used to conceive the child, the surrogate was not the child's natural mother.[147] Therefore, when the surrogate surrendered the child, she would not be exchanging her parental rights for a monetary payment. In that case, the surrogate would simply be fulfilling the terms of the contract. Second, the court determined that the genetic test would be easy to apply. Any dispute with regard to the identity of the natural mother could be easily resolved through DNA testing.[148]

According to the court, the designation of the natural parent might not be the end of the inquiry. A surrogate who did not contribute genetic material to create the child is not the child's natural mother. However, that woman might be found to be the child's legal mother. To become the child's legal mother, the surrogate had to comply with the state's adoption laws. In this case, the court did not have to analyze the steps a gestational surrogate has to take to be adjudicated as the child's legal mother because Carol did not assert her maternal rights.[149]

The court ruled that Anthony and Shelly were the child's natural parents because they contributed the genetic materials used to conceive the child. Furthermore, the court concluded that, because Anthony and Shelly did not relinquish or waive their parental rights, they were the child's legal parents. To summarize, the court determined that the genetic mother is always the natural mother of the child. The natural mother is the child's legal mother unless she takes steps to terminate her maternal rights so that another woman can be identified as the legal mother.[150] The court made it clear that the rights of the woman who supplied the genetic material to conceive the child were superior to those of the woman who gave birth to the child.[151] The court adopted the genetics test to determine maternity in a surrogacy arrangement.

The court endeavored to treat a child conceived in accordance with the terms of a surrogacy arrangement similar to a child who results from sexual intercourse. If a man uses his penis to fertilize a woman's eggs with his sperm, she is clearly the child's natural mother. Under the standard set out in *Belsito*, the outcome would not be different just because the child was conceived using scientific means. Therefore, if a physician fertilizes a woman's eggs with a man's sperm and implants the embryo into another woman's body, the woman who provides the eggs does not lose her genetic connection to the child. A woman who conceives a child naturally can dissolve her legal relationship with the child and put the child up for adoption, so that another woman can become the child's legal mother. The reasoning of the *Belsito* case indicates that the same option is available to a woman who contributes the genetic material in a surrogacy arrangement. That woman can voluntarily relinquish her right to the child, so that the surrogate or another woman can become the child's legal mother. In either case, the law cannot force the woman to turn her biological child over to another woman. However, some courts assert that intentions should outweigh genetics.

The legal mother is the woman who signs the contract with the intent of parenting the child

According to Professor Shultz, courts should adjudicate legal parenthood by considering the parties' intentions.[152] In particular, Professor Shultz contends, "intentions that are voluntarily chosen, deliberate, express and bargained-for ought presumptively to determine legal parenthood."[153] Some courts have applied this logic to conclude that evaluating the parties' intent should be the method used to resolve custody disputes between surrogates and contracting couples. The next case demonstrates that approach.

Johnson v Calvert[154] *(Majority Opinion)*

Mark and Crispina Calvert's plans to become parents were ruined when Crispina had to have a hysterectomy. Because Crispina was still capable of producing eggs, the couple decided to arrange for a surrogate, Anna Johnson, to gestate their child. Under the terms of the agreement the parties signed, Anna would carry the child conceived using the embryo created from Mark's sperm and Crispina's eggs. Once the child was born, Anna was supposed to relinquish her parental rights to the child and to give the child to the Calverts. In exchange for her services, Mark and Crispina agreed to pay Anna ten thousand dollars in installments and to insure Anna's life for two-hundred-thousand dollars. After Anna became pregnant, her relationship with the Calverts deteriorated. Ultimately, Anna asked the Calverts to pay her the rest of the money they owed her. Anna threatened to keep the child if she did not receive all of the money. The Calverts responded by filing a lawsuit to be legally recognized as the parents of the unborn child. Anna countered with her own lawsuit asking the court to recognize her as the child's legal mother. The court combined the cases.[155]

According to blood tests, the Calverts were the child's biological parents. The court had to determine the identity of the child's natural mother under California law. The trial court ruled that the Calverts were the child's "genetic, biological and natural" parents and Anna had no parental rights with regard to the child. The Court of Appeals affirmed the Trial Court's decision, so Anna appealed the case.[156] Anna based her claim to the child on the fact that she gestated and gave birth to the child. The Calverts maintained that because the child was created using her genetic material, Crispina was the child's legal mother.[157] To resolve the case, when allocating maternity, the court had to decide whether to give preference to the woman having the genetic relationship to the child or the woman giving birth to the child. The court decided that both women were able to produce evidence of a mother–child relationship under the provisions of the statute.[158]

Under a section of the UPA, maternity could be proven by the use of genetic evidence gathered through blood testing. Because the blood tests showed that Crispina was the child's genetic mother, she satisfied the evidentiary requirements of the statute. However, a different provision of the law permitted a woman to establish a mother–child relationship by giving birth to the child.[159] Anna was able to show that she gave birth to the child.[160] Therefore, both women met the statutory requirements to prove maternity, so the child appeared to have two natural mothers. However, California would only acknowledge one legal mother.[161]

The court relied upon contract principles to resolve the case. To that end, the court analyzed the terms of the surrogacy agreement. The court ruled that the appropriate test for determining the identity of the legal mother of the child was the "intent" test. Specifically, the court stated "she who intended to procreate the child–that is, she who intended to bring about the birth of a child that she intended to raise as her own-is the natural mother under California law." The Calverts intended to have a child from their genetic material. They carried out that intent by having an embryo created using his sperm and her egg, implanted in Anna. Anna agreed to assist the Calverts in carrying out their intentions. The child would not exist if the Calverts had not acted on their intentions. The court found that Anna's intent to keep the child should not be recognized because it conflicted with the original intentions of the parties.[162] The court seemed to indicate that the existence of a traditional surrogacy arrangement would not have changed the outcome of the case. The main factor in determining maternity was intent and not genetics. Nonetheless, according to some courts, intent and genetics should take a back seat to gestation.

The legal mother is the woman who gives birth to the child

A woman who gestates a child forms a special bond with that child. That connection grows from the moment the embryo is implanted until the child is born. For forty weeks, that woman nurtures and cares for the child.[163] Some commentators have argued that this "sweat equity" should transform the surrogate into a gestational mother.[164] That classification of the surrogate's role acknowledges that the surrogate contributes something of herself to the child. Consequently, she should be regarded as more than a womb or an incubator.[165] Some courts have declared that the surrogate's role as a gestator should factor into the determination of maternity. That point of view is demonstrated by the next case.

A.H.W. v G.H.B.[166]

Gina, an unmarried woman, agreed to act as an unpaid surrogate for her sister, Andrea, and Andrea's husband, Peter. As a result, doctors implanted an embryo created using Peter's sperm and Andrea's eggs into Gina's uterus. Gina became pregnant as a result of the implantation.[167] About two weeks before Gina was to give birth, Peter and Andrea sought a court order adjudicating the maternity and paternity of the unborn child. In particular, the couple asked the court to issue a pre-birth order designating them as the child's legal parents and mandating that their names be placed on the child's birth certificate.[168]

They supported their petition by arguing that because Gina, the gestational surrogate, did not have a genetic connection to the child she should not be recognized as having any parental rights with regard to the child. Moreover, Peter, Andrea, and Gina claimed that Gina was nothing more than an incubator. The court did not agree with that view of the gestational surrogate. According to the court, Gina did more than incubate the child. To support its contention, the court described the bond between a child and the gestational mother. The court referred to Gina as a gestational mother instead of a gestational surrogate. The court felt that title was more appropriate because of the contributions that the gestating woman made to the child's well-being during the pregnancy.[169]

Once the court decided that the gestational mother was the child's legal mother, the court refused to grant the pre-birth order. After reviewing the state statutes and case law, including the *Baby M* case, the court concluded that forcing Gina to give up her parental rights before the child was born was inconsistent with New Jersey law. The court held that Gina could not voluntarily terminate her parental rights until seventy-two hours after she gave birth. New Jersey's adoption statute required a woman to wait seventy-two hours before agreeing to the adoption of her child. The court felt that the same waiting period was appropriate in a case involving a gestational surrogate because the woman might experience the same emotional and physical changes during birth as a woman who gave birth to her biological child. The court also concluded that Gina had the option of changing her mind and filing an action to retain custody of the child.[170]

In reaching its decision, the court emphasized that a strong connection between the woman and the child formed during the pregnancy and at birth.[171] That connection is not weakened by the lack of a biological link. The mother–child relationship develops because of the dependency of the child on the mother. The woman who supplies the eggs that result in the creation of the embryo has a connection to the embryo but not to the resulting child. The woman who provides the nutrients necessary for the embryo to develop into a child is the child's natural and legal mother. That woman is the woman who gestates the child. As a consequence, gestation is the controlling factor in adjudicating maternity. Reproductive technology that makes surrogacy achievable has resulted in two women having the potential to receive maternal rights. Therefore, courts are faced with the daunting task of adjudicating legal maternity. At least one jurist thinks each of those methodologies is unsound because they do not consider what is best for a child.

The legal mother is the person promotes the best interests of the child

Johnson v Calvert *(Dissenting Opinion)*[172]

The dissent in the *Johnson* case argued that the proper way to adjudicate the legal mother of the child is the best interests of the child standard. According to the dissent, the gestational mother and the genetic mother were both the child's natural mothers, so both had an equal claim to the child. However, because the state only allowed one woman to be recognized as the child's legal mother, the court had to determine which woman should be given that status.[173] After reviewing the facts and applicable law, the dissent claimed that the legal issue was which factor to use as the tie-breaker when deciding whether to adjudicate the surrogate or the contracting woman as the child's legal mother. The dissent maintained that the standard should be the "best interests of the child" because that standard would enable the court to reach the decision that was most protective of the child's welfare.[174] In addition, the dissent contended that the intent test was too inflexible to serve the child's best interests.[175] The dissent concluded that the court should evaluate the households and lifestyles of both mothers to determine which placement would be in the child's best interests.[176] The dissent ultimately proposed that courts determine maternity on a case-by-case basis relying on the best interests of the child standard.[177]

Conclusion

The pros and cons of posthumous reproduction are not relevant after a child has actually been conceived using the process. At that time, the debate should cease and the laws should be put in place to ensure that the needs of the child are met. A critical need for any child is the emotional and financial support of a parent. The law is not in a position to guarantee that the child will have a relationship with one or more of its parents. However, courts and legislatures can take steps to make sure that the child has legal parents. In this chapter, I have explored some theories courts can use to adjudicate legal fathers for the child. I have also examined the different ways courts have identified the legal mother in cases involving surrogacy disputes. The next chapter turns to the financial needs of the posthumously conceived child.

Notes

1 Diane Blood registers sons: A widow who fought for the right to have children using her dead husband's sperm is re-registering her two sons' births at www.bbc.co.uk (December 1, 2003).
2 See, e.g., Vernon's Texas Statutes and Code Annotated § 160.201 (West 2016); 750 Illinois Compiled Statutes Annotated § 46/201.
3 *In re Marriage of Broecher*, 528 N.W.2d 510, 513 (Iowa 1998); *Eggmeyer v Eggmeyer*, 554 S.W.2d 137, 139 (Tex. 1977).
4 *In re Certified Question from U.S. Dist. Court for Western Michigan*, 825 N.W.2d 566, 568 (Mich. 2012).
5 Peter M. Cicchino, The Problem Child: An Empirical Survey and Rhetorical Analysis of Child Poverty in the United States, 5 J.L. & Pol'y 5, 36–37 (1996).
6 "Most of us who have had the experience of an early separation from our natural parents appear to possess a sort of vacuum in our life for which we can find no substitute. Let's use the analogy of life being seen as a jig-saw puzzle with bits and pieces fitting together to make it complete except for the adopted child there

are pieces missing. The only explanation he gets is that they just aren't there. For most of us, this is just not adequate. We, too, long to be whole.": quoted in Heidi Hilderbrand, Because They Want to Know: An Examination of the Legal Rights of Adoptees and Their Parents, 24 S.Ill.U.L.J. 515, 528 (2000).

7 Lauren Gill, Who's Your Daddy? Defining Paternity Rights in the Context of Free Private Sperm Donation, 54 Wm. & Mary L. Rev. 1715, 1727–1728 (April 2013).

8 George W. Dent, Jr., Defense of Traditional Marriage, 15 J.L. & Pol. 581, 593–597 (Fall 1999).

9 *Id.*

10 Mary E. Hansen and Josh Gupta-Kagan, Raising the Cut-Off: The Empirical Case For Extending Adoption and Guardianship Subsidies From Age 18 to 21, 13 U.C. Davis J. Juv. L. & Pol'y 1, 7–8 (2009).

11 "Fornication is sexual intercourse between a man, married or single, and an unmarried woman": *State v Johnson*, 69 Ind. 85, 87 (1879).

12 *State v Bigelow*, 92 A. 978, 978 (Vt. 1915) ("[a]ny man, married or single, having voluntary sexual intercourse with a married woman, not his wife, is guilty of adultery.") *Id.*

13 Traci Shalbetter Station, No More Messing Around: Substantive Due Process Challenges to Laws Prohibiting Fornication, 73 Wash. L. Rev. 767, 769 (July 1998); Martin J. Siegel, For Better Or For Worse: Adultery, Crime and the Constitution, 30 J. Fam. L. 45, 47–48 (1991/1992).

14 *Matter of Kathy R. v Steven* S., 47 A.D.2d 680 (1975).

15 *Neil S. v Mary L.*, 131 Cal. Rptr. 3d 51, 56 (Cal. App. 4th 2011).

16 *Brinkley v King*, 701 A.2d 176, 179 (Pa. 1997).

17 *Alisha C. v Jeremy C.*, 808 N.W.2d 875, 880 (Neb. 2012).

18 Niccol Kording, *Nature v. Nurture: Children Left Fatherless and Family-Less When Nature Prevails In Paternity Actions,* 65 U. Pitt. L. Rev. 811, 818 (Summer 2004); Battle Robinson and Susan Paikin, *Who Is Daddy? A Case For the Uniform Parentage Act* (2000), 19-SUM Del. Law 23, 24 (Summer 2001).

19 Debi McRae, Evaluating the Effectiveness of the Best Interests Marital Presumption of Paternity: It Is Actually in the Best Interests of the Child to Divorce the Current Application of the Best Interests Marital Presumption of Paternity, 5 Whittier J. Child & Fam. Advoc. 345, 349 (Spring 2006).

20 Jana Singer, Marriage, Biology, and Paternity: The Case For Revitalizing the Marital Presumption, 65 Md. L. Rev. 246, 248–249 (2006).

21 *Morris v Davies*, (1837) 5 Clark & F 163, 7 (Eng. Reprint 365).

22 Theresa Glennon, Somebody's Child: Evaluating the Erosion of the Marital Presumption of Paternity, 102 W.Va. L. Rev. 547, 563 (Spring 2000).

23 Steve N. Peskind, Who's Your Daddy?: An Analysis of Illinois' Law of Parentage and the Meaning of Parenthood, 35 Loy. U. Chi. 811, 836 (Spring 2004).

24 *Weidenbacker v Dueior*, 661 A.2d 988, 997 (Conn. 1995).

25 *Damien v J.G.*, 957 N.Y.S. 2d 819 (2012) (genetic testing in the children's best interests).

26 "(a) A man is presumed to be the natural father of a child if: (1) He and the child's natural mother are or have been married to each other and the child is born during the marriage, or within three hundred (300) days after the marriage is terminated by death, annulment, or divorce or after a decree of separation is entered by the Court.": Wyo. Stat. Ann. § 14–2–102 (West 2016).

27 *Brinkley v King*, 701 A2d 176, 180–181 (Pa. 1997).

28 *G.F.C. v S.G.*, 686 So.2d 1382 (Fla. 5th D.C.A. 1997) cited in *Bellomo v Gagliano*, 815 So.2d 721, 722 (Fla. 2002); June Calbone, The Legal Definition of Parenthood: Uncertainty At the Core of Family Identity, 65 La. L. Rev. 1295, 1308 (Summer 2005).

29 *C.W. v L.V.*, 788 A2d 1002, 1005 (Pa. Super 2001).
30 *Evans v Wilson*, 856 A.2d 679, 692 (Md. 2004); *Mulligan v Corbert*, 45 A.3d 243, 260 (Md. 2012).
31 See, e.g., A.C.A. § 9–10–201(a) (West 2016); 750 I.C.S.A. § 40/3(a) (West 2016); M.C.A. § 40–6–106(1) (West 2016); R.C. § 3111.95(A) (West 2016).
32 *K.S. v G.S.*, 440 A.2d 64, 66 (N.J. super. Ct. Ch. Div. 1981); *In re Marriage of Witbeck-Wildhagen*, 667 N.E. 2d 122, 126 (Ill. App. Ct. 1996).
33 *Id.*
34 Conn. Gen. Stat. Ann. § 45a–774 (West 2016).
35 Minn. Stat. Ann. § 257.56 (West 2016).
36 912 P.2d 290 (N.M. Ct. App. 1996).
37 *Id.* at 292.
38 *Id.* at 293.
39 *Id.* at 294.
40 912 P.2d. at 295.
41 *Id.*
42 *Id.*
43 *Id.*
44 912 P.2d at 295.
45 *Id.* at 296
46 Md. Code Ann, Est. & Trusts § 1–206(b) (West 2016).
47 Utah Code Ann. § 788–15–704(2) (West 2016).
48 La. Civ. Code Ann. Art. 188 (2016); Mass. Gen. Laws Ann. Ch. 46 § 4B (West 2016); Mich. Comp. Laws Serv. § 333.2824 (West 2016); and Tenn. Code Ann. § 68–3–306 (2016)
49 Unif. Status of Children of Assisted Conception Act § 3 9C U.L.A. 370 (2016); *Id.* §3 cmt., 9C U.L.A. 370–71.
50 Fla. Stat. Ann. § 742.11(1) (West 2016). See also *K.S.*, 440 A. 2d at 68.
51 Ga. Code Ann. § 19–7–21 (West 2016).
52 Del. Code Ann. tit. 13, § 8–705(a) (2016).
53 Tex. Fam. Ann. § 160.705(a) (Vernon 2016) ("Except as otherwise provided by subsection (b), the husband of a wife who gives birth by means of assisted reproduction may not challenge his paternity of the child unless: (1) before the fourth anniversary of the date of learning of the birth of the child he commences a proceeding to adjudicate his paternity; and (2) the court finds that he did not consent to the assisted reproduction before or after the birth of the child.").
54 Unif. Parentage Act (amended 2002) § 705, 9B U.L.A. 64 (2016) ("Except as otherwise provided in subsection (b), the husband of a wife who gives birth to a child by means of assisted reproduction may not challenge his paternity of the child unless: (1) within two years after learning of the birth of the child by means of assisted reproduction he commences a proceeding to adjudicate his paternity; and (2) the court finds that he did not consent to the assisted reproduction, before or after the birth of the child, (b) A proceeding to adjudicate paternity may be maintained at any time if the court determines that (1) the husband did not provide sperm for, or before or after the birth of the child consent to, assisted reproduction by his wife; (2) the husband and the mother of the child have not cohabitated since the probable time of assisted reproduction; and (3) the husband never openly held out the child as his own. (c) The limitation provided in this section applies to a marriage declared invalid after assisted reproduction.").
55 La. Civ. Code Ann. art. 188 (2016).
56 N.H. Rev. Stat. Ann. § 168B:3(1)(a) (West 2016).
57 N.H. Rev. Stat. Ann. § 5-C:30(1) (West 2016).
58 N.H. Rev. Stat. Ann. § 168-B:3 (II) (West 2016).

59 "'Informed consent' occurs when a competent person, while exercising care for his or her own welfare, makes a voluntary decision about whether or not to participate in a proposed medical procedure or contractual arrangement that is based on a full awareness of the relevant facts." *Id.* § 168-B:1(VI).
60 *Id.* § 168-B:13(IV).
61 *Id.* § 168-B:13(IV)(c).
62 *Id.* § 168-B:13(IV).
63 *Id.* § 168-B:13(II).
64 Black's Law Dictionary 1099 (8th ed. 2004) ("the son of no one").
65 I William Blackstone, *Commentaries on the Laws of England* 447 (William S. Hein & Co., Inc., 1992).
66 *Fiallo v Bell*, 430 U.S. 787, 788–89 (1977); *Miller v Albright*, 523 U.S. 420, 424 (1998).
67 *Linda R.S. v Richard D.*, 410 U.S. 614, 615 (1973); *Gomez v Perez*, 409 U.S. 535, 535 (1973); *N.J. Welfare Rights Org. v Cahill*, 411 U.S. 619, 619 (1973); *Mills v Habluetzel*, 456 U.S. 91, 92 (1982).
68 *Mills*, 456 U.S. at 91; *Pickett v Brown*, 462 U.S. 1, 3 (1983); *Clark v Jeter*, 486 U.S. 456, 457 (1988).
69 *Levy v Louisiana*, 391 U.S. 68, 69 (1968); *Glona v Am. Guarantee & Liab. Ins. Co.*, 391 U.S. 73, 73 (1968); *Parham v Hughes*, 441 U.S. 347, 348–49 (1979).
70 *Weber v Aetna Cas. & Sur. Co.*, 406 U.S. 164, 165 (1972).
71 *Labine v Vincent*, 401 U.S. 532, 533 (1971); *Trimble v Gordon*, 430 U.S. 762, 763 (1977); *Lalli v Lalli*, 439 U.S. 259, 261 (1978); *Reed v Campbell*, 476 U.S. 852, 853 (1986).
72 *Jimenez v Weinberger*, 417 U.S. 628, 630 (1974); *Mathews v Lucas*, 427 U.S. 495, 497 (1976); *Califano v Boles*, 443 U.S. 282, 283 (1979); *Beatty v Weinberger*, 478 F.2d 300, 301 (5th Cir. 1973), summarily aff'd, 418 U.S. 901 (1974); *Davis v Richardson*, 342 F. Supp. 588, 589 (D. Conn. 1972), summarily aff'd, 409 U.S. 1069 (1972); *Griffin v Richardson*, 346 F. Supp. 1226, 1228 (D. Md. 1972), summarily aff'd, 409 U.S. 1069 (1972).
73 *Levy*, 391 U.S. at 68; *Glona*, 391 U.S. at 73.
74 *Levy*, 391 U.S. at 72.
75 *Glona*, 391 U.S. at 76.
76 *Gomez*, 409 U.S. at 538.
77 *Id.* at 535–536.
78 *Id.* at 536.
79 *Id* at 536–37.
80 *Gomez*, 409 U.S. at 537.
81 *Id* at 538.
82 *Id.*
83 *Reed v Campbell*, 476 U.S. 852, 854 (1986).
84 *Id.* at 854–55.
85 *Lalli*, 439 U.S. at 275–76.
86 *Trimble*, 430 U.S. at 763.
87 *Id.* at 763–64.
88 *Id.* at 764.
89 *Id.* at 765.
90 *Trimble*, 430 U.S. at 765. The statute allowed non-marital children to inherit by intestate succession only from their mothers without conditions; marital children were permitted to inherit from both their mothers and fathers without conditions. *Id.*
91 *Id.* at 768.
92 *Id.* at 766 See also Trimble, 430 U.S. at 770 (stating that the Illinois Supreme Court held that a state has an "interest in 'establishing a method of property disposition'" (citing *In re Karas' Estate*, 329 N.E.2d 234, 238 (Ill. 1975)).

93 *Trimble*, 430 U.S. at 769–70.
94 *Id.* at 772–73.
95 *Id.* at 772.
96 *Id.* at 776.
97 *Lalli*, 439 U.S. at 261.
98 *Id.* ("(a) For the purposes of this article: (1) An illegitimate child is the legitimate child of his mother so that he and his issue inherit from his mother and from his maternal kindred. (2) An illegitimate child is the legitimate child of his father so that he and his issue inherit from his father if a court of competent jurisdiction has, during the lifetime of the father, made an order of filiation declaring paternity in a proceeding instituted during the pregnancy of the mother or within two years from the birth of the child. (3) The existence of an agreement obligating the father to support the illegitimate child does not qualify such child or his issue to inherit from the father in the absence of an order of filiation made as prescribed by subparagraph (2). (4) A motion for relief from an order of filiation may be made only by the father, and such motion must be made within one year from the entry of such order. (b) If an illegitimate child dies, his surviving spouse, issue, mother, maternal kindred and father inherit and are entitled to letters of administration as if the decedent were legitimate, provided that the father may inherit or obtain such letters only if an order of filiation has been made in accordance with the provisions of subparagraph (2).") *Id.* at 261 n.2 (citing N.Y. Est. Powers & Trusts Law § 4–1.2 (McKinley 1967).
99 *Id.* at 262.
100 *Lalli*, 439 U.S. at 271.
101 *Id.* at 273.
102 *Id.* at 271 ("Accuracy is enhanced by placing paternity disputes in a judicial forum during the lifetime of the father … The administration of an estate will be facilitated, and the possibility of delay and uncertainty minimized, where the entitlement of an illegitimate child to notice and participation is a matter of judicial record before the administration commences.")
103 *Id.* at 273 (noting that unlike the statute in *Trimble*, the statute challenged in this case did not make a large number of non-marital children ineligible to inherit from their fathers.).
104 *Id.* at 271 ("requiring that the order be issued during the father's lifetime permits a man to defend his reputation against 'unjust accusations in paternity claims …'").
105 *Id.* at 271–72.
106 According to the legislative history of the statute, the New York Legislature wanted to " 'grant to illegitimates in so far as practicable rights of inheritance on a par with those enjoyed by legitimate children' … while protecting the important state interests [the Court] described." *Id.* at 274.
107 Richard F. Storrow, Parenthood By Pure Intention: Assisted Reproduction and the Functional Approach to Parentage, 53 Hasting L.J. 597, 607 (March 2002). (citing *Trimble v Gordon*, 430 U.S. 762, 770 (1976)).
108 Unif. Parentage Act § 702 (amended 2002), 9B U.L.A. 335 (2001).
109 E.g., Wyo. Stat. Ann. § 14–2–902 (2016).
110 E.g., Mont. Code Ann. § 40–6–106 (2016).
111 E.g., Or. Rev. Stat. § 109.239(2) ("A child born as a result of the artificial insemination shall have no right, obligation or interest with respect to such donor.")
112 E.g., N.M. Stat. § 40–11–6(B) (2016).
113 For example, the Michigan Legislature has dealt with the legal consequences of the existence of artificially conceived children by passing a statute stating in relevant part: "A child conceived by a married woman with consent of her husband following the utilization of assisted reproductive technology is considered to be the legitimate child of the husband and wife.": Mich. Comp. Law Serv. § 333.2824(6) (West 2016). The statutory provision leads one to conclude that

a sperm donor has no obligation to a child conceived using his sperm if the woman is married. Nonetheless, the legislature has not yet addressed the situation where an unmarried woman conceives a child using donated sperm.

114 The donor is not the child's natural father. Ala. Code § 26–17–702 (West 2016); Cal. Fam. Code § 7613(b) (West 2016) *cited in Steven S. v Deborah D.*, 25 Cal. Rptr. 3d 482, 487 (Cal. Ct. App. 2005); 750 Ill. Comp. Stat. § 40/3(b) (West 2016); Mo. Ann. Stat. § 210.824(2) (West 2016). The donor is not the child's biological father. Minn. Stat. Ann. § 257.56(2) (West 2016).

115 Fla. Stat. Ann. § 742.14 (West 2016). See also *Lamaritata v Lucas*, 823 So. 2d 316, 319 (Fla. Dist. App. 2002).

116 June Carbone & Paige Gottheim, Markets, Subsidies, Regulation, and Trust Building Ethical Understandings into the Market for Fertility Services, 9 J. Gender Race & Just. 509, 535–36 (2009).

117 Wis. Stat. Ann. § 981.40(2) (West 2016).

118 *Id.*

119 Okla. Stat. Ann. tit., 10 § 555 (West 2016) ("An oocyte donor shall have no right, obligation or interest with respect to a child born as a result of a heterologous oocyte donation from such donor. A child born as a result of a heterologous oocyte donation shall have no right, obligation or interest with respect to the person who donated the oocyte which resulted in the birth of the child.").

120 N.H. Rev. Stat. Ann. § 168-B:11 (West 2016).

121 Kan. Stat. Ann. § 38–1114(f) (2016); N.M. Stat. § 40–11–6 (2016).

122 N.J. Stat. Ann. § 9:17–44(b) (West 2016) ("Unless the donor of semen and the woman have entered into a written contract to the contrary, the donor of semen provided to a licensed physician for use in artificial insemination of a woman other than the donor's wife is treated in law as if he were not the father of a child thereby conceived and shall have no rights or duties stemming from the conception of a child.").

123 See *In re K.M.H.*, 169 P. 3d 1025, 1042 (Kan. 2007). The court in *In re K.M.H.* held that the failure of the sperm donor to deposit his sperm with a licensed physician did not take the transaction outside of the artificial insemination statute as long as a licensed physician actually performed the procedure. *Id.* In the case, the man delivered his sperm directly to the woman and she took it to a licensed physician who performed the artificial insemination. *Id.*

124 See, e.g., *Jhordan C. v Mary K.*, 224 Cal. Rptr. 530, 535 (Cal. Ct. App. 1986).

125 John C. Sheldon, Surrogate Mothers, Gestational Carriers, and a Pragmatic Adaptation of the Uniform Parentage Act of 2000, 53 Me. L. Rev. 523, 532–33 (2001).

126 Allison J. Stone, Comment, "Sisters Are Doin' It For Themselves!" Why the Parental Rights of Registered Domestic Partners Must Trump the Parental Rights of Their Known Sperm Donors in California, 41 U.S.F.L. Rev. 505, 510 (2007).

127 The Associated Press, Pa. Sperm Donor to Lesbian Couple Ordered to Pay Child Support, Pittsburgh Trib.-Rev., May 10, 2007, available at www.pittsburghlive.com/x/pittsburghtrib/news/cityregion/s_505968.html.

128 *Jacob v Shultz-Jacob*, 923 A. 2d 473 (Pa. Super. Ct. 2007). See also Jason Miller, Sperm Donor Indispensable Party to Support Proceeding, Law. J. (Allegheny County Bar Ass'n Pittsburgh, Pa.) June 22, 2007, at 2.

129 *Jacob*, 923 A. 2d at 476.

130 *Id.* at 480.

131 *Id.*

132 *Id.* at 480.

133 *Id.*

134 *Id.* at 481.
135 A surrogate gestates and births a child for another person. The two types of surrogacy are traditional and gestational. In a traditional surrogate arrangement, the woman gestates an embryo created with her own eggs and sperm supplied by the contracting party. In a gestational surrogate arrangement, the surrogate's role is limited to gestating and giving birth to the child. She does not have a genetic connection to the child. *In re Baby*, 447 S.W.3d 807, 818 (2014).
136 See *In re C.K.G.*, 173 S.W.3d 714 (2005).
137 See, e.g., § 9–10–108 (West 2016).
138 *In the Matter of Parental Rights as to A.G.*, 295 P.3d 589, 593 (Nevada 2013).
139 Kim A. Feigenbaum, The Changing Family Structure: Challenging Stepchildren's Lack of Inheritance Rights, 66 Brook. L. Rev. 167, 167 (Spring 2000).
140 *Belsito v Clark*, 644 N.E.2d 760 (Ohio Ct. Com. Pl. 1994). For an analysis of *Belsito*, see Dawn Wenk, Note, Belsito v. Clark: Ohio's Battle With "Motherhood," 28 U. Tol. Rev. 247 (1996).
141 *Belsito*, 644 N.E. 2d at 761.
142 See *Id.* at 760–61.
143 *Id.* at 761.
144 *Id.* at 762.
145 *Belsito*, 644 N.E. at 763.
146 *Id.* at 766.
147 *Id.*
148 *Id.* at 766–67.
149 *Id.* at 767.
150 See *Id.*
151 *Id.* ("The birth test becomes subordinate and secondary to genetics.").
152 Marjorie M. Shultz, Reproductive Technology and Intent-Based Parenthood: An Opportunity for Gender Neutrality, 1990 Wis. L. Rev. 287, 302.
153 Shultz, supra note 152 at 323.
154 *Johnson*, 851 P.2d at 776.
155 See *Id.* at 778.
156 *Id.*
157 See *Id.* at 779.
158 *Id.*
159 *Johnson*, 851 P.2d at 781.
160 *Id.* at 780.
161 *Id.* at 781. This is consistent with the state's treatment of paternity. See *Michael H. v Gerald D.*, 491 U.S. 110, 118 (1989) (stating that California law does not permit a child to have two legal fathers.)
162 *Johnson*, 851 P.2d at 782.
163 See Lawrence O. Gostin, *Surrogacy From the Perspectives of Economic and Civil Liberties*, 17 Contemp. Health L. & Pol'y 429, 435 (2001).
164 See, e.g., Scott B. Rae, Parental Rights and the Definition of Motherhood in Surrogate Motherhood, 3 S. Cal. Rev. L. & Women's Stud. 219, 236 (1994).
165 See Gostin, supra note 163 at 435.
166 *A.H.W. v G.H.B.*, 772 A.2d 948 (N.J. 2000). See also *J.F. v D.B.*, 66 Pa. D. & C. 4th 1 (C.P. Ct. of Erie County 2004).
167 *A.H.W.*, 772 A.2d at 949.
168 *Id.* at 950.
169 *Id.* at 953.
170 *Id.* at 954.
171 *A.H.W.*, 772 A.2d at 953.
172 *Johnson*, 851 P.2d at 788 (Kennard, J. dissenting).

173 *Id*. at 789.
174 *Id*. at 799.
175 *Id*. at 795–99.
176 *Johnson*, 851 P.2d at 799–800.
177 *Id*. at 800.

6 Posthumously conceived children (allocating financial support)

When a person of modest means passes away, most of the resources available to provide for the person's family come from life insurance, retirement funds, and government benefits. If the person is not a veteran, the money to help support the person's surviving children comes from the Social Security Administration. After the posthumously conceived child is born, the mother typically applies for Social Security Survivors' benefits on behalf of the child. Consequently, litigation dealing with the inheritance rights of posthumously conceived children usually starts with the denial of that application. One court emphasized that the survivors' benefits program is not intended to function as a welfare program. Therefore, the financial needs of the child are not enough to qualify the child for benefits.[1] The purpose of the survivors' benefits program is to provide monetary benefits to *replace* the financial support the child loses when a parent dies.[2] If the father supplies financial support to the mother during her pregnancy, he is deemed to have provided support to the child.[3]

Under the terms of the Social Security Act(SSA), when a person who is eligible to receive benefits dies, that person's child is entitled to survivors' child's benefits.[4] To qualify for those benefits, the child must be eighteen years old or younger, a student who is younger than twenty-two years old or a child with a permanent disability. The child must also have been dependent at the time the parent dies.[5] The law considers the child to be dependent if he or she is living with the insured parent or receiving financial support from the parent prior to his or her death. A marital child or an acknowledged non-marital child only has to satisfy the age requirements because the law presumes children in those classes to be dependent. A child who is entitled to inherit under the state's intestacy system is also allowed to take advantage of this presumption.[6] To receive benefits, in addition to meeting the age requirements, other non-marital children have to prove that they lived with the deceased or received financial support from him.[7] Because a posthumously conceived child would not be alive until after his or her father's death it would be impossible to show that the child lived with the man or that the child was financially dependent on the man. Nonetheless, that is not the end of the story because courts have given the SSA a liberal construction to ensure that children are financially supported after the death of one or both parents.[8]

On May 21, 2012, the United States Supreme Court decided *Astrue v Capato*,[9] a case involving twins conceived through in vitro fertilization using Robert Capato's frozen sperm over eighteen months after he succumbed to cancer.[10] The Supreme Court concluded that the posthumously conceived twins were not eligible to receive Social Security Survivors' benefits.[11] In its opinion, the Supreme Court indicated that the fate of a posthumously conceived child rests with the state where the wage earner is domiciled when he dies.[12] In essence, the Supreme Court ruled that states can rely upon their individual intestacy systems to determine the posthumously conceived child's rights to benefits under a federal statute. Writing for the Court, Justice Ginsberg concluded that it would not be appropriate to create a uniform federal rule to govern which children are entitled to receive survivors' benefits. The Court chose to leave that task to state intestacy statutes.[13] As a result, this chapter examines the inheritance rights of posthumously conceived children. The first part of the chapter consists of a discussion of the statutory regimes in states that have explicitly addressed the rights of children conceived after the death of their parents. Legislatures in only sixteen states have passed such statutes.[14] Therefore, the second half of the book analyzes court opinions in jurisdictions where the inheritance rights of posthumously conceived children have not been statutorily defined.

Before we turn to how the posthumously conceived child might inherit, let us ponder the question of whether the child should inherit. One court has stated: "The legal relation or status of 'heir' or 'next of kin' arises only upon the death of the ancestor, and it arises immediately."[15] The sentence accurately reflects the legal perspective. For a person to be considered an heir, a death must occur. If the person is to receive that status, it must happen immediately on the happening of the death. This line of reasoning presents a problem for the posthumously conceived child. Even though a death does happen, because the child is not alive at that time he or she cannot instantly obtain the status of heir. The ability to inherit arises from being named an heir. Consequently, since the posthumously conceived child can never be an heir of his or her father, that child should not have the right to inherit under the intestacy system.

There are reasons other than just practical ones why a posthumously conceived child might be prevented from inheriting. Permitting the posthumously conceived child to inherit does not discharge the purpose of the intestacy system. The primary objective of the intestacy system is to create a framework, so the court can effectuate a decedent's likely intent when it comes to the distribution of his property.[16] Intestacy statutes favor children because legislators assume that a man wants to make sure that his children are taken care of when he dies. This is not an issue when the child is not conceived until after the man's death. Prior to his death, it is unlikely that a man would be concerned with the welfare of a child that does not exist and may never exist. The intestacy system was not put in place to deal with situations involving posthumously conceived children.

In addition, from a public policy perspective, it does not make sense to encourage women to create dependent children once the person upon whom they might depend is no longer alive. Finally, the man does not have a legal duty to provide financial support for a posthumously conceived child. A parent's financial responsibility arises when his or her child is born. In the case of the posthumously conceived child, that obligation never occurs because a dead man cannot acquire legal duties. Requiring a portion of the dead man's estate to be set aside for the posthumously conceived child would be like forcing a man to financially support a stranger. That is an action that the law would never permit if the man were alive.

The main reason to permit the posthumously conceived child to inherit from his or her father is because the child exists. As long as the law continues to allow posthumous reproduction, steps should be taken to ensure that the resulting child is financially supported. The child is the innocent party in this situation. In some cases, the man consents to the child's conception knowing that he will be dead before it happens. The woman intentionally conceives a child without a legal father. The law permits the man and the woman to take the respective actions. Because the law is complicit in the child's conception, as a matter of equity, courts should permit the posthumously conceived child to inherit on par with other classes of marital children. Further, any reasonable man who agrees to have a child conceived using his sperm would probably want the child to receive the financial support that he or she needs. If the man is not permitted to provide financial support for his posthumously conceived child, the child's mother may be forced to rely on government assistance. Taxpayers should not be obligated to help financially support a child if the child's parents have the resources necessary to accomplish the task. Lastly, children should never be punished for the actions of their parents or the circumstances of their birth. Courts took this stance when granting greater inheritance rights to non-marital children.

Statutory approaches

The state legislatures that have enacted statutes setting forth the conditions under which posthumously conceived children may inherit have tried to address concerns raised by persons opposed to granting inheritance to those children. The mandates of the statutes differ, but the statutes contain some common provisions. Following the recommendation of the Uniform Parentage Act (UPA), five states permit a posthumously conceived child to inherit as long as the deceased man left a record indicating his agreement to be the child's parent.[17] At the other end of the spectrum, Ohio explicitly denies a posthumously conceived child the opportunity to inherit from his or her father.[18] The language stating that a person had to be alive in order to inherit was placed in the statute before the technology that permits posthumous reproduction even existed. Therefore, the legislators probably did not enact the statutory provision for the purpose of preventing a posthumously conceived child from inheriting property from his or her parent. Nonetheless, because of the statutory language posthumously conceived children cannot inherit under Ohio's intestacy statute. The other ten states with statutes have taken independent approaches and place certain restrictions on the posthumously conceived child's ability to inherit.[19] The Louisiana and Iowa statutes contain unique provisions that permit the existing heirs of the man to challenge the inheritance rights of the posthumously conceived child.[20] This is an attempt to be fair to the children who are born prior to the man's death.

As a result of the statutory regimes created by the states, the following legal requirements impact the ability of a posthumously conceived child to inherit: (1) the deceased man must consent to have children conceived using his sperm; (2) the deceased man's consent must be in writing; (3) the child must be conceived or born within a specified time after the man's death; and (4) the deceased man's sperm can only be used by his surviving spouse. It should be noted that most of the statutes only apply to situations involving married couples. Consequently, in those states, children conceived using fresh sperm extracted and given to parents or significant others may not have the right to inherit from their fathers. I will now briefly discuss the statutory requirements.

Consent

In order to use a dead man's sperm to conceive, a woman usually must have his written consent. Thus, it is not surprising that, for the posthumously conceived child to have the opportunity to inherit from his father, most states require at least a minimum level of consent from the man. For example, under the Texas and Virginia statutes, the decedent will be legally recognized as the father of the posthumously conceived child if, prior to his death, he consented to the artificial insemination of his wife.[21] This approach is consistent with the statutes that deal with children who are conceived through artificial insemination during the life of the woman's husband. If the woman's husband agrees to the artificial insemination of his wife, he is considered the legal father of the child even if the child was conceived using another man's sperm.[22] Hence, it is reasonable to recognize a consenting spouse as the father of a child created using his genetic material after he dies. This supports the public policy argument that children in similar situations should have the same legal rights.

The Maryland statute requires the dead man to take an extra step. In order for a posthumously conceived child to be recognized as his biological father's legal heir, in addition to consenting to the use of his sperm, the man has to agree to be legally deemed to be the resulting child's parent.[23] Under the mandates of the Utah statute, a man must consent to the artificial insemination and to the establishment of the parent–child relationship.[24] These statutes require the mother of the posthumously conceived child to show both that the man agreed to the child's conception and to the recognition of his paternity. This appears to be an unnecessary requirement. If, while he is alive, a man agrees to have his wife conceive a child using his sperm or the sperm of a donor, most states will consider him to be legally responsible for the child. Likewise, the law does not allow men, who agree to have a child artificially conceived, to waive their parental rights and obligations. Therefore, when a man consents to let his sperm be used to conceive a child after he dies, the law should presume that he is also agreeing to be treated as the legal parent of the resulting child.

The Florida statute lacks a consent requirement.[25] The dead man's consent to the conception of the child may be implied by the fact that he provides for the unborn child in his will. The Restatement of Property does not precisely require a man to consent to the child's conception in order for the child to have the right to inherit.[26] Nonetheless, the Restatement does provide that the child has to be born in circumstances indicating that the deceased man would have approved of the child's right to inherit.[27] That statement implies that some type of indication of consent must exist. The consent requirement is usually accompanied by the mandate for some type of writing.

Writing requirement

With regard to the writing requirement, state legislatures have taken two approaches. The majority of states have kept the language of their statutes general, giving the courts in those jurisdictions more flexibility in determining what qualifies as appropriate written consent. The legislatures in the minority of states have specifically worded statutes that contain detailed directions stating the actions that are necessary to satisfy the writing requirement. Some of the states require consent without specifying that it has to be in writing and others mandate the existence of a formal writing. For example, the statutes of Delaware, Maryland, North Dakota, Utah, Wyoming, and Washington require that the dead man's consent be included in a record.[28] The statutes do not contain a definition of what constitutes a record and do not indicate whether the consent has to be in writing. However, from a legal perspective, a record usually refers to a written account of something.[29] In this context, a written agreement between the man and his spouse or the man and the fertility clinic where the sperm is stored would probably suffice. The Colorado statute mandates a signed record, so whatever form the man's consent takes, it must be in writing.[30] According to the Louisiana and Iowa statutes, the man has to give some type of written permission.[31] Nothing in the statutes indicates that this writing has to be formal. Hence, if a woman produces a letter or email from the man agreeing to the posthumous conception of a child with his sperm, that may be enough to satisfy the statutory requirements in those states.

Some state statutes mandate a more formal type of writing. The California state is illustrative of that approach. In order to fulfill the requirements of that statute, the mother of the posthumously conceived child must introduce a detailed writing that is signed and dated by the deceased man.[32] An even more formal writing is required by the Arkansas statute.[33] The required writing must either be notarized or witnessed by a licensed physician or a person acting under the supervision of a licensed physician.[34] Mandating such a writing will protect the man from being unduly influenced or forced to give his consent. It will also be of assistance to the physician and the courts. After the man dies, the physician will be able to prove that he or she acted in accordance with the man's wishes by assisting his wife to conceive his child. From an evidentiary perspective, the existence of a formal writing will enable the court to determine whether or not the posthumously conceived child should have the right to inherit the man's estate. As previously discussed, in Florida, a posthumously conceived child cannot inherit unless the dead man leaves the child a bequest in his will.[35] A will is one of the most formal types of writing recognized by law.

Time restrictions

According to at least one court, allowing a posthumously conceived child to inherit from his or her father is in the child's best interests.[36] However, keeping the man's estate open to give the child the opportunity to be conceived and born may thwart the state's interest in an orderly probate process. It may also interfere with the right of the man's existing heirs. In order for the probate system to operate efficiently, the probate court must close estates within a reasonable period of time.[37] Furthermore, the man's heirs should not have to wait indefinitely to receive their inheritance.[38]

In an attempt to address the above-mentioned concerns, some statutes require the posthumously conceived child to be born within a specified period of time. Under the terms of the California statute, the woman must be pregnant within two years of proof of the man's death.[39] Maryland and Iowa require the woman to actually give birth within two years of her husband's death.[40] This gives the woman time to grieve before she makes the decision to conceive a child using her dead husband's sperm. It also permits time for the woman to decide whether she wants to become a single parent. Other states also restrict the time in which the posthumously conceived child can be conceived or born. For instance, in Louisiana, in order to inherit, the posthumously conceived child must be born within three years of the death of his or her father.[41] Arkansas' statute mandates that the child be conceived within twelve months and born within nineteen months of the man's death.[42] Posthumously conceived children in Colorado are given more time to come into existence. The child has to be conceived within thirty-six months or born within forty-five months after the death of his or her father.[43] The Restatement's approach requires the child to be born within a reasonable time after the man's death in circumstances indicating that the decedent would have approved of the child's right to inherit.[44] The Florida and the Virginia statutes do not put time constraints on the conception or the birth of the posthumously conceived child.[45] Thus, the estates in those jurisdictions have the potential to remain open indefinitely while the woman decides to use the decedent's sperm to conceive a child.

Notice

A notice requirement protects the reproductive rights of the deceased man by making it difficult for him to be classified as the legal father of the posthumously conceived child unless he consents to the child's conception. Further, it protects the man's right to control the distribution of his estate even in the absence of a will. The statutes enacted by both the California and Virginia legislatures have notice requirements that impact the rights of the posthumously conceived child.[46] Under the mandates of those statutes, unless there is written consent on the part of the deceased man, notice must be given to an independent third party.[47]

Notice under the California statute

In California, written notice that the deceased's sperm may be used for posthumous conception must be given to the person in charge of administering the deceased's estate or the holder of the decedent's non-probate assets, including life insurance policies.[48] The notice must be given by the person authorized to control the use of the dead man's sperm within four months of the man's death. The notice must be sent by certified mail.[49] The purpose of the notice requirement appears to be to make sure that the executor of the man's estate knows that there might be another potential heir created. That information will assist the executor in planning the distribution of the man's estate. In addition, the notice requirement promotes the state's interest in the orderly distribution of estates and also protects the interests of the posthumously conceived child by allowing the executor to set aside some portion of the estate for that child. Further, the notice requirement protects the existing heirs by informing them of persons who might have a potential claim against the estate, giving the existing heirs some idea of the amount of their inheritance.

Notice under the Virginia statute

The Virginia statute appears to be designed to address two different sets of circumstances: (1) cases where the man does not sign a written consent and the insemination is performed during his lifetime; and (2) cases where the man consents in writing to have his sperm used to create a child, and he dies before the insemination is performed.[50] In both cases, the man is considered to be the legal parent of the resulting child. Hence, the child has the right to inherit from the man. The notice requirement of the statute deals with the first scenario. For purposes of the Virginia statute, the man is considered to be alive until the physician performing the insemination knows that he is dead.[51] Consequently, if the physician performs the insemination before being notified of the man's death, the insemination is treated as being performed during his lifetime. As a result, the posthumously conceived child is recognized as the man's legal heir. Nevertheless, the Virginia statute appears to state that, absent written consent, if the physician knows or should know of the man's death, he cannot go forward with the procedure.[52] In that case, the procedure is treated as if it never occurred and the child does not have the right to inherit from the dead man.

A key shortcoming of the notice requirement in the Virginia statute is that it might encourage persons to take steps to ensure that the physician is not notified of the man's death until it is too late to stop the procedure. This may be true in a case where a woman wants to conceive a child using a dead man's sperm for less than honorable reasons. In such a situation, the woman may be motivated to keep the physician in the dark about the procedure. The solution to the problem would be to strictly enforce the writing requirement contained in the statute. Thus, the physician should not be able to perform the procedure without the man's written consent.

The New York approach

I have chosen to discuss New York's statute separately because it is the most comprehensive one in the United States. According to the Act, in order for a parent–child relationship between the dead man and the posthumously conceived child to be legally recognized, several things have to be met. Not more than seven years prior to his death, the man has to execute a written instrument in which he explicitly agrees to have his sperm used to posthumously conceive a child and to give a designated person[53] the decision-making authority over his sperm after he dies.[54] After the man dies, the designated person has to give written notice that the man's sperm is available for use. The notice has to be made by certified mail, return receipt requested or personally delivered within seven months from the time the man's estate enters probate to either the executor or administrator of the man's estate. If the man's estate is not probated, the notice has to be delivered within four months of the man's death to the person responsible for disposing of his property and within seven months of the man's death to his intestate heirs.[55] The designated person has seven months from the time of the man's death to record the written instrument in the appropriate surrogate office.[56] Under the provisions of the statute, the child has to be conceived no later than twenty-four months after the man dies and born no later than thirty-three months after his death.[57]

The statute gives specific instructions with regards to the written instrument that is required to show the man's consent.[58] The man must sign the document in front of at least two witnesses who are also required to sign it. The witnesses must both be over the age of eighteen and disinterested in the sense that they have no authority to make decisions with regards to the use of the dead man's sperm.[59] If a man changes his mind before he dies, he can only revoke his consent by another written instrument that is executed with the same formalities.[60] The man cannot amend or revoke the written instrument using a provision in his will.[61] The written instrument requirement cannot be substituted with a contract between the man and his spouse or another person.[62]

The validity of the written instrument depends on it being executed with formalities similar to those required to make an attested will. In his famous article, Professor John H. Langbien set out the purposes of the will formalities.[63] According to Professor Langbien, there are four key Wills Act functions that the writing requirement and the other formalities serve. The writing, signature and witness requirements provide a protective function because they protect the testator from things like fraud, duress, and undue influence. Further, those mandates serve a cautionary function by encouraging the testator to slow down and think about the seriousness of his actions. At the time that a will is admitted to probate, the testator is unavailable. In that instance, the writing has an evidentiary function because it is a permanent record of the man's wishes. The witness requirement also functions as an evidentiary device because the witnesses may be called upon to testify as to what happened during the execution process. The final function Langbien identifies is the channeling function. By adhering to the strict requirements of the Wills Act, the testator helps the probate process go smoothly. Langbien indicates that the formalities act to keep the channels of the probate system clear.[64] A man's choice to permit his sperm to be used for posthumous reproduction is as serious as his decision with regards to the disposition of his property. Therefore, it makes sense to have a writing requirement that serves all of the functions of the Wills Act formalities.

Judicial approaches

Because the majority of American jurisdictions do not have statutes setting forth the inheritance rights of posthumously conceived children the task of determining those rights have been left to the courts. Most of the cases have involved Social Security Survivors' benefits. Courts hearing those cases have taken different approaches. After the United States Supreme Court's decision, it is well-established that the child's ability to receive survivors' benefits is dependent upon his or her capacity to inherit under the relevant state's intestacy system. Nonetheless, litigation continues because the requirements of state intestacy statutes differ, so there is a lack of uniformity. In addition, the outcomes of the cases in jurisdictions with statutes expressly dealing with the inheritance rights of children differ from the ones in states where the law is silent.

Plain meaning approach

Courts using this approach give terms their plain meaning and strictly interpret the relevant statutes. This is the strictest approach and it usually results in the posthumously conceived child not having the right to inherit. When the Court decides that survival is a key component of the right to inherit, the child loses. A child that is not conceived until after the death of his or her father cannot be a "survivor" in the lay or legal sense of the word.[65]

Khabbaz v Comm'r Soc. Sec. Admin.[66]

In September 1989, Donna M. Eng and Rumzi Brian Khabbaz got married. Unfortunately, in April 1997, doctors informed the couple that Khabbaz had a life-threatening illness. Although the couple already had one child, Khabbaz banked his sperm and executed a consent form authorizing Eng to use the sperm to conceive his child. Khabbaz also indicated that he wanted to be acknowledged as the legal father if Eng conceived a child through artificial insemination using his sperm. On May 23, 1998, Khabbaz died. Eng gave birth to a child, Christine, using Khabbaz's sperm in the summer of 2000.[67] Eng tried unsuccessfully to get Social Security survivors' benefits for Christine. The SSA Commissioner denied benefits based upon a determination that Christine would not be eligible to inherit from Khabbaz under New Hampshire's intestacy distribution law. The ALJ and the SSA Appeals Council upheld the Commissioner's decision. In response, Christine appealed the Commissioner's decision to the United States District Court.[68]

First, Eng argued that Christine should be classified as a "surviving issue" based on the language of the intestacy statute.[69] The court rejected that argument, relying on its interpretation of the meaning of "surviving."[70] Relying upon Webster's Dictionary, the court concluded that, in order to be considered a survivor, Christine had to be alive or in existence when her father died. The court reasoned that, because Christine was not conceived until after her father's death, she could not be legally recognized as his survivor. The court went so far as to declare that no "posthumously conceived child is a 'surviving issue' within the plain meaning of the [New Hampshire] statute."[71]

In the alternative, Eng argued that Christine was a non-marital child because, at the time of Christine's conception, Eng was no longer married to Khabbaz. Eng wanted Christine to be treated as a child born out-of-wedlock so she could avail herself of the process the legislature had established for non-marital children to have the opportunity to inherit from their fathers. The court found Eng's argument to be without merit for two reasons. First, the court opined that the legislature intended the statute to deal with children whose parents were not married prior to their births. Because they were a married couple, Eng and Khabbaz were therefore not among the class of persons intended to be covered by the statute. Second, the court concluded that Christine could not be categorized as an illegitimate child because, under New Hampshire's statutory scheme, children conceived by the artificial insemination of a married woman are considered legitimate.[72]

Eng's final argument was based upon public policy. She asserted that a posthumously conceived child who was conceived within a reasonable time after his or her father's death should be permitted to inherit from the father's estate. When putting forth this argument, Eng urged the court to adopt the rationale of the Massachusetts Supreme Judicial Court in *Woodward*. The Supreme Court of New Hampshire sympathized with Eng, but stated that setting public policy was the job of the state legislature and not the court. Consequently, based upon the language of the New Hampshire statute as established by the New Hampshire legislature, the court was compelled to "leave [...] an entire class of posthumous[ly conceived] children unprotected."[73]

The Supreme Court of New Hampshire's strict interpretation of the New Hampshire statute in *Khabbaz* was detrimental to the posthumously conceived child and possibly inconsistent with the deceased's wishes. Although the court felt it was the state legislature's role to make public policy, the court's hypertechnical approach was contrary to the goal of the intestacy system because it defeated the intent of the decedent. The steps Khabbaz took prior to his death indicated that he wanted to be legally responsible for any child conceived using his stored sperm. In light of these facts, and in order to ensure that Khabbaz's estate was distributed in a manner consistent with his wishes, the court should have interpreted the intestacy statute broadly enough to give the posthumously conceived child the opportunity to inherit from her father.

In this case, Khabbaz had a biological child prior to the birth of Christine, the posthumously conceived child. Khabbaz's living heir would not be disadvantaged by permitting the posthumously conceived child to inherit from Khabbaz after his death. Nothing in the facts indicated that Khabbaz would not want his children to inherit on an equal basis. Both children were conceived using Khabbaz's sperm; the only difference between the living heir and the posthumously conceived child was the timing of their conception. In essence, the court penalized Christine because of the circumstances of her birth. The Supreme Court has renounced that approach with regard to non-marital children.[74] This differential treatment should be considered to be against public policy. Over the years, legislatures and courts have sought to ensure that all classes of children are treated similarly with regards to inheriting under the intestacy system. Moreover, since Khabbaz consented in writing to the use of his sperm to conceive a child, his procreative rights are protected and there is limited opportunity for fraud. Additionally, it could be argued that not recognizing Khabbaz as the legal father of the posthumously conceived child intrudes upon Khabbaz's right to procreate in the manner in which he desired.

Afterborn child approach

Courts that use this approach analyze the afterborn child statute to determine if it is broad enough to apply to situations involving posthumously conceived children. A typical afterborn child statute contains the following language: "Relatives of the decedent conceived before his death but born thereafter inherit as if they had been born in the lifetime of the decedent."[75] Most states have enacted some version of an afterborn child statute. The purpose of the statute is to protect "the child who, through mistake or inadvertence, was not provided for by the parent."[76] The majority of the states that have addressed the issue of whether the posthumously conceived child should be considered to be an afterborn child have answered the question in the negative.[77] *Amen v Astrue* illustrates this approach.[78]

Amen v Astrue[79]

Before Joshua and Melissa could get married, doctors diagnosed Joshua with cancer. Prior to undergoing cancer treatment, Joshua had some of his sperm extracted and frozen. The parties later married. While doctors were treating Joshua for cancer, Melissa underwent a fertility treatment cycle with her husband's consent. Unfortunately, Joshua died a short while later before Melissa could conceive his child.[80] About a week after Joshua passed away, Melissa used some of his frozen sperm to conceive a child. After she gave birth, Melissa submitted an application to the Social Security Administration (SSA) to receive mother's insurance benefits and surviving child's insurance benefits on behalf of the posthumously conceived child. SSA denied Melissa's application for benefits.[81] In response to Melissa's request for reconsideration, an administrative law judge (ALJ) ruled that the posthumously conceived child was eligible to receive child's insurance benefits based on her dead father's Social Security record.[82] The ALJ's decision was reversed by the SSA's Appeals Council. The Council reasoned that because the posthumously conceived child was not entitled to inherit from the man under the state's intestacy statute she could not receive survivors' benefits. Melissa appealed the Council's decision in the United States District Court.[83]

The Court had to decide whether a posthumously conceived child was entitled to inherit under Nebraska's intestacy system. The Court determine that, to inherit under the intestacy statute, a person had to survive the decedent. According to the Court, the posthumously conceived child was not a survivor because she did not exist at the time her father died. Therefore, the child could not inherit under the general intestacy provisions.[84] However, the Court concluded that the afterborn child statute created an exception to the rule that a person had to survive the intestate in order to inherit. In order to take advantage of the afterborn child exception, the child had to be conceived prior to his or her father's death. Once the child was conceived, survival was not relevant to the child's ability to inherit. The Court held that the posthumously conceived child was not covered by the afterborn child exception because the child had not been conceived until months after her father's death.[85] The Court acknowledged that its ruling was unfair to the child. Nonetheless, the Court refused to go against the plain language of the statute to figure out a way to permit the child to receive survivors' benefits.[86] At least one Court has used its discretion to interpret an afterborn child statute in a way that benefits the posthumously conceived child.[87]

Estate of Kolacy[88]

On February 7, 1994, doctors informed William Kolacy that he had leukemia. As a consequence, he needed to receive chemotherapy treatments. William worried that, as a result of his chemotherapy treatments, he might be unable to contribute to the creation of children. Thus, in accordance with William's wishes, prior to undergoing chemotherapy and during the treatment, the doctor harvested William's sperm and placed it in a sperm bank. Unfortunately, William died as a result of his cancer on April 15, 1995. More than eighteen months after William's death, his wife, Mariantonia Kolacy, gave birth to twin girls as a result of IVF.[89] In order to receive financial assistance to help care for her children, Mariantonia applied for Social Security dependent benefits.

The Social Security Administration (SSA) denied Mariantonia's application because the panel determined that the twins were not legally William's children, despite the fact that the twins were William's genetic and biological children. An Administrative Law Judge (ALJ) issued a written decision upholding the denial of benefits.[90] Instead of appealing the ALJ's decision, Mariantonia filed an action in the Superior Court of New Jersey to have her twins declared William's legal heirs, making them eligible for Social Security child's insurance benefits.[91] Thus, Mariantonia planned to use the state court's declaration of heirship to help her win her Social Security appeal.[92]

In order to resolve the case, the Superior Court of New Jersey had to decide whether posthumously conceived children qualified as heirs under New Jersey's afterborn child statute.[93] The court approached the issue by exploring why the legislature created an intestacy system that gives preference to children. In light of that exploration, the court determined that the general legislative intent when enacting statutory provisions dealing with intestate succession, including the afterborn heirs statute, was to give children the opportunity to inherit from and through their parents.[94] That determination led the court to conclude that the intestacy statutes should be read broadly enough to give a decedent's posthumously conceived child the chance to inherit from his estate.[95]

The court also considered the competing interests involved when posthumously conceived children seek to inherit from their parents. After considering all of those interests, the court held that the twins were legally William's heirs. William did not have any other heirs who would be disadvantaged by allowing the posthumously conceived twins to inherit from his estate.[96] When balancing the competing interests, the court was persuaded by the fact that the evidence indicated William wanted the children to be conceived posthumously. Therefore, he probably wanted them to have all of the legal protections that would come from being his children.[97]

The outcome of this case is in line with most public policy arguments on the issue of posthumously conceived children. Although the court balanced the three important competing interests of the state, the posthumously conceived child, and the living heirs, it appeared to give the interest of posthumously conceived children priority. Once posthumously conceived children are born, they need to be financially supported by their parents. If the father were alive, he would be required to pay child support to finance the child's needs.[98] After the father's death, the father's Social Security benefits should be used to take care of his children. In light of the fact that William had no other living children, the court's approach was equitable. Under the current Social Security system, if a man dies without survivors, all of the money that he has paid into the system disappears. The man does not have the right to dispose of the money by will. Further, none of the money becomes part of the man's intestate estate.[99] The end result is that the man's money escheats to the federal government. In a case where there are children who are genetically related to the deceased man, it would be unfair for the government to benefit at the expense of those children.

In *Kolacy*, if the court had not allowed the posthumously conceived children to receive William's Social Security benefits, all of the money that he paid into the system would have remained with the government. Therefore, William's children might have been forced to rely on public assistance. This is clearly not the outcome William would have wanted. In addition to considering the multiple competing interests at stake in these cases, there are also sound public policy arguments. For example, because William did not live long enough to recoup the money he paid into the Social Security system, from a public policy perspective it seems equitable that the court allowed his children to receive the money instead. Moreover, another public policy argument supporting the outcome of this case is that receiving their father's benefits prevented the children from being forced to depend upon public assistance.

Balancing approach

The application of this approach permits courts to balance the interests of the state, the dead man, the child and the man's existing heirs. Judges in Massachusetts used this approach to create a test that could be used by future courts.

Woodward[100]

In January 1993, Warren Woodward was diagnosed with leukemia and scheduled to undergo treatment.[101] Because Warren and his wife, Lauren, did not have any children, they were concerned that Warren might be rendered sterile as a result of the treatment. Consequently, the Woodwards had some of Warren's sperm extracted and placed in a sperm bank. In October 1993, Warren died after an unsuccessful bone marrow transplant. Two years later, Lauren gave birth to twin girls who were conceived through artificial insemination using Warren's sperm. Lauren submitted an application for Social Security survivors' benefits on behalf of herself and the children.[102] Lauren relied on Section 402(g)(1) of the Social Security Act to claim mother's benefits based upon her status as a widow with dependent children.[103] Lauren's application for benefits for the twins was based on their status as children of a person who had died fully insured under the Social Security Act. In order to receive mother's benefits, Lauren had to convince the SSA that the children were entitled to survivor's benefits. At the initial stage, the SSA denied Lauren's application after determining the twins were not Warren's children within the meaning of the Social Security Act. While she was appealing the SSA's decision, Lauren petitioned the Massachusetts Probate and Family Court for an order requiring the clerk of court to add Warren's name to the twins' birth certificates. As a result, the Probate and Family Court adjudicated Warren as the twins' father, and issued an order amending their birth certificates to reflect that fact.[104]

Lauren submitted the judgment of paternity and the amended birth certificates to the SSA.[105] Nonetheless, the ALJ concluded that the twins were not eligible for benefits because they would not be considered Warren's heirs under Massachusetts's intestacy and paternity laws. After an unsuccessful appeal to the Appeals Council of the SSA, Lauren filed an appeal in the United States District Court for the District of Massachusetts. The federal court certified the issue to the Supreme Judicial Court of Massachusetts, which had to determine whether posthumously conceived children had a right to inherit under the Massachusetts intestacy system.[106] The parties took dramatically different positions.[107] Lauren argued that posthumously conceived children should always have the right to inherit from their deceased parent as long as there is proof of a genetic connection with the decedent. The government claimed that posthumously conceived children should never have the right to inherit from their deceased parent because they would not be in existence as of the date of the parent's death. The court rejected the positions of both parties as too extreme and searched for a middle ground.[108]

In order to resolve the case, the court reviewed Massachusetts's intestacy law. Because, under that law, only a decedent's "issue" had a right to inherit the decedent's property, the court had to determine whether the twins were Warren's issue. The Massachusetts legislature did not clearly define the term "issue."[109] Thus, the court looked at the legislative purpose behind the Massachusetts intestacy statute to decide if posthumously conceived children should be classified as "issue" for inheritance purposes.[110] As a part of its analysis, the court discussed three competing state interests that need to be considered when addressing the issue of inheritance rights for posthumously conceived children: (1) the state's interest in promoting the best interest of the children, including both posthumously conceived children and children who were alive or conceived prior to the death of the parent; (2) the state's interest in preventing fraud and insuring the orderly administration of probate estates; and (3) the state's interest in protecting the procreative rights of both genetic parents, including the deceased parent.[111]

The Massachusetts court acknowledged that children have the right to receive financial support from their parents and to petition their parents' estate for support.[112] The court determined that the opportunity to inherit should be extended to posthumously conceived children because, in enacting intestacy statutes that gave preference to children, the Massachusetts legislature intended to promote the welfare of all children. The court also emphasized two key points: (1) although the legislature knew that posthumously conceived children existed, it took no action to prevent them from taking under the intestacy system; and (2) the Massachusetts legislature supported the assisted reproductive technologies that were the only means by which posthumously conceived children could come into being. Thus, once they were born, the Massachusetts legislature was obligated to give them the same rights as other children.[113]

The court next addressed Massachusetts's interest in the prompt and accurate administration of probate estates. The court felt that the state was obligated to provide certainty to the decedent's heirs and creditors.[114] Although the court reserved judgment on the resolution of the time constraints in question, the court noted that because posthumously conceived children could be born years after the death of their parent, permitting them to inherit would make it difficult for the state to achieve its administrative goals.[115] Therefore, instead of focusing on the need for finality, the court next dealt with the state's interest in preventing fraud on the probate courts. The court concluded that the probability of fraud would be diminished by the fact that the posthumously conceived children, like other non-marital children, were required to prove paternity before they could inherit.[116] Lastly, the court discussed the state's interest in honoring the right of persons to choose if and when to reproduce.[117] The court decided that the person claiming rights on behalf of the posthumously conceived child had to present convincing evidence that the deceased person consented to the posthumous conception and agreed to support the child that resulted from the procedure.[118] This requirement would protect the procreative rights of the deceased and further promote the state's goal of fraud prevention.[119]

After balancing the competing state interests of promoting the best interests of the children, preventing fraud and ensuring the orderly administration of probate estates, and protecting the procreative rights of both genetic parents, the court held that it was in the best interests of posthumously conceived children to be given the opportunity to inherit from their deceased parents.[120] However, the court recognized that some precautions were necessary to protect the integrity of the probate system and the procreative rights of the deceased parent.[121] Therefore, the *Woodward* court established a three-part test that must be satisfied before the posthumously conceived child can inherit from his or her deceased parent: (1) the person representing the posthumously conceived child must provide evidence that the child and the decedent were genetically related; (2) the representative must prove that the decedent affirmatively agreed to the child's posthumous conception; and (3) the representative must show that the decedent affirmatively consented to provide financial support to any child conceived as a result of the posthumous reproduction.[122] The three-part test created by the *Woodward* court serves as a good model for state legislatures seeking to protect the interests of the posthumously conceived child, the pre-existing heirs, the decedent, and the state. The posthumously conceived child will benefit from the court's decision by having the opportunity to inherit from his or her father.

Inheritance case

In re Martin B.

In re Martin B., one of the few cases to directly address the inheritance rights of posthumously conceived children, dealt with the children's ability to inherit *through* their deceased father.[123] The case involved seven trust instruments (six were governed by the law of the District of Columbia and one was governed by New York law). On December 31, 1969, Martin B. (identified in the case as the Grantor) had seven trust agreements executed.[124] Under the terms of the trusts, Martin B. was entitled to receive income from the trust during his lifetime.[125] The trustees of the trust were instructed to retain the principal while Martin B. was alive. After Martin B.'s death, but before the death of his wife, Abigail, the trustees had the discretion to dispense the principal to and among his issue. The trustees were authorized to distribute the principal after Abigail's death. The distribution was to be to Martin B.'s issue or descendants in accordance with Abigail's directions. If Abigail failed to exercise her right to control the division of the trust principal, the trustee was instructed to distribute the principal to or for the benefit of the issue surviving at the time of Abigail's death. This case dealt with the status of Martin B.'s posthumously conceived grandchildren with regards to the trust.

In July 2001, Martin B. died. His wife, Abigail, their son Lindsay, and Lindsay's two adult children survived Martin B. Martin B.'s other son, James, died in January 2001. James's two young sons, conceived by IVF using James's frozen semen, also survived Martin B. It was clear that "issue" included Lindsay and his two adult children. The dispute arose because of the existence of James's sons. Prior to his death, James deposited a sample of his semen at a laboratory to be frozen. He instructed the laboratory that, in the event of his death, his wife Nancy had the authority to make decisions with regard to the use of the semen.[126] After James died, Nancy used his semen to have one son in 2004 and another son in 2006. The trustees went to court to find out if James's posthumously conceived sons were included in the class of trust beneficiaries. The court, therefore, had to decide whether the posthumously conceived children were descendants and issue for purposes of the trust.

In order to determine if the posthumously conceived children had the right to inherit the trust principal through their father, the court reviewed the intestacy statutes of New York and the District of Columbia.[127] Neither jurisdiction had a statute specifically dealing with the rights of posthumously conceived children. As a result, the court asserted that, in order to resolve the case, it had to rely upon "statutes in other jurisdictions, model codes, scholarly discussions and Restatements of the law."[128] After that review, the court in *Martin* – much like the courts in *Kolacy, Woodward*, and *Khabbaz* – concluded that other state legislatures and courts that had addressed the issue of the inheritance rights of posthumously conceived children had to balance the competing interests of: (1) the public's desire to have a probate system that is efficient, final, and accurate; (2) the state's need to respect the procreative rights of its citizens; and (3) the rights of the children born as a consequence of artificial insemination. The court asserted that it is in the best interests of those children to be treated as the heirs of their father.

After analyzing the various statutes and judicial decisions, the *Martin* court opined that other legislatures and courts had recommended two key mechanisms to promote the interest of all the parties: (1) most state intestacy statutes mandated that the man give written permission to have his genetic material used to create a child after his death; and (2) most state laws required that the child be created within a certain time period following the man's passing. Bearing these two factors in mind, the *Martin* court held that the posthumously conceived children were eligible to inherit through their father because Martin B.'s intent was for all members of his bloodline to get a share of the trust funds.[129]

The court relied upon several factors to justify its holding. First, James satisfied the written consent requirement by leaving instructions with the laboratory telling them that his wife, Nancy, had the right to decide what to do with his semen.[130] Because James gave Nancy such broad discretion, it was not unreasonable to conclude that he would not object to Nancy using the semen to conceive his child. Second, the court noted that, after conceiving her two sons, Nancy permitted the rest of James's sperm to be destroyed. Therefore, at the time of the hearing, the class of James's children was closed, and his estate could be closed with certainty.

Finally, the court reviewed the trust instruments and found them silent in regard to the status of posthumously conceived children.[131] The court decided the failure to mention posthumously conceived children indicated, at the time the trust instruments were drafted, that the Grantor could not have contemplated children could be conceived after the death of their fathers. As a result, the court decided to give the posthumously conceived children the benefit of the doubt and concluded that their grandfather would want them to be treated the same as his other grandchildren. The court's conclusion was supported by the fact that, in the trust instruments, the Grantor provided that, after Abigail died, the trust funds were to benefit the Grantor's sons and their families equally.[132]

Conclusion

Posthumously conceived children have the same financial needs as other children. To get those needs met, the woman usually applies for Social Security Survivors' benefits. Eligibility for those benefits is linked to the child's ability to inherit under the intestacy system where the man was domiciled when he died. Most state intestacy systems require a child to survive in order to inherit. A posthumously conceived child cannot be deemed to have survived his or her father because the child does not exist until after the man has been dead and buried. In the majority of states, posthumously conceived children are unable to avail themselves of the protections provided in afterborn children statutes because they are not in utero prior to the man's death.

Notes

1 *Schaefer v Heckler*, 792 F.2d 81 (7th Cir. 1986).
2 S.Rep. No. 404, 89th Cong., 1st Sess. 110 (1965), 1965 U.S. Code Cong. Admin. News pp. 1943, 2050 cited in *Bennemon on Behalf of William v Sullivan*, 914 F.2d 987, 990 (7th Cir. 1990).
3 *Dubinski v Bowen*, 808 F.2d 611, 612 (7th Cir. 1986).
4 42 U.S.C. § 201; 53 Stat. at 1364–65 (amending section 202(c) of the Social Security Act).
5 *Mathews v Lucas*, 427 U.S. 495, 495 (1976).
6 *Id.*
7 *Id.*
8 *Smith v Heckler*, 820 F.2d 1093, 1095 (9th Cir. 1987).
9 *Astrue v Capato ex. Rel. B.N.C.*, 182 St. Ct. 2021 (2012).
10 *Id.* at 2026.
11 *Id.* at 2034.
12 *Id.* at 2032.
13 *Astrue*, 182 St. Ct. at 2034; *Capato ex. Rel. B.N.C. v Commr. Soc. Sec.*, 532 Fed. Appx. 251 (2013).
14 **Tex. Fam. Code Ann.** § 160.707 (Vernon 2016) ("If a spouse dies before the placement of eggs, sperm, or embryos, the deceased spouse is not a parent of the resulting child unless the deceased spouse consented in a record kept by a licensed physician that if assisted reproduction were to occur after death the deceased

spouse would be a parent of the child"); **Del. Code Ann.** tit. 13, § 8–707 (West 2016) ("If an individual who consented in a record to be a parent by assisted reproduction dies before placement of eggs, sperm, or embryos, the deceased individual is not a parent of the resulting child unless the deceased individual consented in a record that if assisted reproduction were to occur after death, the deceased individual would be a parent of the child."); **N.D. Cent. Code** § 14–20–65 (707) (West 2016) (same); **Utah Code Ann.** § 78B-15–707 (2016) (same); **Wyo. Stat. Ann.** 1977 § 14–2–907 (West 2016) (same); **Wash. Rev. Code** § 26.26.730 (West 2016) (same); **Cal. Prob. Code** § 249.5 (West 2016) ("For purposes of determining rights to property to be distributed upon the death of a decedent, a child of the decedent conceived and born after the death of the decedent shall be deemed to have been born in the lifetime of the decedent, and after the execution of all of the decedent's testamentary instruments, if the child or his or her representative proves by clear and convincing evidence that all of the following conditions are satisfied: (a) The decedent, in writing, specifies that his or her genetic material shall be used for the posthumous conception of a child of the decedent, subject to the following: (1) The specification shall be signed by the decedent and dated. (2) The specification may be revoked or amended only by a writing, signed by the decedent and dated. (3) A person is designated by the decedent to control the use of the genetic material. (b) The person designated by the decedent to control the use of the genetic material has given written notice by certified mail, return receipt requested, that the decedent's genetic material was available for the purpose of posthumous conception. The notice shall have been given to a person who has the power to control the distribution of either the decedent's property or death benefits payable by reason of the decedent's death, within four months of the date of issuance of a certificate of the decedent's death or entry of a judgment determining the fact of the decedent's death, whichever event occurs first. (c) The child was in utero using the decedent's genetic material and was in utero within two years of the date of issuance of a certificate of the decedent's death or entry of a judgment determining the fact of the decedent's death, whichever event occurs first."); **Ohio Rev. Code Ann.** § 2105.14 (West 2016) (" Descendants of an intestate begotten before the intestate's death, but born after the intestate's death, in all cases will inherit as if born in the lifetime of the intestate and surviving the intestate; but in no other case can a person inherit unless living at the time of the death of the intestate."); **La. Rev. Stat. Ann.** § 9:391.1A (West 2016) ("A. Notwithstanding the provisions of any law to the contrary, any child conceived after the death of a decedent, who specifically authorized in writing his surviving spouse to use his gametes, shall be deemed the child of such decedent with all rights, including the capacity to inherit from the decedent, as the child would have had if the child had been in existence at the time of the death of the deceased parent, provided the child was born to the surviving spouse, using the gametes of the decedent, within three years of the death of the decedent."); **Va. Code Ann.** § 20–158B (West 2016) ("B. Death of spouse. – Any child resulting from the insemination of a wife's ovum using her husband's sperm, with his consent, is the child of the husband and wife notwithstanding that, during the ten-month period immediately preceding the birth, either party died. However, any person who dies before in utero implantation of an embryo resulting from the union of his sperm or her ovum with another gamete, whether or not the other gamete is that of the person's spouse, is not the parent of any resulting child unless (i) implantation occurs before notice of the death can reasonably be communicated to the physician performing the procedure or (ii) the person consents to be a parent in writing executed before the implantation."); **Fla. Stat. Ann.** § 742.17(4) (West 2016) ("(4) A child conceived from the eggs or sperm of a person or persons who died before the transfer of their eggs, sperm, or preembryos to a woman's body shall not be eligible for a claim against the decedent's estate unless the child has been provided for by the decedent's will."); **Ark. Code Ann.** § 28–9–221(a) (West 2016) ("(a) Notwithstanding the provisions of any law to the contrary, a child conceived after the death of a decedent who specifically authorized the decedent's surviving spouse, in a writing that is either notarized or witnessed by a licensed physician or a person acting under the supervision of a licensed physician, to use the decedent's gametes after the decedent's death shall be deemed the child of the decedent with the right to inherit from the decedent if the child is conceived within twelve (12) months following the death of the decedent and born within nineteen (19) months following the death of the decedent."); **MD. Code, Estates and Trusts**, § 3–107(b)(1)–(3) (West 2016) ("(b) No other after-born relation may be considered as entitled to distribution in the relation's own right unless: (1) The decedent had consented in a written record to use of the decedent's genetic material for posthumous conception ****; (2) The decedent consented in a written record to be the parent of a child posthumously conceived using the person's genetic material; and (3) The child posthumously conceived using the decedent's genetic material is born within 2 years after the death of the decedent."); **Colo. Rev. Stat. Ann**. § 15–11–120(11) (West 2016) ("(11) When posthumously conceived child treated as in gestation. If, under this section, an individual is a parent of a child of assisted reproduction who is conceived after the individual's death, the child is treated as in gestation at the time of the individual's death *** if the child is: (a) In utero not later than thirty-six months after the individual's death; or (b) Born not later than forty-five months after the individual's death."); **Iowa Code Ann** § 633.220A(1) (West 2016) ("For the purposes of rules relating to intestate succession, a child of an intestate conceived and born after the intestate's death or born as the result of the implantation of an embryo after the death of the intestate is deemed a child of the intestate as if the child had been born during the lifetime of the intestate and had survived the intestate, if all of the following conditions are met: a. A genetic parent-child relationship between the child and the intestate is established. b. The intestate, in a signed writing, authorized the intestate's surviving spouse to use the deceased parent's genetic material to initiate the posthumous procedure that resulted in the child's birth. c. The child is born within two years of the death of the intestate."); **McKinney's EPTL** § 4–1.3 (West 2016) (the provisions of the New York statute will be discussed in the body of the book.)

15 *In re Fretheim's Estate*, 194 N.W. 766, 768 (Minn. 1923).

16 *Estate of Britel*, 186 Cal. Rptr. 3d 321, 329 (Cal. App. 4th 2015).

17 Unif. Parentage Act § 707 (West 2016). Those states are Delaware, North Dakota, Utah, Washington and Wyoming.

18 Ohio Rev. Code Ann. § 2105.14 (West 2016).

19 Those states are Arkansas, California, Colorado, Florida, Iowa, Louisiana, Maryland, New York, Texas and Virginia.

20 LA. Rev. Stat. Ann. § 391.B (West 2016) ("B. Any heir or legatee of the decedent whose interest in the succession of the decedent will be reduced by the birth of a child conceived as provided in Subsection A of this Section shall have one year from the birth of such child within which to bring an action to disavow paternity."); Iowa Code Ann § 633.220A(2) (West 2016) ("Any heir of the intestate whose interest in the intestate's estate would be reduced by the birth of a child born as provided in subsection 1 shall have one year from the birth of the child within which to bring an action challenging the child's right to inherit under this chapter.").

21 Tex. Fam. Code Ann. § 160.707 (Vernon 2016); Va. Code Ann. § 20–158B (West 2016).

22 Karin Mika & Bonnie Hurst, One Way to Be Born? Legislative Inaction and the Posthumous Child, 79 Marq. L. Rev. 993, 997 (1996).
23 MD. Code, Estates and Trusts, § 3–107(b)(1)-(3) (West 2016).
24 Utah Code Ann. § 78B-15–707 (2016).
25 Fla. Stat. Ann. § 742.17(4) (West 2016).
26 Restatement (Third) Property § 251 (1999).
27 *Id.*
28 Del. Code Ann. tit. 13, § 8–707 (West 2016); N.D. Cent. Code § 14–20–65 (707) (West 2016); Utah Code Ann. § 78B-15–707 (2016); Wyo. Stat. Ann. 1977 § 14–2–907 (West 2016); Wash. Rev. Code § 26.26.730 (West 2016).
29 See Utah Code Ann. § 78B-15–102(18) (defining "record" as "information that is inscribed in a tangible medium or that is stored in an electronic or other medium and is retrievable in perceivable form.").
30 Colo. Rev. Stat. Ann. § 15–11–120(11) (West 2016).
31 La. Rev. Stat. Ann. § 9:391.1A (West 2016); Iowa Code Ann § 633.220A(1) (West 2016).
32 Cal. Prob. Code § 249.5 (West 2016).
33 Ark. Code Ann. § 28–9–221(a) (West 2016).
34 *Id.*
35 Fla. Stat. Ann. § 742.17(4)(West 2016).
36 See, e.g., *Woodward v Comm'r of Soc. Sec.*, 760 N.E. 2d 257, 265 (Mass. 2002) (recognizing that courts must consider the best interests of the children when contributing the distribution of inheritance rights).
37 See, e.g., *Fazilat v Feldstein*, 848 A.2d 761, 766 (N.J. 2004) (recognizing that the state has an interest in the prompt settlement of estates.).
38 See, e.g., *Woodward*, 760 N.E. 2d at 266 (speculating that posthumously conceived children may draw resources from other heirs who have the right to the prompt and accurate administration of estates).
39 Cal. Prob. Code § 249.5 (West 2016).
40 MD. Code, Estates and Trusts, § 3–107(b)(3) (West 2016); Iowa Code Ann § 633.220A(1)(c) (West 2016).
41 La. Rev. Stat. Ann. § 9:391.1A (West 2016).
42 Ark. Code Ann. § 28–9–221(a) (West 2016).
43 Colo. Rev. Stat. Ann. § 15–11–120(11) (West 2016).
44 Restatement (Third) of Property § 2.5 cmt. 1 (1999) ("[T]o inherit from the decedent, a child produced from genetic material of the decedent by assisted reproductive technology must be born within a reasonable time after the decedent's death in circumstances indicating that the decedent would have approved of the child's right to inherit.").
45 Fla. Stat. Ann. § 742.17(4) (West 2016); Va. Code Ann. § 20–158B (West 2016).
46 Cal. Prob. Code § 249.5 (West 2016); Va. Code Ann. § 20–158B (West 2016).
47 *Id.*
48 Cal. Prob. Code § 249.5 (West 2016).
49 *Id.*
50 Va. Code Ann. § 20–158B (West 2016).
51 *Id.*
52 *Id.*
53 The designated person can be the man's spouse. However, if the marriage is legally invalidated in any way, including by divorce, annulment or separation, the spouse's authority as the designated person is revoked. McKinney's EPTL § 4–1–3 (d) (West 2016).
54 McKinney's EPTL at § 4–1–3 (b)(1)(A) and (B).
55 *Id.* at § 4–1–3 (b)(2)(A) and (B).

56 *Id.* at § 4–1–3 (b)(3).
57 *Id.* at § 4–1–3 (b)(4).
58 The statute includes a sample form of the instrument. *Id.* at § 4–1–3 (c)(5).
59 *Id.* at § 4–1–3 (c)(1).
60 *Id.* at § 4–1–3 (c)(2).
61 *Id.* at § 4–1–3 (c)(3).
62 *Id.* at § 4–1–3 (i).
63 John H. Langbien, Substantial Compliance With the Wills Act, 88 Harv. L. Rev. 489, 516–518 (1975).
64 Langbien, supra note 580 at 516–518.
65 *In re Certified Question from U.S. District Court for Western Michigan*, 825 N.W. 2d 566, 569 (2012).
66 930 A.2d 1180 (N.H. 2007).
67 *Khabbaz*, 930 A.2d at 1182.
68 *Id.*
69 *Id.* at 1183.
70 *Id.* at 1183–84.
71 *Id.* at 1184.
72 *Khabbaz*, 930 A.2d at 1185.
73 *Id.* at 1186.
74 *Trimble*, 430 U.S. at 769–70.
75 Neb. Rev. Stat. § 30–2308 (Reissue 2008).
76 *DeCoste v Superior Court in and For Maricopa County*, 470 P.2d 457, 459 (Ariz. 1970).
77 *See Vernoff v Astrue*, 568 F3d 1102 (9th Cir. 2009); *Beeler v Astrue*, 651 F3d 954 (8th Cir. 2011) cert. denied, 132 S. Ct. 2679 (2012); *Stephen v Commr. of Soc. Sec.*, 386 F.Supp. 2d 1257 (M.D. Fla 2015); *Finley v Astrue*, 270 S.W. 3d 849 (2008); *Seaman v Colvin*, 2015 WL 5112975 (2015).
78 822 N.W. 2d 419 (2012).
79 *Id.* at 419.
80 *Amen*, 822 N.W. 2d at 422.
81 *Id.*
82 *Id.*
83 *Id.*
84 *Amen*, 822 N.W. 2d at 422.
85 *Id.*
86 *Id.*
87 *In re Estate of Kolacy*, 753 A.2d 1257 (N.J. 2000).
88 753 A 2d at 1257.
89 *Kolacy*, 753 A.2d at 1258.
90 *Id.* at 1259.
91 *Id.*
92 *Id.* at 1260.
93 *Id.* at 1262.
94 *Id.* at 1261–62.
95 *Kolacy*, 753 A.2d at 1263–64.
96 *Id.*
97 *Id.* at 1263.
98 Gloria Banks, Traditional Concepts and Nontraditional Conceptions: Social Security Survivors' Benefits For Posthumously Conceived Children, 32 Loy. L.A. L. Rev. 251, 299 (1999).
99 Richard W. Pingel, Note, Should Social Security Retire?: A Study of Personal Retirement Accounts in the American Probate System, 20 Quinnipiac Prob. L.J. 99, 111 (2006).

100 760 N.E. 2d 257 (Mass. 2002).
101 *Woodward*, 760 N.E. 2d at 260.
102 *Id.*
103 *Id.* at 260 n.3
104 *Id.* at 260.
105 *Woodward*, 760 N.E. 2d at 261.
106 *Id.*
107 *Id.* at 262.
108 *Id.*
109 *Woodward*, 760 N.E. 2d at 263.
110 *Id.* at 264.
111 *Id.* at 264–65.
112 *Id.* at 264.
113 *Woodward*, 760 N.E. 2d at 264–65.
114 *Id.* at 266.
115 *Id.* at 268.
116 *Id.* at 266–67.
117 *Woodward*, 760 N.E. 2d at 268.
118 *Id.* at 269.
119 *Id.* at 267.
120 *Id.* at 266.
121 *Woodward*, 760 N.E. 2d at 272.
122 *Id.* at 270.
123 *Martin*, 841 N.Y.S.2d at 208.
124 *Id.* at 207–208.
125 *Id.* at 208.
126 *Id.* at 207–208.
127 *Id.* at 207–208.
128 *Martin*, 841 N.Y.S.2d at 209.
129 *Id.* at 211.
130 *Id.* at 208.
131 *Id.* at 211.
132 *Id.* at 212.

Part IV

The balance

7 Finding the balance

The purpose of this chapter is to discuss the balance between protecting the reproductive rights of the dead man and promoting the best interests of the posthumously conceived child. The government will probably not ban the use of posthumous reproduction. Therefore, rules need to be put in place in order to address the ethical consequences that may occur because of the availability and use of posthumous reproduction. This chapter starts with a brief answer to the question of whether or not posthumous reproduction should be legally permitted. Nonetheless, most of the chapter is dedicated to an exploration of the regulations that are needed to protect the integrity of the process. I make recommendations that I think will help to protect the interests of all parties involved in the process. At the end of the chapter, I include my proposals for creating a system that protects the reproductive rights of the dead man and supports the needs of the posthumously conceived child. Posthumous reproduction should only be permitted if it can be done in a way that addresses the main ethical concerns. The fact that the law allows a woman to become pregnant through posthumous reproduction should not automatically make the resulting child eligible to inherit from the man. Prior to conception, the child's mother should have to take actions to enable the child to inherit.

There are several reasons why the government will probably not prohibit the conception of children using the sperm of dead men. First, the law permits the use of other controversial forms of assisted reproductive technology, including reproductive tissue transplantation[1] and mitochondrial manipulation therapy,[2] that raise ethical concerns similar to those that stem from the availability of posthumous reproduction. Second, the government is reluctant to impede on reproductive rights because of the legally recognized right to privacy.[3] Although state legislatures are consistently trying to regulate abortions, ethical and legal issues involving the use of assisted reproduction technology continue to be unresolved.[4] The dearth of regulation in this area may stem from the fact that most state legislatures are not comprised of doctors and scientists. In fact, most state legislators have backgrounds in business and law.[5] The lack of medical expertise may prevent lawmakers from tackling issues relating to the growing advances in assisted reproductive technology. Third, the American public still places a high value on children and family and the rate of infertility is growing. Therefore, infertility treatment is a billion dollar industry.[6] As long as companies can make a profit off of infertility, scientists will continue to push the envelope when it comes to inventing assisted reproductive technology.[7] Lastly, legislators are politicians, so they have to cater to the needs of their constituents. Infertile people are voters who will express their displeasure at the polls if they fear that the government is unduly interfering with their rights to procreate. For the aforementioned reasons, I am convinced that the use of posthumous reproduction will continue to grow. The question is whether that growth should be permitted.

Should posthumous reproduction be allowed?

Thoughts from the crowd

While I was writing this book, I spent a great deal of time talking about posthumous reproduction in both formal and informal settings. Regardless of the make-up of my audience, everyone had strong opinions about posthumous reproduction. Some of those views were positive and some of them were negative. I will summarize a few of those sentiments. I will start with some of the comments from persons who support keeping posthumous reproduction legal and available.

An overwhelming number of people I spoke with thought that posthumous reproduction was beneficial because it left family planning in the hands of the parties. As long as both the man and the woman agrees to the use of his sperm to conceive a child after his death, the government should not intervene. Posthumous reproduction presents no more risks than other forms of assisted reproduction, so it should be treated in a similar manner. A woman can become pregnant through artificial insemination with a man's sperm while he is alive. The man's death should not change the woman's ability to use his sperm if he consents to the process. Conceiving a child should be a collaborative process between the supplier of the eggs and the sperm. When one of the parties is no longer alive, the government should speak for the missing party. Therefore, the law should only allow posthumous reproduction when it is able to ascertain the wishes of the dead man.

In a sea of cheerleaders, I ran into detractors who thought that posthumous reproduction should be banned or strictly restricted. Some of the critics I encountered were especially troubled by postmortem sperm retrieval and sperm extraction from incapacitated men. They felt that the procedure showed a lack of respect for the dead and the debilitated. In addition, in some cases, the sperm harvesting may be against the man's expressed or unexpressed wishes. For example, situations discussed in this book have involved men who only agreed to procreate because they were trying to please their wives or save their marriages. Once the man's death prevents him from achieving those goals, the law should consider any consent he might have given while he was alive to be null and void.

My thoughts

A dead man will suffer no legal harm from posthumous reproduction and any ethical harm can be minimized. The child benefits from being conceived, so the balance weighs in favor of allowing posthumous reproduction. When evaluating the suitability of posthumous reproduction, courts should consider the interests of the man's existing children. Permitting more children to be conceived from a dead man's sperm may adversely impact his surviving children economically, socially and psychologically. If the man dies intestate or executes a will leaving his estate to his "children," the amount that his surviving children receive from the estate may be reduced if his sperm is used to create other potential heirs. Furthermore, depending on the age of the surviving children, having siblings conceived using their dead father's sperm may cause the man's children to be bullied and denigrated. Some infertile couples are so afraid of being stigmatized because of their infertility that they do not tell even close family members that they conceived using assisted reproductive technology.[8] Therefore, it is not unreasonable to believe that children may be humiliated by the fact that their mother becomes pregnant after the death of their fathers. The embarrassment may result from the fact that people might believe that the woman got pregnant by sleeping with another man soon after her husband's death or that she was impregnated using the sperm of a dead man. The dead man probably would not agree to posthumous reproduction using his sperm if he knew of these unintended consequences. The man might sacrifice potential children to protect the children that he knows and loves. From a psychological perspective, if the existing children are waiting around for their mother or their father's wife to conceive, they may not be able to grieve and to get the closure that is necessary to move forward without their father.

The conception of children using the sperm of a dead man might also have negative consequences for the state. The importance of the state's interest in protecting the integrity of the probate system has been legally recognized.[9] It can take years to probate a large estate. The probate process is challenging because of will contests and other litigation brought by dissatisfied family members. The probate courts have the task of ensuring that the property of the dead is distributed in a timely and orderly manner. The availability of posthumous reproduction may wreak havoc on that undertaking for several reasons. In order to give the posthumously conceived child time to be conceived and born, the probate court may have to keep the man's probate estate opened indefinitely. This could give the dead man too much control over the actions of the living. One of the purposes of the common law Rule Against Perpetuities (RAP) was to limit the control the "dead hand" had over property disposition. That task was accomplished by voiding property interests that had the potential to vest too remotely.[10] Even though the RAP would not be implicated, the availability of posthumous reproduction has the potential to create a situation where the "dead man" controls the disposition of his property long after his death. The possibility of a posthumously conceived child creates uncertainty for the probate court because the woman may or may not use the dead man's sperm to have children. In order to make sure that all of the man's heirs have the opportunity to inherit, the probate court would be in the position of having to wait and see what the woman decides to do. The end result might be backlogs in probate courts.

In spite of the potential negative consequences of posthumous reproduction, I think, with appropriate regulations put in place, the process should be permitted. Justice is represented by a scale that is supposed to symbolize the evenhandedness of the law. To live up to that attribute, judges are to weigh all of the material facts and come up with a balanced and fair resolution.[11] With regards to posthumous reproduction, one side of the scales may hold the harms to the reproductive rights of the dead man and the other side may hold the benefits to the posthumously conceived child. The scale would immediately tip in favor of the child because the benefit to the child of being able to exist would outweigh any harm to the dead man's reproductive rights. Some courts have rejected wrongful life causes of actions because of the difficulties of calculating damages. It is much too complicated to compare the relative benefits of life and non-existence.[12] In fact, one court opined "[w]hether it is better never to have been born at all than to have been born with even gross deficiencies is a mystery more properly to be left to the philosophers and the theologians. Surely the law can assert no competence to resolve the issue, particularly in view of the very nearly uniform high value which the law and mankind has placed on human life, rather than its absence."[13] Even in cases involving disabled children, courts have rejected the notion that non-life is preferable to living.[14]

Because this is such a one-sided situation the balancing process I am proposing is not balancing the child's right to live against the man's right to not be reproduced without his consent. When I refer to getting to the balance, I mean putting legal regulations in place to ensure that posthumous reproduction is done in an ethical manner. In the remainder of this chapter, I will recommend a two-part system that I feel will help achieve that goal. The first part of the proposal deals with the permissibility of posthumous reproduction and the second part pertains to the ability of the posthumously conceived child to inherit from the dead man's estate. The process will call for the man to execute one writing in which he consents to the posthumous reproduction and a second writing agreeing to the creation of a legal father–child relationship between him and the resulting child. The existence of that relationship will permit the child to inherit a portion of his or her dead father's intestacy estate.

Proposal part one (permitting posthumous reproduction)

The main ethical goals this part of my proposal seeks to accomplish are the following: (1) preventing a dead man from being reproduced without his consent; (2) reducing any hardships that may be placed upon the man's existing heirs; (3) avoiding possible interference with the probate process; and (4) decreasing any potential adverse consequences to the posthumously conceived child. The items in this section are the things that must take place in order for the woman to get to conceive using posthumous reproduction.

The man's preparations

Posthumous reproduction should be limited to the use of sperm that the man had frozen prior to his death. Sperm should not be permitted to be harvested from the body of a dead man or a man in a vegetative state *unless* the man has executed an advanced directive consenting to the procedure. These mandates are necessary to make sure that the man has thought about the possibility of having children after his death. Moreover, the man will have the opportunity to state what he wants done with his frozen sperm, and to make the necessary arrangements to ensure that his health care provider adheres to those wishes. He will also be afforded the opportunity to state his opposition to posthumous reproduction without being pressured by his spouse.

When fresh sperm is involved the situation is too rushed. In order for the sperm to be viable, it has to be retrieved in a relatively short period of time if the man is dead. Therefore, the health care provider may harvest the sperm before taking the time to determine if the man would have wanted his sperm extracted. If the facts later show that the man did not want his sperm retrieved posthumously, the damage would have already been done. That man's body would have been mutilated without his consent and his surviving spouse would have been looking forward to parenting his child. If he or she is denied use of the sperm, the sperm will have to be destroyed. For the spouse, that might be like losing the man a second time.

When a man has his sperm frozen, it is usually because he is facing a medical emergency or some other life-changing situation that endangers his fertility. At that time, the man is going through a frightening and stressful ordeal, so he does not have the time to think about the possibility of children being conceived using his sperm in the event that he dies. He is just trying to safeguard his future and his fertility. Thus, there should be a waiting period between the time the man has his sperm frozen and the time that he is asked whether he wants his sperm to be used to conceive children posthumously.[15] During that time period, the man should have to undergo counseling.[16] The purpose of the counseling would be to help the man handle the situation that he is facing and to permit him to talk about matters related to his possible demise.

The man's first written consent

If the man decides that he wants his sperm to be used to conceive a child after he dies, his agreement to the process must be in writing. It is crucial that the man's consent be in writing. However, the writing requirement should not be able to be satisfied by the standard consent form that the man signs with the fertility clinic or the hospital when he has his sperm extracted and frozen. The man may not read all of the boilerplate language in the fertility contract which usually consists of several pages and contains provisions that are not relevant to posthumous reproduction. The man should have to sign an independent agreement expressing his desire for his wife to use his sperm after he dies. The writing should be signed in front of the man's physician and kept on file with the man's medical records. The writing should be revocable by the man or a person he designates at any time prior to the man's death or incapacitation. The man should be able to revoke his consent in writing or orally. If the man chooses an oral revocation, that revocation must be performed in front of two disinterested witnesses, one of whom must be the man's physician. By signing this writing, the man creates a rebuttal presumption that he wants to be legally recognized as the child's father. This recognition is similar to the acknowledgement that is required to legitimize a non-marital child. The consent in this writing should not be interpreted as explicit consent to parent or to have the child classified as the man's heir.

In order to satisfy the written consent requirement, the writing does not have to be formal. There are several options available that would not be unduly burdensome on the man and his family. The legislature could create a statutory consent form that the man could fill out authorizing the use of his sperm to conceive a child prior to or after his death. Another option is for the medical facility withdrawing the man's sperm to provide a form for him to fill out prior to the procedure. Currently, before surgery or admittance to a hospital, patients are asked to fill out numerous types of forms, including living wills. Therefore, it would not be a burden for the hospital to generate another type of form to cover situations involving extraction of sperm. In fact, some states already require a licensed physician to obtain consent from a woman's husband before inseminating her with donor sperm. Those states could amend their statutes to require the woman to present a written consent form signed by the deceased man prior to releasing his previously stored sperm to the woman or removing sperm from the man's dead body. In addition, the man could be encouraged to leave provisions in his will for the distribution of his sperm to the person he wants to use it to conceive his child.

The spouse's preparations

Even if the man takes all of the steps that he is required to take, posthumous reproduction should not be permitted unless the spouse does his or her part. The first thing the spouse should have to do is to participate in grief counseling. Losing a spouse is a devastating experience, so when the man first dies, the spouse may automatically decide that he or she would like to have his child. In several of the cases discussed in this book, after taking time out to grieve, the person requesting posthumous reproduction had a change of heart. Counseling may also be beneficial in situations where the spouse is feeling pressure from the man's family to have his child. A person should not conceive out of guilt or a sense of obligation. That decision should be made when the person can decide the best course for her and the potential child. Spending time talking with an independent health care professional will afford the spouse the opportunity to reflect before having to decide what to do with the man's frozen sperm.

If the spouse decides to go forward with the posthumous reproduction, there are other steps she should have to take. Prior to undergoing the procedure, the spouse should have to designate a guardian for the child. The child would have already lost one parent. In the unlikely event that the woman dies in childbirth, there should be another adult ready, willing and able to step in to parent the child. This requirement is necessary regardless of the health or age of the woman because any female can suffer pregnancy complications, especially when assisted reproductive technology is involved. One might argue that this mandate interferes with a person's right to procreate. Nonetheless, the courts have made it clear that the right to procreate does not include the right to procreate using assisted reproductive technology. In the writing, the woman should include a financial plan for the support of the posthumously conceived children. That plan may include cash from a savings account, a certain percentage of the man's estate or a specific amount of the man's non-probate assets. The plan cannot be based upon the child's ability to inherit under the intestacy system or to receive Social Security Survivors' benefits.

For informational purposes, the woman should be required to notify the probate court and the man's adult existing heirs of her decision to conceive posthumously. Contrary to the mandates of the Louisiana law examined earlier, I do not think that the man's existing heirs should have the legal right to object to the posthumous reproduction or the resulting child's ability to inherit under the intestacy system. Once the man agrees that his spouse should have additional children using his sperm, his already born children should not have standing to object. Probate law is clear. A person does not have the right to inherit. The authority to dispose of property belongs to the person who accumulates it.

Proposal[17] *(inheritance rights of the posthumously conceived child)*

The question of the ability of a posthumously conceived child to inherit from his or her deceased father may come up in two types of situations. **Case One:** Prior to his death, a man has his doctor extract and freeze his sperm, and he dies before the conception of a child using that sperm. **Case Two:** Fresh sperm that is harvested from the body of a man who is dead or in a vegetative state is used to conceive a child. Both circumstances require courts to answer the following two questions: (1) Whether the resulting child should be given the chance to inherit from his or her father? and (2) What, if any, stipulations should the law put on the child's right to inherit from his or her father? The second scenario mentioned would not be permissible under my proposal unless the man gave written informed consent for post-mortem sperm extraction. To appropriately balance all of the rival interests, states that presently have not enacted statutes regulating the inheritance rights of posthumously conceived children should pass laws that include a written consent requirement, time restrictions, and other appropriate restrictions. States which currently have statutes setting forth the rights of posthumously conceived children should modify them accordingly if they do not already contain these critical components.

Opportunity to inherit

If the man signs the writing agreeing to posthumous reproduction and the child is conceived, the posthumously conceived child should be presumed to be the legal heir of the dead man for intestacy purposes. The presumption should be rebuttable in order to protect the rights of the man's living heirs. It is should also be rebuttable because agreeing to posthumous reproduction is not deemed the same thing as agreeing to provide financial support for the resulting child. Giving the posthumously conceived child the chance to inherit from his or her father will not infringe on the man's reproductive rights by forcing parental responsibilities on him. The man's reproductive rights are protected by some action taken by the man during his lifetime indicating that he wanted a child to be conceived using his sperm. The man's death should not prevent his reproductive wishes from being fulfilled. Furthermore, if the man had his sperm removed when he was facing a life-threatening illness or a situation that would leave him sterile, that affirmative action indicates that the man had his sperm removed because he was contemplating the conception of a child or children using his sperm. This indicates his desire to be a father.

At a minimum, unless contrary evidence is presented, the court should presume that the man would have wanted any child conceived posthumously using his sperm to inherit from his estate.[18] This approach will not discount the man's reproductive rights because, after the withdrawal of his sperm and the signing of the first written consent form, the man has the opportunity to change his mind and to have the stored sperm destroyed. For instance, the man could make arrangements to have the stored sperm destroyed during his lifetime or he could include a provision in his will ordering the destruction of his sperm. The involvement of a neutral third party in the withdrawal of the man's sperm reduces the possibility of fraud or misuse of the sperm. As *Kievernagel* indicates,[19] if the man makes his wishes known, the courts will order the medical facility to comply with the instructions that he leaves regarding the use of his sperm. Litigation over the use of a dead man's sperm usually occurs when he does not leave clear instructions about the disposal of his sperm.

Conditions to inherit

The opportunity to inherit should not be a guarantee of inheritance rights. Consequently, the living parent of the posthumously conceived child should have to show that certain conditions were met in order for the child to actually obtain the right to inherit. Those conditions should be geared toward protecting: (1) the interests of the posthumously conceived child; (2) the procreative rights of the dead man; (3) the interests of the man's other heirs; (4) and the interests of the state.

Written consent

At the time that the man agrees to posthumous reproduction, he should be given the opportunity to decide whether or not he wants to be legally recognized as the child's father. The man should have to indicate his consent by signing a second writing in which he states that any child that results from the use of his sperm should be presumed to be his marital child. The posthumously conceived child should not be able to inherit from the deceased man if the man does not sign the second written agreement. The second writing places more legal responsibility on the man's estate so it should be a more formal writing. The writing should have to be witnessed or notarized. The witnesses should be disinterested and one of the witnesses should be selected by a member of the man's family other than his spouse. Those requirements protect the man from undue pressure and give concerned parties the opportunity to report suspected abuse.

This writing agreeing to paternity should be more formal than the writing consenting to conception. Nonetheless, the formalities should fall short of those mandated by the Wills Acts. In Florida, the posthumously conceived child can only inherit if his or her father provides for the child in a will. A substantial number of people die without leaving wills. The children of those people are protected by the intestacy system. The states do not punish children because their parents die intestate. That makes sense from a public policy perspective because a child cannot force his or her parents to draft a will. The Florida will requirement treats posthumously conceived children differently from other children. If a child were born posthumously, Florida would permit that child to inherit under the state's intestacy system without requiring any action from the father.

Requiring a woman to obtain the man's written consent to use his sperm to conceive his child after he dies and to have him recognized as the father ensures that the man has seriously thought about the process. The written consent requirement also helps protects against fraud, and creates a safe harbor which provides the man with the assurance that the court will carry out his wishes. Additionally, in the case of artificial insemination performed while the man is alive, some jurisdictions permit a man's consent to be presumed or implied.[20] In light of the fact that a deceased man will not be around to speak on his own behalf in the context of posthumous conception, the mother of the child should be required to acquire the man's written consent.[21] If the woman does not produce proof of both the man's written consent to the posthumous conception and to be legally recognized as the father, the resulting child should not be able to inherit from his estate.

The writing requirement, like a will, serves several useful purposes. Requiring a writing forces a man to give serious consideration to his decision to agree to permit the use of his genetic material to create a child. The ritual of reading and signing a document usually impresses upon the person that he is making an important, and often binding, commitment. Therefore, he will be able to give informed consent to the procedure. Given the legal responsibilities that spring from conceiving a child, it is critical that the decision is not hastily made. The writing requirement also serves an evidentiary function. The writing signed by the man will serve as a reliable source of proof. As a result, when the woman petitions the probate court on behalf of the posthumously conceived child, she will be able to prove that the man consented to the conception of the child and agreed to be the child's legal father. Since the events all take place after the man is dead, a writing signed by his hand is the best available evidence of his wishes.

Moreover, the writing requirement serves a protective function. It enables the probate court to function smoothly by reducing the number of fraudulent claims that are filed. It also protects the procreative rights of the deceased man by not making him responsible for a child unless he agreed in writing to the conception and the paternal recognition. The writing provides a safeguard against the misuse of frozen sperm. The man may have frozen his sperm to use at a later time in his life. He may not want the sperm to be used to create a child that he will never know.

The final function of the writing requirement is to create a safe harbor that provides the man with the assurance that the court will carry out his wishes. The probate court is supposed to bring about the presumed intent of the decedent when it comes to distributing his property. The writing requirement provides the court with the directions it needs to perform that task. This is especially true in Florida where the writing requirement can only be satisfied by a will. The man's right to decide if he wants to be financially responsible for a child is protected because if he does not provide for the posthumously conceived child in his will, the child is not his heir. This is consistent with the manner in which the testacy system treats all children. A man has a right to disinherit his existing children, so he should have the right not to provide for his posthumously conceived child.

The writing requirement is fair to all of the parties impacted by the birth of the posthumously conceived child. It promotes the state's interests in making sure that the financial needs of minor children are met. Prior to the child's birth, the writing requirement permits the state to have a person it can hold responsible for the support of the child. If the man gives written consent for the child to be conceived, that writing can be used by the state to obtain financial support for the child from the man's estate or his Social Security benefits. The writing requirement helps the child by giving him or her tangible proof of paternity. That proof can be presented to the probate court or the Social Security Administration on behalf of the child. The writing requirement also protects the existing heirs by reducing the number of persons who can make a claim against the man's estate. The writing requirement creates a bright-line rule. If the child does not have the requisite written authorization, he or she does not have a right to inherit from the man's estate.

There has been much dispute about whether a man's sperm should be recognized as property.[22] The written consent requirement should apply regardless of which view is adopted. If the court decides to treat the dead man's sperm as just another body part, it still should not be extracted without written permission from the decedent. For example, a hospital does not harvest a person's organs unless that person has filled out an organ donor card or the hospital receives written consent from the person's next of kin.[23] The harvesting of sperm should be more restricted because sperm has the potential to create a human life that the deceased man's resources may be used to support.[24] In addition, the decision to be a parent is a personal one that should be made by the man during his lifetime. Consequently, a man's sperm should not be extracted from his body posthumously without some type of written permission from him.

The court in *Hecht*[25] indicated sperm should be treated as property a man can dispose of in his will. In jurisdictions that choose to follow that approach, the written consent requirement is still appropriate. Distribution by a written instrument signed by the decedent is the law's preferred method of disposing of property. The courts and legislatures recognize that a man should have the right to dispose of his property in accordance with his wishes. Thus, if a man leaves a will, the court will take steps to honor the instructions that he includes in that instrument. If the man dies without executing a will, the intestacy system is in place to distribute his property in a manner consistent with his presumed intent. Consequently, a posthumously conceived child should only have the right to inherit from a man's estate if the man intended to have his sperm used to create that child and agreed to be the child's legal father. The most reliable indicator of that intent is a written instrument evidencing the man's consent to the posthumous conception and his agreement to be adjudicated the child's parent.

Time restrictions

It is very important that the probate court close the estates of decedents as quickly and efficiently as possible. The probate court and the man's existing heirs should not have to sit back and wait for the man's widow to decide that she wants to conceive his child. Consequently, in order to inherit, the posthumously conceived child should have to be conceived within a certain time period. The time restrictions imposed by the Louisiana and the California systems are fair to all the parties involved. The time frame permitted affords the woman the opportunity to conceive and give birth to the child. A shorter time period would be unrealistic because it typically takes several fertility treatments for the woman to conceive. In addition, the woman may have a miscarriage or other complications. The woman should be given time to grieve and to conceive. The two-to-three-year window of opportunity gives the woman more than one chance to conceive using the dead man's sperm. A longer time period would not be fair to the existing heirs. They should not have to wait indefinitely to receive an inheritance.

The Restatement approach permits flexibility because the court can determine what is a "reasonable" amount of time based upon the circumstances of a particular case. However, the "reasonable" language is so vague it may not promote judicial economy because the court might be constantly called upon to decide if the child was born within a reasonable period of time. A specific time should be stated in order for the child to be conceived. After that time period has expired, the class of the decedent's heirs should be closed. The time limit should be long enough to give the woman a realistic opportunity to conceive and give birth. Nonetheless, the time period should be short enough to prevent numerous additional heirs from being conceived and to allow the existing heirs to receive their inheritance in a timely manner. The time frame can be based upon the average time it takes to probate an estate of that size in that jurisdiction.

Other restrictions

Because the man is making the determination before he dies, the law should not dictate the relationship that the person using the sperm has to the man. If a man wants to permit his sperm to be used by his spouse, significant other or parents, that should be his choice. He should also have the option to donate his sperm. Most current statutes only permit the man to consent to the use of his sperm by his spouse. That approach has some merit. If the use of the process is not limited to married couples, nothing limits the number of times that a man can consent to the afterdeath use of his sperm to conceive a child. Consequently, it is conceivable that several women might conceive children using the sperm of the dead man. The end result could be numerous heirs filing claims against the man's estate. This would put a strain on the probate court and it would be unfair to the man's existing heirs. Therefore, the legislatures need some way to control the number of children posthumously conceived using a man's sperm. One way to achieve that task is to limit the pool of persons who have the right to create a man's heir after his death to his spouse. That decision makes sense because it is reasonable for a man to want his surviving spouse to bear his child. In addition, only permitting spouses to file claims against a man's estate will promote judicial economy.

Notwithstanding the benefits of restricting the application of the statutes to only spouses, that approach has some serious drawbacks. First, it is out of step with the evolution of the American family. More and more persons are choosing to have long-term committed relationships without the benefit of marriage, as recognized by the court in *Hecht*. Even though Hecht was not Kane's wife, the court acknowledged his right to leave her his sperm so that she could conceive his child after he died. By only giving a married man the right to consent to the posthumous use of his sperm, the legislatures disregard the wishes of men in long-term committed relationships.

Additionally, the statutes appear to punish posthumously conceived children whose parents chose not to marry before their conception. When legislatures enacted statutes that deprived non-marital children of the opportunity to inherit from their fathers, the United States Supreme Court found those statutes to be unconstitutional. As a result, because death ends the marriage, a child conceived posthumously has a great deal in common with a non-marital child. Thus, a similar Equal Protection argument can be made on behalf of the posthumously conceived children of unmarried couples. That argument might be successful because there appears to be no compelling reason to treat those children differently from the posthumously conceived children of married couples. Statutes that are not limited to married couples are broad enough to cover most circumstances. Therefore, under those types of statutes, more posthumously conceived children will have the opportunity to inherit from their fathers. Hence, this approach appears to be in the best interests of the conceived children.

Conclusion

Currently, the average person is not comfortable with the conception of children using the gametes of dead or incapacitated men. Nonetheless, the process will probably continue to be available and used. Because the procedures necessary to conceive a child using posthumous reproduction are costly and often not covered by health insurance the number of persons who utilize the process may be limited. However, the desire to have children for men who are dead or incompetent may cause some persons to do whatever is necessary to raise the money to pay for posthumous reproduction. Therefore, the government needs to regulate the procedure to ensure that the reproductive rights of the dead man are not violated. A person's death does not automatically deprive that person of the right to be treated with dignity. Nevertheless, attempts to protect the dead should not be taken at the expense of the living. If done properly, posthumous reproduction should remain legal and available. In addition, the law should take steps to protect the rights of posthumously conceived children.

Notes

1 Valarie K. Blake, Ovaries, Testicles, and Uteruses, Oh My!: Regulating Reproductive Tissue Transplants, 19 Wm. & Mary J. Women & L. 353, 353 (Winter 2013).
2 Judith Daar, Multi-Party Parenting in Genetics and Law: A View From Succession, 49 Fam. L.Q. 71 (Spring 2015).
3 *Litchez v Haritgan*, 735 F.Supp. 1361, 1376 (N.D. Illinois 1998).
4 Steve P. Calandrillo, In vitro Fertilization and the Law: How Legal and Regulatory Neglect Compromised a Medical Breakthrough, 57 Ariz. L. Rev. 311, 329 (2015).
5 Karl Kurtz, Not As Diverse As the American Public, State Lawmakers Are a Varied Lot, State Legislatures Magazine at www.ncsl.org/research/about-state-legislatures/who-we-elect.aspx (December 1, 2015).
6 Maggie Davis, Who Should Reproduce?: Perpetuating Archaic Value Judgments of Procreation in the Patient Protection and Affordable Care Act, 16 Scholar: St. Mary's L. Rev & Soc. Just. 255, 267 (2004).
7 Maya Sabatello, Posthumously Conceived Children: An International and Human Rights Perspective, 27 J.L. & Health 29, 36 (2015).
8 David Orenflicher, Discrimination Out of Dismissiveness: The Example of Infertility, 85 Ind. L.J. 143, 174 (2010).
9 *Lalli*, 439 U.S. at 268 cited in *Turner v Nesby*, 848 S.W.2d 872, 877 (Ct. App. Tex. 1993) and *Estate of Britel*, 186 Cal. Rptr. 3d at 337.
10 *Atlantic Richfield Company v Whiting Oil and Gas Corporation*, 320 P.3d 1179, 1180 (Colo. 2014).
11 Rebecca K. Lee, Justice For All?, 65 Vand. L. Rev. En Banc. 217, 224 (2012).
12 *Nelson v Krusen*, 678 S.W.2d 918, 925 (Tex. 1984).
13 *Becker v Schwartz*, 386 N.E. 2d 807, 812 (N.Y. 1978).
14 *Clark v Children's Memorial Hosp.*, 955 N.E. 2d 1065, 1084 (Ill. 2011).
15 Physician-assisted statutes require a waiting period between the time the terminally ill person requests the medicine and receives the lethal dose of medication. The law recognizes that time is need to think about the seriousness of a life-changing or life-ending decision. Browne Lewis, A Graceful Exit: Redefining Terminal to Expand the Availability of Physician-Facilitated Suicide, 91 Or. L. Rev. 457, 471 (2012).
16 Some states have mandated counseling for women seeking abortions. Bebe J. Anderson, Litigating Abortion Cases in the Post-Windsor World, 29 Colum. J. Gender & L. 143, 146 (2015).
17 This proposal was first presented in Browne Lewis, Dead Men Reproducing: Responding to the Existence of Afterdeath Children, 16 Geo. Mason L. Rev. 403, 435 (2009).
18 Robert J. Kerekes, My Child But Not My Heir: Technology, the Law and Post-Mortem Conception, 31 Real. Prop. Prob. & Tr. J. 213, 240 (1996) ("It is

illogical to assume that a decedent would desire to prevent a biological child from sharing in his estate.").

19 *In re Estate of Kievernagel*, 83 Cal. Rptr. 3d 311, 317–18 (Cal. Ct. App. 2008) (noting that only the decedent has a right to the determination of the use of his sperm, which must be governed by his intent when this is clear).

20 See, e.g., MD. Code Ann., Estates & Trusts, § 1–206(b) (West 2016); see also, e.g., *In re Baby Doe*, 353 S.E.2d 877, 879 (S.C. 1987) (citing *R.S. v R.S.*, 670 P.2d 923, 926 (Kan. Ct. App. 1983) ("Husband's consent to his wife's impregnation by artificial insemination may be express, or it may be implied from conduct which evidences knowledge of the procedure and failure to object.").

21 *See K.S. v G.S.*, 440 A.2d 64, 66 (N.J. Super. Ct. Ch. Div. 1981); see also *In re Marriage of Witbeck-Wildhagen*, 667 N.E.2d 122, 125–126 (Ill. App. Ct. 1996) (holding that it is against public policy to require a man to provide financial support for a child that his wife conceives by artificial insemination without his consent).

22 Jennifer Long Collins, Note, *Hecht v Superior Court*: Recognizing a Property Right in Reproductive Material, 33 Y. Louisville J. Fam. L. 661, 673–78 (1995); see also Bonnie Steinbock, Sperm as Property, 6 Stan. L. & Pol'y Rev. 57, 66 (1995). But see John A. Robertson, Posthumous Reproduction, 69 Ind. L.J. 1027, 1038–39 (1994) (citing *Moore v Regents of the Univ. of Calif.*, 793 P.2d 479, 489 (Cal. 1990) (discussing different viewpoints about the treatment of body parts, especially sperm, as property)).

23 Kristin Cook, Familial Consent for Registered Organ Donors: A Legally Rejected Concept, 17 Health Matrix 117, 121–22 (2007); see also Lloyd R. Cohen, Increasing the Supply of Transplant Organs: The Virtues of a Futures Market, 58 Geo. Wash. L. Rev. 1, 19 (1989).

24 Bruce Wilder, Posthumous and Post-Incompetency Reproduction: Legal Ramifications for Family Law and for the Law of Probate, 13 Divorce Litig. 57, 58 (2001).

25 *Hecht*, 20 Cal. Rptr. at 283.

Index

For Product Safety Concerns and Information please contact our EU representative GPSR@taylorandfrancis.com
Taylor & Francis Verlag GmbH, Kaufingerstraße 24, 80331 München, Germany

www.ingramcontent.com/pod-product-compliance
Ingram Content Group UK Ltd.
Pitfield, Milton Keynes, MK11 3LW, UK
UKHW022123190926
475702UK00013B/1616
9780367075637